A NATURALIST'S GUIDE
TO CANYON COUNTRY

A NATURALIST'S GUIDE
TO CANYON COUNTRY

CANYONLANDS
Natural History Association

Second edition

David B. Williams

Illustrated by Gloria Brown and Todd Telander

FALCONGUIDES

GUILFORD, CONNECTICUT
HELENA, MONTANA
AN IMPRINT OF ROWMAN & LITTLEFIELD

Copyright © 2013 Rowman & Littlefield
Illustrations © Gloria Brown except where otherwise credited
Previously published in 2000 by Falcon Publishing, Inc.

Published in cooperation with Canyonlands Natural History Association

FalconGuides is an imprint of Rowman & Littlefield.
Falcon, FalconGuides, and Outfit Your Mind are registered trademarks of Rowman & Littlefield.

Map © Rowman & Littlefield

The Library of Congress has catalogued a previous edition as follows:
Williams, David B., 1965-
A naturalist's guide to canyon country / by David B. Williams; Illustrated by Gloria Brown
         p. cm.
Includes bibliographical references (p.).
ISBN 1-56044-783-4
1. Natural history—Colorado Plateau—Guidebooks. 2. Mountain ecology—Colorado Plateau—Guidebooks. 3. Colorado plateau—Guidebooks. I. Title.
QH104.5.C58 W56 2000
508.792'5—dc21   99-056384

ISBN 978-0-7627-8071-6

Printed in the United States of America

Distributed by NATIONAL BOOK NETWORK

CONTENTS

PREFACE

I remember my first trip to canyon country. I had driven over from Colorado with a group of friends to go backpacking. We arrived in the Needles district of Canyonlands National Park at about 11 p.m., pulled off the road, set up camp, and went to sleep. The next morning I awoke to the most astounding sight I had ever seen. The sun, which had just crept over the La Sal Mountains, lit the rocks so intensely it looked like the light was coming from within the rocks. Like many people who visit canyon country, I was immediately addicted to this region.

Two years later I moved to Moab to work for a small educational nonprofit organization, Canyonlands Field Institute (CFI). My original plan was to stay for 3 months. I left 9 years later.

I initially viewed the landscape with a geologist's eyes. I concentrated on the rocks and learned about the waxing and waning of deserts and seas that once covered this area.

The plants and animals of canyon country often suffer such a fate, for this place is truly a geologist's paradise. Over time though, my focus began to change and I started to see the smaller parts of the landscape. Canyon country contains a diverse and fascinating range of flora and fauna.

I was fortunate in working at CFI for several reasons. I got to spend most of my time out in the field attending educational workshops. The passion of the instructors opened up the natural world to me. I began to see the interactions between the plants, animals, and geology and discovered that I could not look at this landscape without wanting to know more about these relationships.

I was also fortunate in working with some wonderful people at CFI. Their deep love for this landscape was a model for me. They encouraged and supported me in my efforts to learn more about the natural world.

AUTHOR'S ACKNOWLEDGMENTS

A host of people have helped me put this book together. First and foremost is my wife, Marjorie. Gloria Brown's continuous support from the beginning was also essential. Thanks to David Lee of Falcon Publishing for his patience, editing, and support. Thanks to Diane Allen, chief of interpretation at Arches National Park, and Brad Wallis, director of the Canyonlands Natural History Association, for their editing and comments.

Others who read part of the text or answered key questions of mine include David Armstrong, Jayne Belnap, Hellmut Doelling, Alice Drogin, Damian Fagan, Lee Goodman, Tim Graham, Richard Hill, Boris Kondratieff, Andy Nettell, Dave Ross, Raven Tennyson, Susan Tweit, and Tara Williams. I could not have written this book without their patience, knowledge, and support.

I would also like to thank the CFI staff members for their help: Sue Bellagamba, Barry Miller, Mary Moran, Marian Ottinger, and Karla VanderZanden. I would especially like to honor the person I miss most from those days, Robin Wilson, who helped foster my deep love for the Moab area.

I began this book while I worked at CFI and even though I have not worked there in 7 years, I could not have written the book without those early years of education.

Revised Edition

Again, I have been fortunate to have many people help me with this revision: Mary Barkworth, Mark Bierner, Dean Blinn, Mario Boisvert, Matt Bowker, Elmar Buchner, Brenda Casper, Shawn Clark, Ted Cochrane, Jay Cole, Pete Eeles, Becky Flowers, David Giblin, Terry Griswold, Bill Grogan, Bill Heinrich, Tim Higgs, David Inouye, Scott Johnson, Josh Kapfer, Adam Leache, Mark Milligan, Joel Pederson, Frank Parker, Wright Robinson, Stan Smith, Larry St. Clair, Llo Stark, Todd Stout, Fredric Vencl, David Weissman, Alan Whittemore, and Kevin Williams.

And finally, I would like to thank Jessica Haberman for all of her support in bringing this new edition to fruition.

—David B. Williams

ILLUSTRATOR'S ACKNOWLEDGMENTS

A frequent refrain echoing throughout the canyons has been that there existed no book of this nature for the region. Upon embarking on a search for visual references for it, one of the many reasons for this became clear. Without the assistance of numerous people and institutions generously contributing their time, resources, collections, libraries, photography, and knowledge, the artwork would not have been possible. These illustrations express my sincere appreciation for their assistance and represent a fragment of dedicated lifetimes.

I am most grateful to David Williams and Bill Schneider for their original visions, and Globe Pequot Press and the remarkable Jessica Haberman—without whom all hope would have been lost.

Special recognition is extended to Ron Wittmann for delightfully bringing mosses to life; Dina Clark and Tim Hogan at the University of Colorado Museum of Natural History Herbarium; Larry St. Clair at the Monte L. Bean Life Science Museum, Brigham Young University; the Bureau of Land Management Moab District, notably Lynn Jackson, Bob Milton, Linda Seibert, Daryl Trotter, Dave Williams, and Alex van Hemert, with Joshua Huffman at Eagle Lake; Tim Graham, USGS–BRD Canyonlands Field Station; Jim Dougan, Natural Bridges National Monument; Jayne Belnap, Neal Herbert, Mary Moran, Charlie Schelz, and Vicki Webster, Canyonlands National Park; Diane Allen and Denise D'Agnese, Arches National Park; Brad Wallis, Canyonlands Natural History Association; Grand Canyon Association; Museum of Moab; Red Butte Garden; Bill Alther, Denver Museum of Natural History; the wonderful worlds of Boris Kondratieff, Darrel Snyder, and Bruce Wunder, Colorado State University; Craig Evoney, Sonya Norman, and Ken Stockton, Arizona-Sonora Desert Museum; Tom Powell, Colorado Division of Wildlife; Mark Milligan, Utah Geological Survey; the astute eye of Lee Goodman; humor from Doug Fiske; the photographic assistance of J. Scott Altenbach, Chris Bellingham, Alice Drogin, Damian Fagan, Richard Forbes, Nick Fuzessery, Geoffrey Hammerson, Dave Johnson, Roger Jones, Edwin Knight, Chris Parish, Khaleel Abdul Razak, Raven Tennyson, and Joel Tuhy; and for the support of my family and friends, especially the artistic insights of Deborah Kelley-Galin. Also to Todd Telander, who provided art when a bicycle accident made some illustrations impossible for me to complete.

Heartfelt thanks go to Jeanne Treadway for the shuttle, Larry Frederick for the map, the Stengel family for sharing their camp, and my mother for instilling an enduring love for the environment and art.

—Gloria Brown

INTRODUCTION

A *Naturalist's Guide to Canyon Country* is a comprehensive guide to the geology, shrubs, trees, flowers, mammals, birds, fish, reptiles, amphibians, insects, and arachnids of the northern Colorado Plateau. It covers an elevation range roughly between 4,000 and 7,500 feet and is a handy guide to the plants and animals that you might typically encounter while exploring this region.

Over the last two decades, the Colorado Plateau has experienced an unprecedented boom in visitation. Some claim the landscape is literally being loved to death. While this viewpoint may be extreme, human impacts on fragile desert ecosystems are becoming more commonplace. In this land of little rain, plant and animal communities do not quickly return to full health after they have been trampled, developed, or overused.

One of my main goals in writing *A Naturalist's Guide to Canyon Country* is to educate you about the desert's fragility. This guide will also give you the keys to identifying the region's plants and animals, and it describes the interrelationships between plants, animals, and their physical environments. As John Muir wrote: "When we try to pick out anything by itself, we find it hitched to everything else in the Universe."

A Naturalist's Guide to Canyon Country focuses on understanding the natural history of the Colorado Plateau, a physiographic province that totals roughly 130,000 square miles with the densest concentration of national park units in the lower 48 states. Although the plateau covers a vast area, it is unified by both geology and ecology, thus making one single field guide applicable to the region.

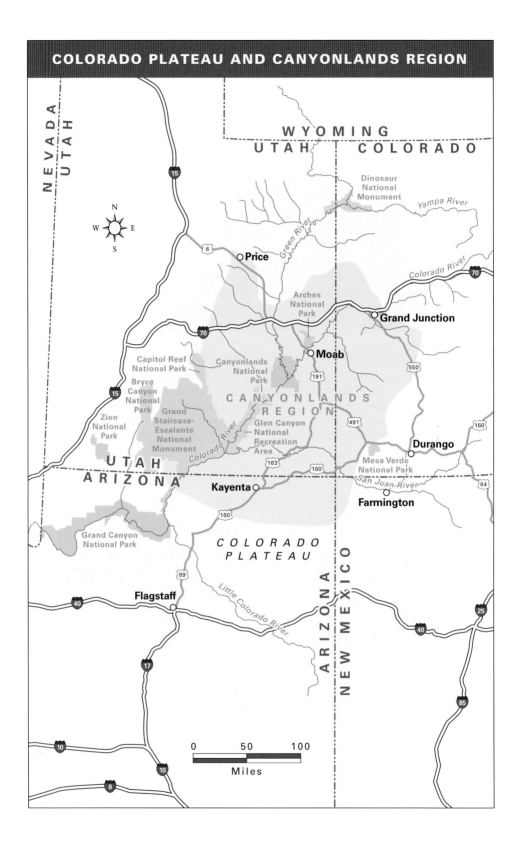

COLORADO PLATEAU AND CANYONLANDS REGION

GEOLOGY

The simplicity of its structure, the thoroughness of its drainage, which rarely permits detritus to accumulate in its valleys, its barrenness, and the wonderful natural sections exposed in its cañons, conspire to render it indeed "the paradise of the geologist." There he can trace the slow lithological mutations of strata continuously visible for hundreds of miles; can examine, in visible contact, the strata of nearly the entire geological series, and detect every nonconformity, however slight, and can study the simpler initiatory phases of an embryo mountain system.

—Grove Karl Gilbert, *Report upon Geographical and Geological Explorations and Surveys West of the One Hundred Meridian*, 1875

Understanding the geology of canyon country requires understanding one of the basics of science: What goes up must come back down. Geology fundamentally involves a battle between uplift and erosion, making us cognizant of the power of gravity. Geologic evidence shows that the Colorado Plateau was last at sea level more than 65 million years ago. Since then it has been uplifted at least 6,500 feet, but erosion is now the dominant force, with several thousand feet of rock removed in the last 30 million years. The stunning layers of exposed canyon country rock records this slow battle of gravity.

Visible changes between rock units (a contact zone) indicate that a change in depositional environment has occurred. Canyon country's geology displays numerous contact zones, which reveal that sea levels rose and fell, how winds deposited sands, and where rivers ran.

Learning the names and descriptions of most of the rock layers in this region is not difficult. At most locations only about five or six different layers are visible. The key is recognition of the dominant layers: Wingate Sandstone, Navajo Sandstone, and Entrada Sandstone. Although it is often hard to distinguish these large, cliff-forming layers from each other, if one recognizes the distinctive layers above and below each dominant layer, the problem of identification becomes easier to solve. The following chronological descriptions, and the stratigraphic column on pages 4-5, will help you understand and identify different layers.

The information below addresses rocks found around Moab, Utah. I felt that focusing on one area would create a clearer picture of how a landscape forms. Many of the rocks around Moab occur across the geographic area covered by this book. More important, the broad outline of this story with its deserts, seas, and tidal flats, and the corresponding uplift, weathering, and erosion is quite similar to the story that could be told about any area covered by this book.

Precambrian Era (4.6 Billion Years Ago [Bya]–542 Million Years Ago [Mya])

Precambrian rocks are exposed in only a few places in canyon country. The closest areas to Moab to find these black, metamorphosed rocks are in Westwater and Ruby Canyons on the Colorado River, the first just west, and the second just east of the Utah-Colorado border. These hard gneisses (banded rocks) and schists (foliated rocks) hardened during deep burial by heat and pressure between

Close-up

The Enigma of the Colorado Plateau

The red rocks record a great enigma: What caused the Colorado Plateau not only to rise but also to remain internally undeformed, especially compared to the adjacent Rocky Mountain and Basin and Range provinces? The unusual topography prompted Clarence Dutton in 1885 to write in his *Mount Taylor and the Zuñi Plateau* of "many short abrupt ranges, or ridges, looking upon the map like an army of caterpillars crawling northward. At length, about 150 miles north of the Mexican boundary, this army divides into two columns, one marching northwest, the other north-northeast.... This split in the main chain of cordilleras, forming the Basin range on the west and the Rockies on the east, leaves between them the vast area of the Plateau country."

In attempting to understand the region, geologists initially proposed that a river meandered across the region, and as uplift proceeded, the river cut down into the rocks to form the canyons. In other words, the uplift is younger than the river.

More recently, geologists recognize the Colorado Plateau as "a place where the cutting is younger than the uplift," says Joel Pederson of Utah State University. Geologic studies in the past decade or so show that the uplift began around 65 million years ago during what is known as the Laramide Orogeny. During this period, a tongue of one of the earth's plates extended at a shallow angle from the west under the region to about what is now Colorado. Not only did the tongue, known as the Farallon Plate, help buoy up the plateau, but it also led to the greater uplift of the Rocky Mountains. Over time, as the Farallon changed position, it allowed for hot molten rock to ooze into the area under the plateau and drive an additional rise, dated around 30 million years ago.

Further uplift in the plateau also came from what is known as isostatic rebound. Most often associated with the melting of glaciers, isostatic rebound involves a rise in the land due to the removal of a heavy mass that pushed down upon the land. With the weight gone, the land bounces back, or rebounds upward. On the Colorado Plateau, the erosion of 6,000 to 9,000 feet of sediments led to about 3,000 feet of uplift. Finally, canyon cutting began around 6 million years ago.

This description provides one alternative to explain the rise of the Colorado Plateau. Although other geologists disagree, they do agree that the anomalous uplift will require further study to ferret out the full story.

1.8 and 1.4 billion years ago. They were originally deposited as sediments on the newly forming North American continent. In some places, they melted beneath the surface and formed granitic rocks after they cooled. Precambrian rocks can also be found in the San Juan Mountains, on the Uncompahgre Plateau of Colorado, and in the bottom of Grand Canyon National Park.

Cambrian to Mississippian Period (542–323 Mya)

No rocks from these time periods exist at the surface in the Moab area. From subsurface cores and exposures in nearby national parks, however, geologists know that Utah was located near the equator, that an ocean lay to the west, and, as in modern equatorial regions, warm waters supported numerous marine organisms. Rocks from the Grand Canyon record the deposition of shallow marine and continental deposits, reflecting fluctuating sea levels. Oil drilling has revealed Cambrian, Devonian, and Mississippian rocks beneath both Canyonlands and Arches National Parks. Rocks from the Ordovician and Silurian periods are not present in this area. They may have been deposited during these two periods but later eroded.

Pennsylvanian Period (323–299 Mya)

The Utah region, with an ocean on its western border, still sat near the equator, but a dramatic change occurred when a large mountain chain, known as the Uncompahgre Uplift, began rising in eastern Utah and western Colorado. The Uncompahgre formed one arm of a series of mountain ranges known as the Ancestral Rockies and reached elevations that rivaled the modern-day Rockies. As the mountains pushed higher, the Paradox Basin, a northwest-southeast trending trough, formed and allowed water to flow into the area. The interplay between the erosion of the Uncompahgre Uplift and deposition in the Paradox Basin dominated the geologic picture for the next 100 million years.

The basin deepened along earthquake faults on an intermittent basis. When the faults deepened, water flowed into the basin, forming a restricted sea protected by a sandbar or reef. In the hot equatorial environment, when the faults were quiet, water began to evaporate and minerals settled to the bottom of the basin. Carbonates (limestone and dolomite) sank to the bottom first, followed by gypsum, and eventually by rock salt (halite [NaCl] and sylvite [KCl]). With fault reactivation, the reef or sandbar lowered and fresh water rushed into the basin, initiating the process again. In the Paradox Basin, at least twenty-nine cycles occurred, leaving an estimated 5,000 to 6,000 feet of salt, with some individual beds as thick as 700 feet. The salt of the Paradox Formation, as it is now called, will become one of the principal players in the geologic story of canyon country.

The salts of the Paradox Formation are not exposed at the surface. Groundwater dissolves them and carries them away down to the deep water table that currently prevails in the area. However, a cap rock composed of the less soluble residue of the Paradox is exposed along the margin of Moab Valley, in the middle of Salt Valley in Arches National Park, and in several other places around Moab. Salt reaches to within about 500 feet of the surface beneath the cap rock.

The Pennsylvanian period ended as a better connection opened between the ocean and the inland basin. Sea level continued to fluctuate, and the unrestricted sea deposited the fossiliferous limestones, marine sandstones, and siltstones of the Honaker Trail Formation. Fossils in this unit include crinoids, brachiopods, corals, and bryozoans.

The sands and silts came from the eroding Uncompahgre: the first example of the battle between uplift and erosion. The limestones precipitated from the seawater. The best exposures of the 1,000-foot-thick Honaker Trail Formation occur at Goose-

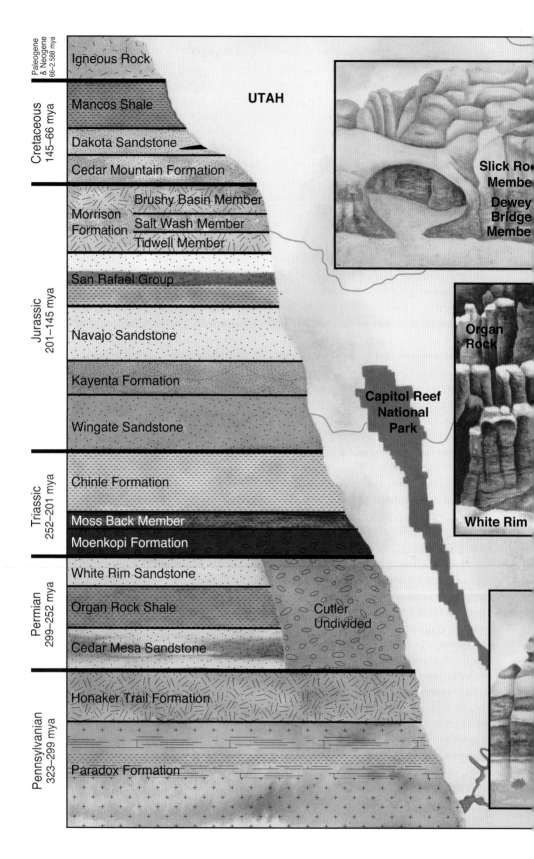

Paleogene & Neogene 66–2.588 mya

Igneous Rock

UTAH

Cretaceous 145–66 mya

Mancos Shale

Dakota Sandstone

Cedar Mountain Formation

Morrison Formation
- Brushy Basin Member
- Salt Wash Member
- Tidwell Member

Jurassic 201–145 mya

San Rafael Group

Navajo Sandstone

Kayenta Formation

Wingate Sandstone

Slick Rock Member
Dewey Bridge Member

Organ Rock

Capitol Reef National Park

Triassic 252–201 mya

Chinle Formation

Moss Back Member

Moenkopi Formation

White Rim

Permian 299–252 mya

White Rim Sandstone

Organ Rock Shale

Cedar Mesa Sandstone

Cutler Undivided

Pennsylvanian 323–299 mya

Honaker Trail Formation

Paradox Formation

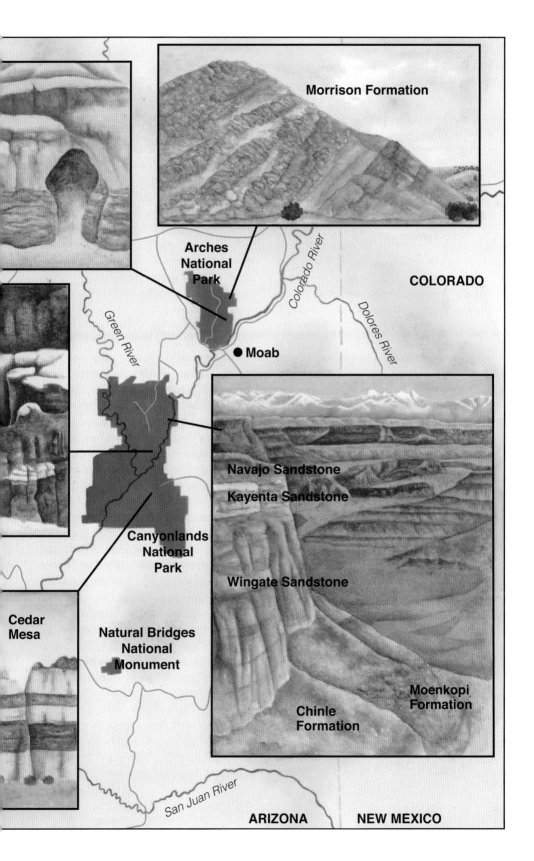

Morrison Formation

Arches
National
Park

COLORADO

Colorado River

Dolores River

Green River

● Moab

Navajo Sandstone

Kayenta Sandstone

Wingate Sandstone

Canyonlands
National
Park

Cedar
Mesa

Natural Bridges
National
Monument

Moenkopi
Formation

Chinle
Formation

San Juan River

ARIZONA   NEW MEXICO

necks of the San Juan State Park and in Cataract Canyon in Canyonlands National Park. The grayish unit consists of interbedded sandstone, siltstone, and limestone ledges and slopes. It also outcrops along US 191, near the Arches National Park visitor center.

As sediments from the mountains piled atop the Paradox Formation, an unusual geologic event started to occur—the underlying salt began to move and deform. Salt has two extraordinary properties: Under pressure it flows like wet putty, and because it is usually less dense than the surrounding material, it tends to rise upward, creating domes and ridges. Continued movement of the linear faults weakened the overlying rocks. In the Moab area, salt moved away from the mountains into these weaker zones. The linear belts of thickened salt are called diapirs. Salt movement continued for the next 100 million years and played a central role in the creation of the landscape we see today.

Permian Period (299–252 Mya)

The combination of fluctuating sea levels and the Uncompahgre's shedding of sediments toward a sea that advanced and retreated from the west produced the region's most confusing and most distinctive rock unit, the Cutler Group. All this activity created many environments and consequently many interbedded rock units, which exhibit great variation in color, thickness, and grain size on both a horizontal and vertical scale.

Cross-bedding

Eroding mountains created a reddish feldspar-rich sediment, which streams deposited as a dark reddish-brown rock unit, known as the Undivided Cutler or Cutler Undifferentiated. These deposits form a giant wedge, thickest (up to 10,000 feet) near the mountains, and thinning (about 1,200 feet) toward the south and west. Continued movement of the underlying Paradox further altered the thickness of the Cutler. Deposition continued throughout the Permian period, and the present-day sediments form the Fisher Towers, 23 miles up the Colorado River from Moab, and the lower cliffs on the western side of US 191 starting about 1.5 miles north of the turnoff to Arches National Park.

Southwest of Moab, the Cutler picture becomes confusing. Shallow waters from a sea to the west pushed into the area, producing a series of red-brown, shaly mudstones and fine-grained sandstones known as the Halgaito Shale. This unit has its best exposures near Mexican Hat, Utah.

After a drop in sea level, winds from the northwest began pushing sands into canyon country. These winds deposited a white to pale reddish-brown cross-bedded unit, the Cedar Mesa Sandstone. Changing wind directions can create a complex set of beds as sand dunes move over one another, migrating across a landscape. The Cedar Mesa forms the canyons of the Maze District of Canyonlands National Park and the Cedar Mesa region of San Juan County.

As the Cedar Mesa sands moved toward the Cutler sands, a great "push-of-war" of sedimentation occurred. First, the Cedar Mesa advanced toward the mountains, depositing great beds of white sand. Then, with changing environmental conditions, the Cutler moved back west, depositing beds of red sand. After a few hundred thousand or million years, the Cedar Mesa would push back, starting the process over again with each layer varying in thickness. This battle produced the spectacular red and white banding of the Needles District of Canyonlands National Park.

Eventually the supply of white sediments tapered off, but red sediments from the Uncompahgre Uplift continued to reach the canyon country. These sediments settled in an environment dominated by tidal flats, floodplains, and streams. As tides and streams moved these fine-grained muds and silts, they left behind numerous layers of varying thickness of the purplish red Organ Rock Shale, a unit equivalent to the Grand Canyon's Hermit Shale.

The final Permian rock unit is the White Rim Sandstone. Coastal winds on the eastern margin of a sea deposited this cross-bedded unit. The marine equivalent of this unit to the west is the Kaibab Formation. The White Rim Sandstone, as its name suggests, forms a prominent white bench in the Island in the Sky District of Canyonlands National Park. This unit is thickest to the northwest and, except for a small exposure in Castle Valley (10 miles northeast of Moab), gradually thins eastward and terminates at the Colorado River. An extended episode of hyperaridity that produced wind-sculpted ridges brought this period to an end. Geologists estimate that at least 20 million years of time passed before deposition of the overlying Moenkopi Formation began.

The interrelationship between the Organ Rock Shale and the overlying White Rim Sandstone provides an excellent example of the canyon-forming process. Erosion of the softer Organ Rock from underneath the White Rim forms alcoves. The alcove eventually collapses, pushing the canyon farther back, and the process begins again. In some places, the White Rim Sandstone provides a protective cap rock for the shale, creating ephemeral mushroom-shaped towers. The process can be seen in the Monument Basin area below White Rim Road in Canyonlands National Park.

Triassic Period (252–201 Mya)

Northward movement of the North American continent moved Utah into a climate that was generally warm with monsoons and intermittent seasonally dry periods. The deeper ocean still lay to the west. The Triassic ended as continental conditions returned and streams removed sediments and plant debris from the Ancestral Rockies.

Tides from a sea that covered an area to the west and north spread sediments across an extensive mud flat, producing the Moenkopi Formation. The chocolate-brown siltstones and sandstones display the Moenkopi's characteristic ripple marks, worm burrows, and mud cracks. In some places the Moenkopi still looks wet. The Moenkopi varies in thickness across the region, averaging between 300 and 500 feet thick. Paradox salt continued to move at this time, and, like the Cutler, Moenkopi sediments thin over salt diapirs and thicken between them. Good exposures exist along the Colorado River at Big Bend and in Professor Valley along SR 128. Moenkopi rocks cover the entire southern part of the state.

After another brief period of erosion, the highly varied Chinle Formation was deposited. During Chinle deposition, sufficient moisture fell to create streams, lakes, and marshes; at times flooding occurred, depositing silts, muds, and fine sands. Early in the Chinle's depositional history, thick soils developed on these sediments; today they have a mottled appearance of purple, white, yellow, and brown. Root casts and worm burrows are common in the lower part of the formation. Later a steady stream of red-brown fine sand was deposited over the land, punctuated by layers of volcanic ash that blew in from volcanoes active to the west. Chinle rocks form the soft slopes beneath the massive cliffs of the Wingate Sandstone and occur as far south as Petrified Forest National Park in Arizona.

New research in the Chinle has revealed many interesting fossils. The sediments that washed out of the Uncompahgre highlands contained vast amounts of wood. The most common plant fossils are conifers, ferns, and horsetails. Vertebrate fossils include reptiles and amphibians. One unusual trace fossil discovery may represent the burrow of a lungfish, an animal that possessed both lungs and gills.

Like the units laid down previously, the Chinle was affected by the underlying salt, but this marks the end of the major salt movement. Salt movement would not play an important role in the area's geology for another 100 to 150 million years.

The uranium stampede to canyon country began when Charlie Steen discovered uranium in the lowest part of the Chinle, the Moss Back Member. Sometime after Chinle deposition, uranium-rich ground water, possibly leached from the volcanic ashes, started to move through the porous sands. As it percolated through the rock, the water encountered organic material and precipitated uranium minerals, especially uraninite, a dull black, dense material also known as pitchblende.

Jurassic Period (201–145 Mya)

During the Jurassic, the Uncompahgres were finally reduced to inconsequential hills. New mountains, which began rising in the west and south during the Triassic, started to contribute significant amounts of sediments. Continued northerly drift pushed the continent into drier and drier climatic zones. Windblown (eolian) sand dunes dominated the landscape for the next 40 million years, producing over 1,000 feet of vertical cliffs. A few short interludes of wetter climates periodically broke up this sea of sand.

The Wingate Sandstone preserves the first of these eolian dunes. The light brown to reddish brown, 300-foot-thick unit forms the sheer cliffs that dominate skylines for hundreds of miles in this region. Although the Wingate appears to be a formidable unit, the layers above and below it, the Chinle

and Kayenta, are responsible for its appearance. Similar to the Organ Rock Shale–White Rim Sandstone contact, the erosion of the softer underlying Chinle undercuts the harder Wingate above until it collapses. This is one of the more prominent and easily recognizable geologic contacts in the area and one you should learn to identify first. Surprisingly, the overlying Kayenta, which does not form prominent cliffs but is more resistant to erosion, protects the Wingate. Without the Kayenta the Wingate would not be so formidable.

A short interlude of increased precipitation created the fluvial (stream) deposits of the Kayenta Formation. This light-colored hard, ledgy layer represents the final episode in the battle between uplift and erosion in the Uncompahgre Uplift. After this period, it would be more correct to compare the Uncompahgres to the Adirondacks than to the Rockies. The transition between the Kayenta and the Navajo, which is well exposed along Potash Road (SR 279), displays windblown, fluvial, and lake deposits.

More arid conditions returned, producing wind-deposited sand dunes that stretched from the middle of Wyoming to northern Arizona and west to Nevada. Curiously, all of this sand started life in the Appalachian Mountains and was carried west by continent-crossing river systems. This great area of sand (possibly the largest ever) is known as the Navajo Sandstone in our area, the Nugget Sandstone to the northeast, and the Aztec Sandstone in Nevada. The whitish to pale reddish, cross-bedded Navajo erodes into rounded domes and knolls. The vertical cliffs reach heights of 2,000 feet in Zion National Park, but are only 400 to 500 feet high near Moab. Around Moab, the Navajo forms the ups and downs of the Slickrock Trail and the "Petrified Dunes" section of Arches National Park.

In the middle of the Jurassic period, Utah remained at low elevations. A sea intermittently encroached into central Utah,

Close-up

Oases in the Desert

The standard picture of the desert preserved by the Navajo Sandstone is of a sand sea stretching from horizon to horizon, with few animals or plants existing anywhere. During the rainy season, however, streams flowing off nearby mountains traveled under the sand, percolated to the surface in low points of the dune field, and created small seasonal lakes. Additional lakes also formed during multi-decadal periods of heavier-than-normal precipitation, which led to a rise in groundwater and subsequent lake or pond development.

Like oases in modern deserts, these Navajo paleo-oases drew in animals, creating a sanctuary of life. Tracks, fossils, and petrified wood, preserved in the rock, provide tantalizing evidence to a diverse array of life.

Dinosaurs often visited these lakes. Tracks range in size from a few inches to a foot or more and include three- and four-toed, bipedal and quadrapedal dinosaurs. On one well-preserved slab, numerous tracks crisscross, possibly representing over a dozen different animals. Insects also thrived in the oases and left behind tracks and burrows.

The water also provided an area for plants to grow. Non-flowering plants included algae and a precursor of *Equisetum*, our modern-day horsetail or scouring rush. Horsetails still grow in Utah, only the modern ones are much smaller; Jurassic-age *Equisetum* relatives were 20 feet tall. Some of the petrified wood found in these ancient watery refuges is several feet long and more than a foot in diameter.

The paleo-oases are preserved in the rock record as 1- to 4-foot-thick lenses of either reddish or gray, fine-grained carbonate material. These limestone layers are always harder and sharper (some geologists call this material "tearpants-limestone") than the surrounding tannish to reddish sandstone.

connecting with the open ocean to the north. The climate was semiarid. Eastern Utah, including the present-day canyon country, lay east of the sea but was greatly influenced by its presence. Rising sea levels created tidal flats or a similar kind of coastal environment. A receding sea returned the area to desert or steppe conditions.

All of these units were deposited either just offshore or just onshore of a broad seaway, which occupied much of the western United States. The units west of the Green River represent offshore environments, and the eastern units represent onshore environments. Thus, the Carmel Formation is a marine unit that includes the Dewey Bridge Member, deposited on a muddy flat. Coastal dunes formed the Entrada Sandstone and its eastern facies, the Slick Rock Member. As the sea moved back into the area, it produced the marine Curtis Formation, which includes the coastal dunes of its Moab Tongue Member. A marginal marine mud flat resulted in deposition of the Summerville.

The Carmel outcrops in a protean suite of limestone, sandstone, gypsum, and siltstone. Dewey Bridge rocks are red-brown, muddy, and irregular with locally contorted beds. Both always occur above the cross-bedded Navajo. The western Entrada weathers into smooth cliffs or unusual shapes, characterized by the plethora of shapes, referred to as "hoodoos" or "goblins," found at Goblin Valley State Park.

Smooth cliffs dominate east of the Green River as the Slick Rock Member, most commonly in Arches National Park. The Curtis Formation consists of greenish yellow sandstone, overlain by thin, muddy, greenish to red sandstone. To the east the Moab Tongue Member looks like a thin equivalent of the Navajo. The Summerville Formation, a brown, thin- to medium-bedded sandstone, normally forms steep slopes.

These rock layers are found mostly north of Canyonlands National Park, along an east-west line that terminates at the Colorado River. The best exposures of the Carmel, Curtis, and Summerville Formations occur in the vicinity of the San Rafael Swell. The majority of the larger arches in Arches National Park have formed at the contacts between the separate members of the Entrada. These units make up the San Rafael Group.

The Tidwell Member of the Morrison Formation, a thin-bedded red sandstone and shale interspersed with gray limestone ledges, formed in quiet lakes on a broad floodplain. It contains abundant white chert (cryptocrystalline quartz, sometimes referred to as chalcedony, flint, or jasper) nodules and boulders. The Tidwell forms a distinct red ribbon on the white Moab Tongue, especially along the trail to Delicate Arch.

Relative calm returned to the region in the late Jurassic as mountains in the west started to lose the erosion-uplift battle and streams began to carry away the sediments. The first unit deposited by these streams, the Salt Wash Member of the Morrison Formation, has produced many of the finest dinosaur fossils in the world. The best-known quarries are in Dinosaur National Monument and at the Cleveland-Lloyd Quarry, south of Price, Utah. Uranium and vanadium (a steel-hardening metal) are also found in the Salt Wash concentrated in fossilized plant debris. This is a light gray or grayish-yellow sandstone with intermittent beds of green, muddy siltstone.

Continued erosion in the west resulted in the next layer in the area, the Brushy Basin Member of the Morrison Formation. Large sluggish rivers, like the modern Mississippi, flowed out of the highlands carrying fine silts and sands. In low-lying areas, the river periodically pushed out into a floodplain commonly inundated and covered by lakes. Volcanic ash, spewed from western volcanoes, fell into this landscape of lakes and large, slow-moving rivers. The varicolored slopes of the Brushy Basin are bright green where the ash fell into the lakes and maroon in areas where the ash fell on the floodplains. The green color comes from iron in the ash that altered in the oxygen-free environment at the bottom of the lake. The best bright green layers occur at the Delicate Arch trailhead in Arches National Park.

Cretaceous Period (145–66 Mya)

Sediments continued to wash off the western mountains, and North America was still progressing north during the beginning of the Cretaceous. Toward the end of this period a great seaway split North America in half. The waters stretched from Alaska to Mexico with deposition of several thousand feet of fine-grained materials in the Moab area. Uplift of the Rocky Mountains brought this period to an end.

The younger layers of this period are hard to distinguish from each other. They form low, inconspicuous ledges and slopes found mostly north of Arches National Park. Cedar Mountain Formation sandstones outcrop as brownish-gray ledges with lavender and light green mudstones both above and below. They are the product of streams washing off mountains. Some sediments also settled in shallow lakes. East of the Colorado River, geologists call the Cedar Mountain the Burro Canyon Formation, a unit with larger sediments, indicating a closer proximity to the mountain source.

Rock Varnish

Beautiful streaks of rock varnish often coat the vertical walls of rocks in canyon country. Also known as desert varnish, this micro-thin patina (up to about 200 micrometers, or about the width of two strands of hair) covers the surface of many rocks. Although clay makes up 70 percent of the varnish, the color is influenced by manganese and iron oxides. It varies in color from reddish brown (iron-rich) to black (manganese-rich).

Two theories exist to explain how desert varnish is formed. Both propose that the constituent materials are derived from external sources, either windblown dust or rain with trace amounts of iron and manganese. The controversy arises in how the materials are cemented to the rock surface.

In the first scenario rainwater mixes with the clays on the rock surface. Water combines with the iron and manganese to create oxides, which bond to the surface. It is a purely chemical reaction. The second scenario proposes that bacteria are necessary for the creation of varnish. As the bacteria begin to grow on the wet, nutrient-poor rocks, they concentrate the iron and manganese and cement the oxides to the surface. It is likely that the process is a combination of the two scenarios, depending upon the environmental factors at the surface of the rock.

Throughout the study of desert varnish, people have tried to use it as a tool. If the varnish developed in a consistent and predictable manner, some proposed a correlation between thickness and age. Researchers discovered, however, that varnish accumulation depended upon climatic conditions. For example, layers with 5 to 15 percent manganese oxides formed during dry periods, and those with 25 to 45 percent developed during wet periods. Those layers in between the extremes formed during periods of transition from very wet to very dry.

This information has allowed some work on comparing the microscopic layers of varnish. In essence, rock varnish layers could be used like tree rings, proxies for wetter and dryer periods. Researchers have established a chart, correlating specific layers with specific time periods, so that if one can match sequences of layers, one can obtain a date when the varnish formed. There is still some controversy with this method.

Perhaps more exciting is that rock varnish could be used to help understand life on other planets. If microbes are definitely involved in the formation of varnish, then any varnish found on Mars, for example, would imply that there was life on Mars. A planned space mission to Mars in 2018 is supposed to contain equipment that can detect rock varnish.

The Dakota Sandstone was the last layer deposited prior to inundation by the midcontinental seaway. Streams slowly crossing a broad coastal plain laid down the Dakota's yellowish-gray sands. In some areas, marine water inundation created lagoons, beaches, and other shoreline features, resulting in gray marine shale and local coal beds. This unit makes up the final hard ledge below the soft Mancos slopes.

The midcontinental sea produced several thousand feet of gray to yellowish-gray fine-grained sediments. The Mancos Shale harbors numerous marine fossils, including oysters, shark teeth, and ammonites. It forms the badlands topography along US 191, north of the Moab Airport. Water-absorbing clays within this rock wreak havoc with roads by cracking pavement and turning dirt roads into impassable gumbo.

Close-up

Upheaval at Upheaval Dome

Upheaval Dome in the Island in the Sky district of Canyonlands National Park is one of the most enigmatic geological features in canyon country. From above, it looks like a bull's-eye target, with concentric rings of colored rock. Up close, it is even more striking, with gray and red upturned and crenulated beds of shale and sandstone.

Geologists have proposed three modes of origin for Upheaval Dome: cryptovolcanic, salt tectonics, or meteor impact. The cryptovolcanic theory developed soon after Upheaval Dome's discovery on Christmas Day 1925. In this theory the dome resulted from the "sudden liberation of pent-up volcanic gases" associated with a shallow intrusion of molten rock. Later studies found no igneous material under Upheaval.

The salt tectonics theory postulates that a massive subterranean blister of salt bowed up the surrounding sediments, most of which have eroded away in the 100 million years since the salt stopped rising. A recent variation on this theme proposes a column of salt pushing up into surrounding sediments and eventually piercing the surface, where it flowed like an ice glacier, and then eroded away.

The meteor-impact theory states that a ⅓-mile-wide meteor crashed into the earth 60 million years ago. Subsequent erosion of a mile of sediment has revealed how the meteor pushed deep into ground and how the rock rebounded in reaction. This is why the rocks in Upheaval Dome point up, as if some force was pushing from below.

Over the last decade, the meteor crater theory has gained more traction with geologists. Proponents have found geologic features that only form under the intense pressure of an extraterrestrial collision. They have also conducted seismic studies, which show that underground faults and folds plunge and bend in accordance with faults and folds found at other known meteor craters.

Both sides admit that their theory does not explain all the features found at Upheaval Dome. Neither has been able to find the knockout blow that allows them to conclusively reject the opposing theory. For the foreseeable future, Upheaval Dome will remain one of North America's most unusual geologic features.

As the sea retreated, other sediments continued to be deposited. These rocks do exist, but they occur north of canyon country in the Book Cliffs and Uinta Basin. Perhaps they were deposited around Moab but later eroded away. Therefore, the Mancos Shale brought to an end the 260-million-year record of deposition in this region.

Paleogene and Neogene Periods (66–2.588 Mya)

Author note: *Recently, those genial folks in charge of naming geologic time periods have eliminated the well-known Tertiary, replacing it with the Paleogene and Neogene. You will still encounter the term Tertiary in many scientific and nonscientific publications.*

Extensive lakes covered large areas of the Colorado Plateau during the Paleogene. One of the most prominent produced the sediments of the Claron Formation, which makes up the orangish red hoodoos of Bryce Canyon National Park. They did not, however, extend into southeastern Utah. A major period of igneous activity initiated 35 million years ago started the mountain forming process. Uplift of the plateau began about 30 million years ago and was followed by rapid downcutting of the Colorado and Green Rivers.

Three mountain ranges rise high above canyon country: the La Sals, Henrys, and Abajos. These mountains, referred to as laccoliths, formed when magma cooled within the earth. As this magma reached a zone of weakness on its upward thrust, it spread laterally between sedimentary layers and, its energy still not diminished, continued to push upward, forming mushroom-like structures. Over time, softer sediments eroded away, leaving behind rounded mountains, which glaciers eventually carved into jagged peaks. Magma emplacement occurred during the following times: La Sal Mountains, 28 to 25 mya; Abajo Mountains, 32 to 22 mya; and Henry Mountains, 31 to 23 mya.

Throughout most of geologic history (up until about 65 mya), the Colorado Plateau was near sea level. About 30 million years ago, though, the region began a new period of uplift. Not until 24 million years or so later did a river began to carve and entrench its path, forming the deep canyons of today. As erosion proceeded deep enough, groundwater leaked into the thick salt diapirs and the salt started to move again.

Quaternary Period (2.588 Mya to Present)

The Colorado Plateau continued to rise. The Colorado River and its tributaries still continued to erode. Salt Valley and Moab Valley formed as water continued to percolate down into and dissolve the salt, facilitating the collapse of the overlying rocks. Other features associated with salt movement include the sandstone fins of Arches National Park and the needles of Canyonlands National Park. Geologists estimate that erosion has removed up to 10,000 feet of sediments in the past few million years.

ECOLOGY

What Is a Desert?

The American Heritage Dictionary defines a desert as "a region rendered barren or partially barren by environmental extremes." Definitions are never that easy in the natural world; too many factors contribute to an ecosystem to allow such a simple declaration.

How then can we define a desert in more practical terminology? Early scientists described a desert merely as a place having an average of 10 inches or fewer of precipitation per year. This is also too simple; Tucson, Arizona, in the heart of the Sonoran Desert, averages more than 10 inches of rain annually, and some grasslands average fewer than 10 inches of annual precipitation.

A definition of what is a desert does revolve around water, but it is a complicated picture. How much precipitation falls in a year affects available water, which in turn is affected by the amount of yearly sunshine, soil types, desiccating winds, and seasonal precipitation.

One key to the amount of moisture available lies in the unpredictable nature of when, where, and how much precipitation falls. Moab averages 7 to 9 inches of precipitation per year, which usually arrives in winter snows when many plants cannot use the water. More rain falls in summer thunderstorms, when much of it washes away; and some comes as spring showers, when it has maximum absorption and use by plants. If it rained across the Colorado Plateau on a consistent, predictable basis, this landscape would be much greener.

A further clue lies in how temperature and sunshine influence water availability. Deserts are lands of extreme temperatures. The generally clear skies and sparse, widespread vegetation allow an estimated 90 percent of available sunlight to reach the earth's surface, compared to 40 percent in more temperate zones. At night, the lack of moisture in the air reverses the process, and 90 percent of the heat escapes. These effects combine to create vast temperature fluctuations on both a daily and yearly basis. In the Moab area the yearly temperature can range from minus 10°F to 110°F. On a daily basis, 40° temperature differences are common.

These extremes affect how much moisture will escape back into the air from plant transpiration and soil evaporation. This process of evapotranspiration is so successful in the desert that areas receiving as little as 5 inches of precipitation may lose 120 inches of moisture back into the atmosphere each year. This places plants under extreme stress; thus, even when precipitation falls, plants may not be able to use it.

The inconsistent availability of water is the limiting factor in desert biological processes. Water determines where plants and animals live, when they reproduce, and what they consume. Observe the desert in springtime and watch the abundance of life that flourishes with spring rains and you will discover the importance and beauty of water.

Knowing how to define deserts doesn't explain why they exist. Warm air absorbs and retains moisture. Cool air releases moisture. This simple phenomenon bears the primary responsibility for desert formation. Whether the air temperature is controlled by air currents, water currents, or mountain ranges, the effects are the same: Moisture is removed from a region, leaving a desert.

Global air circulation patterns produce a region of dryness between 15 and 35 degrees latitude, north and south of the equator. Warm air rises at the equator, cools and releases its moisture, and moves toward the poles. As it approaches the 30 degree parallels, the descending air begins to heat up and increases its ability to retain moisture; like a giant sponge, it sucks the earth dry. This phenomenon is the primary factor in producing the two largest deserts of the world: the Sahara and the Australian.

Global water circulation can also affect air temperatures. Cold ocean currents travel away from the poles alongside continents. As air moves over this water, it is cooled, decreasing its water retention ability. When the air reaches land, it may produce mist or fog but rarely rain. The driest spot on earth, the Atacama Desert on the Pacific coast of Chile, averages 0.5 inch of rain per year. The California current, off the coast of Baja California, produces a similar effect in Baja.

A third agent of change in air masses is the presence of mountain ranges. As warm, moisture-rich air encounters mountains, it rises and cools, leading to a subsequent release of rain or snow. By the time this air has climbed the peaks, it has lost most of its moisture and descends to lower elevations as warm, evaporative air. The Sierra Nevada blocks Pacific Ocean currents and produces the rain shadow responsible for the largest North American desert, the Great Basin Desert.

Deserts are complex and beautiful environments. Plants and animals have evolved and adapted to fill particular niches, but their apparent hardiness belies their fragility. Limited water means that it is a resource more valuable than gold, and small changes can translate into large-scale effects.

This information provides broad details about deserts and desert formation, but if we take a closer look at the area around Moab, the picture becomes even more complicated. Canyon country is not all desert; several other ecosystems exist. These include the large-scale La Sal Mountain and Colorado River communities; the smaller scale Mill Creek, Pack Creek, and Negro Bill Canyon riparian communities; and the Scott M. Matheson Wetlands Preserve.

Close-up

Chert

Chert is a catch-all term that describes many varieties of cryptocrystalline (i.e., crystals can only be seen through a microscope) quartz. It is generally dense and smooth with fractures that resemble broken glass. Chert comes in a wide range of colors including white, red, yellow, black, and green. Varieties of cryptocrystalline quartz include jasper, chalcedony (kal-sed'n-e), agate, onyx, and flint. They cannot be distinguished in the field. Some geologists and archaeologists have proposed that flint should only be used in reference to artifacts such as arrowheads and spear points.

Chert forms in two ways. The first is when quartz is carried in solution in water and precipitated in rock cavities. This type is common, but not restricted, to limestone rocks. Chert also comes from the deposition of microscopic organisms such as radiolarians and diatoms that have quartz skeletons. Sedimentary rocks are the most common place to find chert formed by both methods.

Humans have used chert for thousands of years for tools and projectile points. Some of the earliest artifacts in the Southwest are from cultures that inhabited this region more than 10,000 years ago. Bones and other rocks were the primary tools used to make razor-sharp, long-lasting points.

On the smallest scale are the microclimates: hanging gardens, potholes, and seeps, to name a few. Each one is an important reservoir of increased biodiversity. Several species of shrimp, tadpoles, and beetles thrive in the ephemeral potholes. Douglas fir, aspen, and columbine grow in the protected hanging garden alcoves. These habitats also offer additional food, water, and shelter for other desert organisms.

All of these ecosystems are interrelated. The La Sals contribute additional moisture to the desert by creating summer thunderstorms, through stream runoff, and by recharging groundwater aquifers. The stream canyons provide important travel corridors for large mammals and birds. The recharging of the aquifers provides water for the wetlands, which in turn offer a haven for migrating bird species.

Biological Soil Crusts

Author note: Over the years, these crusts have had many names including cryptobiotic, cryptogamic, and microbiotic. Recently, biological soil crusts has become the preferred term, as the crusts are not hidden and they are full of living organisms.

Biological soil crusts are complex communities composed of cyanobacteria, green algae, lichens, fungi, and mosses that form a living cover on many ground surfaces. They grow in most semiarid and arid ecosystems on this planet, from hot deserts to polar regions. These living crusts are the topsoil of the desert. Although most people think of the crusts as dark and bumpy, they can be reddish or brown and smooth and are nearly invisible when they first develop.

Crusts perform several functions critical to productive desert environments. They stabilize the soil, increase the soil's water absorption, aid in nutrient availability (particularly nitrogen) for vascular plants, and can enhance seedling establishment. Unfortunately, due to their extreme fragility, most of the crusts'

functions are severely curtailed when they are trampled. This problem is further exacerbated by the 15 to 250 years it takes for small areas to recover from being crushed. Large areas may take longer to recover.

Biological crusts are everywhere; therefore, you will damage them if you venture off the trail. If you must walk or ride off marked trails, hop from rock to rock or stick to slickrock and washes. Be creative and think of it as a game to "tiptoe around the crypto." If you are in a group, do not spread out; walk in each other's footsteps. This still damages the crusts, so stay on trails.

Biological soil crusts stabilize soil by sending out a mass of filaments that wind their way both under and on the ground surface, leaving behind a sticky, mucilaginous trail that adheres to soil particles. This trail is produced from the sheaths and filaments of the crusts' major constituent, cyanobacteria. Cyanobacteria, formerly known as blue-green algae, is one of the earth's oldest known life forms. One species of cyanobacteria, *Microcoleus vaginatus*, represents up to 95 percent of the biomass of biological crusts in Utah deserts.

The sheaths and filaments wind their way through the soil, grabbing hold of rock and soil particles. These filaments are inactive when dry, but become active soon after water reaches them. When moistened, numerous filaments spurt out from the *Microcoleus* sheath. As the ground surface dries, these living filaments secrete a polysaccharide material (the sheath) that sticks to the soil components and which, even when dry, firmly adheres to whatever it has encountered during the moisture cycle. Soil crusts build up thousands of these sheaths over time, all active in holding soil and rock particles together.

Another important function of sheaths is also water triggered. Sheaths can swell up to ten times their dry size when wet. Thus the sheaths act as sponges, sopping up and storing the desert's limited rain. In one study at

Arches National Park, water infiltration rates (the amount of water that soaks into the soil) were 90 percent less in trampled areas than in untrammeled areas. This results in less water for plants and increased erosion. The bumpy ground surface also restricts water movement, allowing more water to soak into the ground.

Although these sheaths provide excellent tensile strength (the ability to stretch) in holding the soil together, they cannot withstand the compressional strength (downward crushing) of feet, hooves, or tires. Think of the tubes of a bike frame, or of fiberglass sheaths. They have exceptional tensile strength; they can withstand thousands of miles of punishment. But if you put those tubes into a vise, it does not take much to crush the tubes to a useless mass.

Although plants need nitrogen to live, none can obtain it from the air. They need to obtain it from nitrogen-fixing lichen and bacteria, which remove nitrogen from the air and convert it to a usable form. Some plants have nitrogen-fixing nodules on their roots, but most plants on the Colorado Plateau do not. To obtain nitrogen, many plants rely on biological soil crusts.

A microscopic examination of a cross section of biological soil crust reveals numerous small air holes. These holes play a critical role in soil fertility by letting water and gases flow into the soil, providing space for microorganisms to live and facilitating root penetration. Without these holes, less light would reach the subsurface cyanobacteria, reducing photosynthesis within the soil. This in turn would result in fewer nutrients in an already nutrient-limited system. Without these crusts, most native flowers, shrubs, and trees would not thrive in the desert, and this region would quickly lose its plant diversity.

Cryptos also function as a plant nursery for the desert. Seeds that fall into a crypto patch gain a roothold because the crusts hold moisture, block desiccating winds, and pull nutrients out of the atmosphere. In the words of one researcher, "[Crusts] are the glue holding this place together."

Large-scale destruction of crusts may also lead to alteration of local weather patterns. Trampling by feet, hooves, and vehicles creates loose sand, which is then spread by winds, creating dunes. One small-scale example of dune replacement is the Sand Flats area near the Slickrock Bike Trail, where increased visitation has contributed to widespread crust destruction and a subsequent proliferation of dunes. This increases the surface reflectivity (sand is lighter colored than crusts), or albedo. Instead of the ground absorbing sunlight, it now reflects the sunlight back into the atmosphere. Rising columns of warm, dry air push clouds away, which in turn leads to fewer clouds and less localized rainfall.

This alteration of surface cover can also lead to less water infiltration. Water escapes from the ecosystem instead of remaining to benefit plants and animals. Less water soaks into the ground and less water is available for evaporation, which results in less water available for rainfall. Thus the cycle of land degradation builds on itself.

Some people think that they have seen crusts recover in as little as 3 years. Unfortunately, what they have seen is a minimal recovery of the top 2 to 4 millimeters of the crust. One to two species of cyanobacteria may be present, compared with fourteen to fifteen cyanobacteria species and many lichens, algae, and mosses in healthy crusts. And, more important, the underlying *Microcoleus* sheaths are destroyed and can no longer adhere to soil and rock particles or fix nitrogen.

Remember this when you hike, bike, or drive on biological soil crusts; you don't kill them, but you severely restrict all processes and functions. The recovery process takes from 50 to 250 years. Once the crusts are disturbed, other people follow the tracks, areas start to erode, gullies begin to form, barren sand dunes take over the region, and a productive ecosystem is destroyed.

Biological Soil Crusts

1500X	1500X	300X
YOUNG CRYPTOS: 0 TO 3 YEARS	MIDLIFE CRYPTOS: 3 TO 10 YEARS	MATURE CRYPTOS: 10+ YEARS

Cyanobacteria float through air and fall to the ground, crawl across the surface, or are carried by bugs and animals. They remain on the surface to catch sunlight and photosynthesize for their life processes.

Cyanobacteria secrete sticky sheaths that stick to sand particles. When buried by soil, the cyanobacteria move to the surface, shedding the sheaths below, which in time build up the soil depth. With frost heaving, sheaths form a contorted surface.

Lichens, mosses, fungi grow on surface; water debris and seeds become entrapped in pockets; seeds root, which further strengthens soil.

SHRUBS AND TREES

One of the great botanical features in southern Utah's deserts is that the woody plants generally grow on a human-size scale. In addition, walking or hiking to these plants is easy; no dense forests or snarling vines block your access. These two benefits make the task of getting to know the shrubs and trees a bit easier.

That this desert even has large plants comes as a surprise to some first-time visitors. How could these shrubs and trees survive in a land with so little rain and such high temperatures? Several adaptations in their leaves or roots enable the plants to live here. Almost all desert shrubs have small leaves. The smaller surface area means that less water is lost through transpiration. The few plants with large leaves, like cottonwoods, are limited to riparian ecosystems along washes, streams, and rivers. One plant that does have relatively large leaves (about 1 inch across), the singleleaf ash, has a reduced number of leaves compared to ashes found in wetter climates.

Size is not the only way desert plants have modified their leaves. Some have waxy leaves, which slow transpiration. Others have curled or hairy leaves. Many also drop their leaves during the hottest part of the summer and escape having to deal with being too hot. And finally, two plant groups, the cacti and the conifers, have modified leaves of spines and needles, respectively.

Preventing moisture loss is one problem and obtaining water is another. Many plants have long taproots, which reach deep underground to find water. Others have numerous small roots near the surface that absorb any moisture that reaches the ground. Some plants have taproots and surface roots and can take advantage of practically any water that falls.

Organizing the shrub and tree section presents a problem because many plants grow in several different plant communities. This book restricts itself to plants and animals that roughly inhabit an elevation range of 4,000 to 7,500 feet. The dominant ecosystem within this zone is the piñon-juniper woodland, but within this broad community one can find other communities based on soil type and depth, aspect, and moisture. To make it easier to determine what you are looking at in the field, this section is organized into four broad categories:

1. Salt desert scrub: Characterized by plants that can withstand highly alkaline and saline soils.

2. Riparian or protected: Characterized by plants that live along watercourse banks or that live in restricted habitats like protected canyons or alcoves.

3. Mixed desert scrub: Characterized by sandy and rocky soils. This covers a wide range of plants that may also inhabit the piñon-juniper woodland.

4. Piñon-juniper woodland: The most widespread community. Characterized by plants that grow in rocky soils or straight out of the bedrock in joints and fissures.

Please note: Many plants have edible parts. You should always exercise caution when eating any wild plant because several poisonous plants closely resemble the edible ones.

Scientific names in this section conform to the USDA Plants Database (http://plants.usda .gov/java/), and family names conform to Angiosperm Phylogeny Database (www.mobot .org/mobot/research/apweb/welcome.html).

Salt Desert Scrub

The following plants fall into the salt desert scrub category and are characterized by plants that can withstand highly alkaline and saline soils.

MORMON TEA
Ephedra viridis
Ephedra family (Ephedraceae)
1–5 feet

Most plants photosynthesize through their leaves; Mormon tea does not. It has adapted to a desert environment by reducing its leaves to inconspicuous scale-like parts and photosynthesizing through the chlorophyll in its green, jointed stems.

In the spring, when the plants set seed, they appear to be flowering plants; they are not. Mormon tea is a gymnosperm, the group of nonflowering plants that includes pines and junipers. Ephedras produce small cones with males and females on separate plants.

Males, whose pollen is dispersed by wind, occur on steeper, drier spots, where wind prevails. Females, which require more moisture and nutrients for seed production, occur on wetter sites.

Native people and early pioneers made a medicinal tea from the stems and leaves. Mormon tea contains pseudoephedrine, a drug commonly used in nasal decongestants and closely related to ephedrine. Old World varieties of Ephedra contain ephedrine.

FOUR-WING SALTBUSH
Atriplex canescens
Amaranth family (Amaranthaceae)
2–3 feet

Four-wing saltbush has the widest distribution of any saltbush, growing from South Dakota to Mexico and west to California. It is an important forage plant for a variety of wildlife because the plants are evergreen and lack spines. The common name refers to the four-winged fruit. Four-wing saltbush plants have 1-inch-long linear leaves, in contrast to the more rounded, smaller leaves of the closely related shadscale (*A. confertifolia*).

One defining characteristic of desert ecosystems is that potential evapotranspiration (the amount of moisture escaping back into the air from plant transpiration and soil evaporation) exceeds annual precipitation. If this difference is large enough, then water does not leach salt to great depths and soils can accumulate salt in the root zone. As the name implies, saltbush can survive on these salty soils, although they generally grow on sandy soils and even sand dunes. *Atriplex* sp. pump excess salts into hair-bladders on the leaf surface; eventual rupture of these hairs excretes the salt.

Most plants either have both sexes on the same plant (monoecious: Latin for "one home") or on separate plants (dioecious: Latin for "two homes"). Four-wing saltbush is generally dioecious, but in some situations they may be monoecious or even transsexual and can reverse themselves, switching from male to female and back again.

The Amaranth family recently absorbed the goosefoot family (Chenopodiaceae), other members of which include spinach, beet, and chard.

GREASEWOOD

Sarcobatus vermiculatus

Amaranth family (Amaranthaceae)

3–8 feet

Despite growing in the harsh environment of alkali or saline flats, greasewood has bright green, fleshy leaves and can reach heights of 8 feet. Many native animals forage on the young shoots and use the thorny plant for protection. Some livestock may also eat it, but too much can be toxic. Greasewood survives in soils inhospitable to most plants by having deeply penetrating roots that can reach down to 57 feet to obtain groundwater.

Both male and female floral parts occur on the same plant. To ensure that an individual plant does not self-pollinate, the male stamens mature and dry several weeks before the female pistillate flowers mature. Cross-fertilization leads to greater genetic diversity and thus a greater ability to adapt. (See plateau striped whiptail, page 166, for more information.)

Some people use the term greasewood to refer to creosote bush (*Larrea tridentata*), a ubiquitous plant of hot deserts. *Sarcobatus* refers to the plant's thorny growth: *sarkos* (fleshy) and *batos* (thorn).

RUSSIAN THISTLE
Salsola tragus
Amaranth family (Amaranthaceae)
Up to 3 feet or taller

Most people can identify mature Russian thistle, also known as tumbleweed, which looks like the skeleton of a normal shrub and can range in size from a soccer ball to a Volkswagen Beetle. Fewer people recognize the seedling and juvenile plants' bright green, succulent, grass-like shoots, which are usually red or purple striped. The inconspicuous green flowers grow at axils (where leaves branch off the stem) of the upper leaves, each one accompanied by a pair of spiny bracts. Mice, bighorn sheep, pronghorn, and some people eat the tender shoots.

As the plants roll down a desert road, they disperse upward of 250,000 seeds per plant. They are unusual in that they lack any protective coat or stored food reserves. Instead, each seed is a coiled, embryonic plant wrapped in a thin membrane. To survive winter without a warm coat, the plant does not germinate until warm weather arrives.

When moisture hits and the temperature is between 28°F and 110°F, the seed uncoils and germinates, shooting out two needle-like leaves. By autumn the plant has reached maximum size, flowered, and begun to dry out. A specialized layer of cells in the stem facilitates the easy break between plant and root and the journey begins anew.

Like many alien weeds, tumbleweed exploited the destruction of native ecosystems. When farmers removed prairie grasses, they created a perfect environment, smooth and flat, for a plant that could roll across the landscape dispersing seeds. Herbicides now control the spread of Russian thistle by disrupting the maturation process of the plant.

Native to the arid steppes of the Ural Mountains in Russia, tumbleweeds were first reported in the United States around 1877 in Bon Homme County, South Dakota, apparently transported in flaxseed imported by Ukrainian farmers. Within two decades it had tumbled into a dozen states and by 1900 had reached the Pacific Coast.

SHADSCALE
Atriplex confertifolia
Amaranth family (Amaranthaceae)
1–3 feet

BROOM SNAKEWEED
Gutierrezia sarothrae
Sunflower family (Asteraceae)
Up to 3 feet

Shadscale grows on hard, stony alkaline soils throughout the arid West. It is often the dominant plant in such environments. Ranchers regard it as important winter browse for domestic grazers. Shadscale's low growth, usually less than 3 feet tall, and edible fruits and leaves make the plant an important food source for small rodents and jackrabbits. The small rounded leaves are gray and often tinged with red. Unlike the closely related four-wing saltbush, shadscale has two-winged seeds. Spiny saltbush, another common name, refers to the pointed branches that protect the plant from herbivores.

Like rabbitbrush, snakeweed produces yellow flowers in the fall and commonly occurs along roadsides and overgrazed or disturbed soils. These two plants are often mistaken for each other, though snakeweed is generally half the size of rabbitbrush, has slender stems, and flowers with both rays and disks (see page 46 for discussion of rays and disks). Snakeweed leaves are 1 to 3 inches long and often sticky.

All plants adapt to their environment, and snakeweed is no exception. In areas where spring precipitation predominates (north), snakeweed plants develop a high root density in the topsoil to help them obtain and use the moisture from light rains. By contrast, southern populations develop deeper and thicker roots to obtain water stored from fall and winter precipitation, which allows for survival during drier springs. A corollary to this deep root development is that these southern plants have larger canopies and drop fewer leaves during the summer than their northern counterparts.

The generic name refers to Pedro Gutierrez, a nineteenth-century correspondent for the Botanic Garden in Madrid.

BUSH ENCELIA
Encelia frutescens
Sunflower family (Asteraceae)
1–4 feet

RABBITBRUSH
Ericameria nauseosa
Sunflower family (Asteraceae)
1–7 feet

Most shrubby composites bloom in summer or fall; bush encelia is an exception, flowering in late spring instead. The yellow flowers grow at the end of a several-inch-long yellowish stem. Unlike other desert species of *Encelia,* bush encelia does not have hairy leaves, which increase light reflection, resulting in lower leaf temperatures. The plant instead depends upon higher water loss through its leaves (transpirational cooling) to survive in hotter weather. Although it often grow along roadsides, bush encelia also can be found on talus and slickrock associated with blackbrush and shadscale.

The genus name honors Christopher Encel, an English botanist who wrote a book on oak galls in 1577.

In late summer a yellow border begins to appear along many roads in the arid southwest. Taking advantage of extra roadside runoff, rabbitbrush quickly colonizes this man-made environment, as well as riparian habitats and the piñon-juniper zone. They are the most conspicuous plant in the fall and easily identified by their abundant flowers, 3-inch-long linear leaves, and strong scent.

Rabbitbrush's color and fragrance also attract numerous insects and spiders. Some come to feed on the abundant nectar while others come to feed on these pollinators. Two common rabbitbrush dwellers are the golden crab spider and the red-and-black longhorn beetle. The spiders do not build webs; instead, they catch their quarry with a quick rush followed by a paralyzing bite. Rabbitbrush was formerly in the genus *Chrysothamnus.*

Riparian or Protected

The following section is characterized by plants that live along watercourse banks or that live in restricted habitats like protected canyons or alcoves.

POISON IVY
Toxicodendron rydbergii
Cashew family (Anacardiaceae)
Up to 3 feet

Poison ivy was one of the earliest plants noted by the first colonists of the United States. Captain John Smith is credited with bestowing the common name because he thought it resembled English or Boston ivy. He also observed that the plant "caused itchynge and blisters."

At least ten species and subspecies, ranging from eastern Asia to Guatemala, bear the common name poison ivy. Our local representative is known as *Toxicodendron rydbergii*. The generic epithet comes from the Greek *toxikos* (poisonous) and *dendron* (tree). The species name honors Per Axel Rydberg (1860–1930), a Swedish-born botanist who wrote two important books on the flora of the Rocky Mountains.

Like the better known eastern species (*T. radicans*), *T. rydbergii* has three leaflets growing together, orange to red fall foliage, and small, cream-colored berries. The western variety grows as a small shrub and does not have a viny structure. The local species grows in protected or moist environments. Locations to be aware of include hanging gardens, streamsides, and shady canyons.

Plants can reach heights of 10 feet or more.

More than 2 million people per year have a reaction to poison ivy. Symptoms most often occur between 24 and 48 hours after exposure. The active ingredient, urushiol oil, *T. vernicifluum,* occurs in the sap, and breaking or crushing the plant is usually necessary to induce infection, although touching the leaves can also trigger a reaction. In sensitive people, as little as 0.001 milligram can cause a reaction.

"Treatment" for poison ivy dermatitis ranges across the spectrum. Some more novel approaches include kerosene, buttermilk, strychnine, and everyone's favorite medicine, cream and marshmallows.

Washing with soap and water immediately after touching a plant is the recommended first line of therapy, although added moisturizers and oils in typical soap may actually spread the urushiol oil. Tecnu Oak-N-Ivy Brand Outdoor Skin Cleanser, a mixture of organic solvents and wood pulp byproducts, does effectively wash off urushiol. It was originally developed in 1961 to remove radioactive fallout dust.

NETLEAF HACKBERRY
Celtis reticulata
Hemp family (Cannabaceae)
15–20 feet

RUSSIAN OLIVE
Elaeagnus angustifolia
Oleaster family (Elaeagnaceae)
Up to 40 feet

Netleaf hackberry ranges from riparian woodlands to rocky uplands, but grows best in sheltered areas, such as washes, rocky outcrops, and narrow canyons. In these microhabitats this small tree exploits the surface and subsurface water—especially the water that accumulates in rock cracks. They seldom form large groves, usually occurring as small or highly localized thickets.

Netleaf hackberry receives its common name and specific epithet from the netlike veins found on the leaves. The toothed, asymmetrical leaves feel like crunchy, fine-grained sandpaper. A wide variety of animals use hackberry trees for cover and nesting sites. Birds and mammals eat the reddish, fleshy fruit.

Russian olive, an alien species, germinates in a wide range of soil types over a wide range of seasons. The trees normally become established in or near a cottonwood stand. Over time the shade-tolerant Russian olives can supplant the native cottonwoods and willows, creating dense thickets of thorny trees that can exclude wildlife. Fewer insects are also found in the thickets, which means fewer insectivorous birds. In addition, many cavity-nesting animals lose potential sites when Russian olives grow instead of cottonwoods.

These 20- to 40-foot-tall trees, which take up to 10 years to mature to seed production, are easily recognizable by their thorns and lance-shaped gray-green leaves. Yellow flowers appear in spring, producing a strong odor relished by few. In contrast to the tree's negative effects, the sweet fruit provides a food source for birds throughout the winter.

Russian olive was introduced into this country as early as the 1850s as a windbreak and for erosion control. It escaped cultivation in Utah around 1924 and is now considered to be a noxious weed in some counties.

DESERT OLIVE
Forestiera pubescens
Olive family (Oleaceae)
6 feet or taller

DOUGLAS FIR
Pseudotsuga menziesii
Pine family (Pineaceae)
Up to 130 feet

Coyote bush, New Mexican forestiera, or desert olive, as it is also known, grows along riparian corridors, often forming dense thickets. In spring, the large shrub produces yellow flowers that lack petals. Unisexual and bisexual flowers are on the same plant. Two to four stamens give the flower its yellow color. Simple, opposite leaves appear after flowering. In summer and fall, birds visit the plant seeking the tart, blue-black fruit. When foxes and coyotes eat the berries, they produce purple-stained, seed-filled fecal matter, often found far from its riparian source.

The generic name refers to Charles Le Forestier, an early nineteenth-century French physician and naturalist.

Douglas fir grows in a few scattered alcoves and other protected sites throughout the region. Although only a handful exist, they provide important insight into the last ice age. From evidence gathered in pack rat middens, ecologists propose that Douglas fir and limber pine (*Pinus flexilis*) were the dominant trees in canyon country between 20,000 and 12,000 years ago.

Two types of relict communities occur in canyon country: vestigial remnants of formerly widespread flora or fauna that have persisted through the warming and drying of the intermountain region, or areas that have not been affected by human activities, particularly livestock grazing. By definition most of these are small-scale ecosystems. Isolated buttes and mesas contain grasses and biological soil crusts that have never been grazed. Douglas fir and aspen that grow at low elevations are forest islands in a desert sea.

The available clues point to continuous habitation over the last 20,000 years. The limited data from pack rat middens shows Douglas fir growing abundantly near present-day locations as recently as 6,000 years ago. The modern trees mostly grow in well-protected, north-facing sites that have a source of water—an environment that resembles ice age climates. Look for their cones with their characteristic three-pronged bracts.

BIRCHLEAF BUCKTHORN
Rhamnus betulifolia
Buckthorn family (Rhamnaceae)
Up to 15 feet

Birchleaf buckthorn generally occurs in the mountainous areas of the northern Sonoran and Chihuahuan Deserts, but creeps up along the Colorado River into southeast Utah. It grows along riparian areas, and favorable microhabitats including overhangs and cracks in rocks. Buckthorn has 3- to 4-inch-long, dark green leaves with deep veins and finely toothed margins. The older bark is smooth and gray, whereas young twigs are greenish to reddish. Many birds eat the green to purple-black berries.

FRÉMONT'S COTTONWOOD
Populus fremontii
Willow family (Salicaceae)
Up to 90 feet

Cottonwoods once formed extensive stands on riparian corridors throughout the Southwest, lending their Spanish name, *alamo,* to many places. At present, dam building, livestock grazing, extensive clear-cutting, and stream channelization have reduced the original forests by 90 percent. On the other hand, because branch cuttings root easily in moist soil and the trees grow quickly, many new cottonwoods have been planted throughout human-populated areas. Males are the preferred sex to plant because female plants' seeds release white cotton, which many people dislike.

Cottonwoods affect the entire riparian community. Their deep roots prevent erosion and keep soils porous, allowing water to percolate downward. The large trees provide nesting sites for great blue herons, ravens, and hawks; dam building material for beavers; and holes for owls, raccoons, and other cavity dwellers.

Three species of cottonwood grow throughout the region; Frémont's cottonwood is the most common. It has large, triangular leaves with rounded teeth. In fall they turn golden yellow. The other two species, narrowleaf cottonwood (*P. angustifolia*) and lanceleaf cottonwood (*P. x acuminata*), have narrower leaves and usually occur at higher elevations, generally above 6,500 feet. *P. x acuminata* is a hybrid of crosses of *P. fremontii* and *P. angustifolia*.

According to one cattleman, cottonwoods provided a natural remedy for bad water consumed on the trail. Cowboys would take the bark, boil it, and consume the tea, which is "a hell of a drink, a wonderful astringent, and a bitter dose."

COYOTE WILLOW
Salix exigua
Willow family (Salicaceae)
6–9 feet

Along with cottonwoods, willows are the dominant native plant in streamside (riparian) environments. Both plants require abundant water near the ground's surface. Willows, unlike cottonwoods, are insect pollinated, a feature not commonly associated with small-flowered plants. They reproduce by seeds and through root suckering.

Coyote willows have long, narrow, toothed leaves and rarely reach heights of more than 10 feet. Gray hairs cover the top side of the leaves. Apetalous flowers occur in catkins, short spikes of inconspicuous flowers. The plants are dioecious; male catkins are more prominent due to silky hairs. Beaver, deer, and livestock forage on the plants.

Several species of *Salix* grow in the riparian habitats of the Southwest; they are notoriously hard to tell apart. Another common species, the peachleaf willow (*S. amygdaloides*), reaches heights of 30 feet. All species contain salicin in the bark and stems. When eaten, this compound breaks down into salicylic acid, the base ingredient of aspirin.

BOXELDER
Acer negundo
Soapberry family (Sapindaceae)
12–38 feet

Although boxelders commonly grow along streambanks throughout the Southwest, they may be more familiar to people as an ornamental tree in towns, where people desire their fast growth and yellow fall foliage. The common name came about because people used to box, or tap, the trees for their sap. There is some debate about the origin of *Acer*, the ancient name for maples. "Ac" means "sharp," and is used in a variety of plant names, such as Acacia, and more common words, such as acerbic. Some believe that the reference to sharp comes from the pointed leaves, whereas others state that it refers to the use of maple in the heads of pikes and lances.

Similar to many other plant species (see greasewood and four-wing saltbush), male plants dominate in drier, nonstreamside habitats, and females thrive on wetter sites. This distribution has led to distinct growth habits. Males are more efficient at using water on both a long-term and short-term scale but have a lower rate of photosynthesis. Therefore males are more drought resistant but are outcompeted in a moist habitat because females grow faster. A further advantage of drier sites for males is that pollen spreads farther and more easily on drier sites than wetter sites.

TAMARISK
Tamarix chinensis
Tamarisk family (Tamaricaceae)
Up to 20 feet

Salt-cedar, or tamarisk as it is more commonly known, was introduced into the United States from the Middle East in the early 1800s for erosion control. Nurseries in California began to sell the plant in 1861, and by 1880 wild tamarisk appeared in Utah. One geographer estimated that tamarisks moved up the rivers at a rate of 12 miles per year. They still are a prevalent streamside plant, characterized by minute, scaly leaves; fragrant, white to pinkish flowers; and dense, woody growth.

Tamarisks have several adaptations that helped the plants spread so far, so quickly. A single mature plant can produce 500,000 seeds each year, which can germinate within 24 hours of becoming wet. Tamarisks bloom from April through October, and seeds can establish themselves in fall when other species' seeds are not present. Once they become established, tamarisks have further adaptations to resist invasion by other species. A dense thicket of tamarisk has little bare soil underneath in which other plants can set seeds. In addition, tamarisks excrete salt from leaf openings, which falls to the ground, creating a hypersaline condition that kills grasses and seedlings.

Despite all these adaptations, tamarisk may not be able to maintain its dominance over native willows and cottonwoods. Some researchers now believe that tamarisk has reached its maximum distribution. At this point, though, we only have about 50 years of data on tamarisks, much of it conjectural. Ecologists are just starting to learn about the tamarisk life cycle and its place in the riparian ecosystem. Tamarisk invasion occurred at a time when humans were significantly altering western waterways. Will it continue to thrive in its current state or will native species reestablish themselves? Fifty years is not a long time in the natural world.

A different species of tamarisk, *T. aphylla*, grows more as a tree, up to 65 feet tall with a 3-foot-diameter trunk. Known as athel, it is not considered to be an invasive species. They are common at Lake Powell.

Close-up

Biological Control of Tamarisk

Ecologists have long known the downside of the pervasive invasion of tamarisk. The plants increase soil salinity, dry up springs, lower water tables, make wildfire more frequent, and outcompete native plants. One study estimated the water costs of tamarisk annually at $133 million to $285 million. Because of these drastic changes, there has been a widespread attempt to control and/or eliminate tamarisk. Attempts have included herbicide, hand cutting and stump removal, and bulldozing and burning, but they have either been too expensive, too labor intensive, or too ineffective.

In the 1980s, ecologist Jack DeLoach begin to investigate the possibility of using native enemies to biologically control tamarisk. His team's research found that a species of beetle, *Diorhabda carinulata,* completely defoliated tamarisk in its native habitat. They are part of the leaf beetle family, Chrysomdelidae, other members of which have been used successfully for controlling St. Johns wort and purple loosestrife.

After determining that the beetles did not feed on any other native plants, they were released in open fields in six states beginning in 1999. The yellow- and black-striped bugs are now found on an estimated 10 million acres of land in southern Utah and western Colorado.

At about 0.25 inch in length, tamarisk beetles are not conspicuous, but they can gather in immense groups, attracted by the plant's aroma and by the males' pheromones. Predators include birds, assassin bugs, and ants. A female tamarisk beetle can lay up to 700 eggs during her two-month life. The larvae hatch in a week, eating voraciously until they descend to the ground and pupate into yellow cocoons, which develop into adults about a week later.

Adults, which don't fly well till the temperature reaches 80°F, start to enter dormancy when the days shorten to 14.5 hours of sunlight. They emerge in spring when tamarisk have begun to sprout new leaves. Females can lay up to four generations of eggs in a single season, though two or three is more common.

Tamarisk beetles generally do not kill tamarisk in a single season. Defoliation prevents plants from photosynthesizing, but they can produce again in the same or following season. With continued defoliation over several years, the plants usually cannot recover and die. Defoliation also may make it easier for land managers to come in and remove the tamarisk.

One of the best places to see these effects is around Moab. Anyone traveling in the area can see miles of defoliated and/or dead tamarisk along riparian areas. It remains difficult, however, to measure the success of releasing tamarisk beetles.

Defoliation of the plants does not necessarily mean success. Plants can produce new leaves, and if the beetles don't remain and eat the new foliage, you have a bunch of ugly tamarisk, soon to spring back to life. If the plants die, then new tamarisk, or other nonnative invasives such as knapweed or thistles, might simply replace the previous invaders.

Animal species see the effects, too. Species such as the southwestern willow flycatcher, an endangered species, have thrived in the tamarisk. Will their numbers drop? How will other species of birds and reptiles respond to tamarisk defoliation and death?

The best definition of success I heard is reducing the number of tamarisk plants so that the ecological community is more in balance and the plants are no longer so widely dominant in the ecosystem.

The introduction of tamarisk beetles is an ongoing experiment writ large across a vast swath of landscape. We have just a few years of data for what will be a long-term process of change. Stay tuned.

Mixed Desert Scrub

The following plants are characterized by existing in sandy and rocky soils. This covers a wide range of plants that may also inhabit the piñon-juniper woodland.

WINTERFAT

Krascheninnikovia lanata
Amaranth family (Amaranthaceae)
Mostly 3 feet or taller

The common name alludes to the plant's importance as a winter browse for wildlife and livestock. Heavy overgrazing, though, has drastically reduced the small shrub's abundance throughout its range. Winterfat can form relatively pure stands but is more often associated with sagebrush, rabbitbrush, piñon pine, and junipers. Like many desert shrubs, winterfat depends upon an extensive fibrous root system and a taproot that can penetrate as deep as 25 feet to survive drought conditions.

The plants produce inconspicuous flowers in the summer. Cottony hairs, which cover the ripened fruits and soften the look of the pointy branches, aid in wind pollination. The scientific name honors eighteenth-century Russian traveler and naturalist Stepan Krascheninnikov, who made extensive studies in Siberia.

SKUNKBUSH

Rhus trilobata
Cashew family (Anacardiaceae)
2–8 feet

Like other members of the cashew family, which includes poison ivy, pistachio nuts, and mangos, skunkbush leaves turn rusty red in autumn. These large shrubs are easy to identify by their trilobed leaves, which when crushed emit a distinct odor (hence skunkbush) disliked by many people. Unlike poison ivy, the leaves do not produce allergic reactions. Another name, lemonbush, refers to the flavor of the red, sticky berries. Many desert travelers add the corn-kernel-size, vitamin C–rich fruit to their water bottles.

Despite its normally gnarled and crooked growth habit, many people used, and still use, the branches for arrows and baskets. Cutting back or burning the plant stimulates the growth of straight, supple shoots.

SAND SAGEBRUSH
Artemisia filifolia
Sunflower family (Asteraceae)
Up to 5 feet

LONG-FLOWER SNOWBERRY
Symphoricarpos longiflorus
Honeysuckle family (Caprifoliaceae)
Up to 3 feet

The common name, sand sagebrush, refers to this shrub's propensity to grow in sandy soils. Another common name, old man sage, alludes to the grayish hairlike leaves. Although not common, these medium-size plants can form large stands in sandy areas.

A debate exists about whom the generic epithet commemorates. Some claim Queen Artemisia, the wife of Mausoleus, who supposedly discovered the medicinal qualities of the genus. Others prefer Artemis, the Greek goddess of the moon and hunt.

Snowberry plants produce a creamy white berry in autumn. Many birds and small mammals consume the pea-size berries. The 1- to 3-foot-tall shrubs grow on dry, rocky slopes throughout the entire region. Like the closely related Utah honeysuckle (*Lonicera utahensis*), the $1/2$-inch-long tubular flowers grow in groups of two. The honeysuckle's fruit is black or red.

Another species of snowberry also grows across the region. Mountain snowberry (*S. oreophilus*) generally grows at higher elevations, although it may creep down into sagebrush regions. It also has white fruit. Both species are deciduous.

FENDLERBUSH
Fendlera rupicola
Hydrangea family (Hydrangeaceae)
3–6 feet

FROSTED MINT
Poliomintha incana
Mint family (Laminaceae)
1–4 feet

Fendlerbush is an inconspicuous shrub until it blooms in April and May when it produces showy, white four-petaled flowers. Deer and bighorn sheep browse on the narrow, 1-inch-long leaves. The plants grow on rocky slopes, preferring cracks and crevices. When the roots push down into cracks, they begin a process known as biological weathering, where plants and/or animals contribute to the chemical and mechanical breakdown of rocks.

Formerly a member of the saxifrage family, fendlerbush honors August Fendler (1813–1883), a German-born naturalist who was one of the first botanists to collect plants in New Mexico and Texas.

This fragrant shrub is also known as purple sage. Crushing its hirsute leaves releases the aromatic oils, a characteristic of the mint family. The frosted appellation refers to the hairy flowers.

Frosted mint also displays two other aspects of the mint family. It has square stems with opposite leaves, and the flowers are bilaterally symmetrical. Looking straight into a mint flower reveals an almost mouth-like shape with the lower three petals fused to form a lower lip, the stamens protruding like teeth, and the top two petals united into a stiff upper lip. Purple dots on the lower lip act as guides for pollinators seeking the nectar within.

SINGLELEAF ASH
Fraxinus anomala
Olive family (Oleaceae)
4–13 feet

CORYMBED BUCKWHEAT
Eriogonum corymbosum
Buckwheat family (Polygonaceae)
Up to 4 feet

Unlike other ashes, singleleaf ash trees only have one leaf per stem. This adaptation is helpful in an environment of high temperatures and little rain. Fewer leaves mean less surface area available for water loss through transpiration.

Small, bright green shoots begin to sprout soon after the snow disappears. They eventually develop into 1- to 1$^1/_2$-inch-long leaves. The inconspicuous flowers appear soon after the leaves develop and turn into winged fruit in late spring. Despite the summer heat, the leaves remain until they turn a brilliant yellow-gold in fall. This ash grows in piñon-juniper woodlands, blackbrush flats, and mixed desert scrublands. *Fraxinus* originates from the Greek word phraxis, which means "parting" or "splitting," most likely in reference to ease of splitting the ash wood.

Corymbed buckwheat has a sporadic distribution from southern Wyoming through Utah to Arizona, growing on clayey, sandy, and silty soils. Some varieties produce yellow flowers, but most have white blossoms and all bloom in late summer to fall. Individual flowers are inconspicuous and grow in a terminal umbel that gives the impression of a large flowering head. In good years this buckwheat superficially resembles a giant head of cauliflower.

Corymbed buckwheat, also known as Frémont's buckwheat, grows in mixed desert scrub or piñon-juniper communities. The Republican Party's initial presidential candidate, John C. Frémont, was the first to collect a specimen of this buckwheat. He was in Colorado on his third expedition to California in 1845. His pioneering explorations earned Frémont the name "The Pathfinder."

BLACKBRUSH

Coleogyne ramosissima
Rose family (Rosaceae)
Up to 3 feet

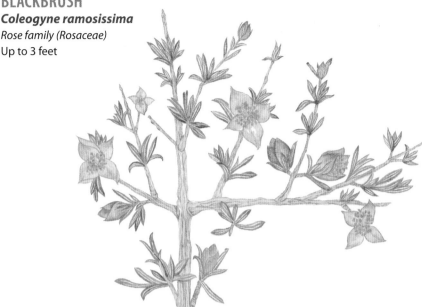

Blackbrush often forms extensive, practically monotypic stands on shallow soils between 3,500 and 6,000 feet along the valleys of the Colorado River and adjacent drainages in southeast Utah. This shrub grows on benchlands with shallow soils, avoiding bottomlands where cold air accumulates. Growth and flowering occur in the vernal months, although summer precipitation can produce an additional growth period. To save water, blackbrush drops its older, outermost leaves at the onset of its summer dormancy.

The generally round and spiny plant rarely reaches heights of more than 3-feet tall. Despite its thorny nature, blackbrush forms a major part of the late fall and winter diet of bighorn sheep, which eat the narrow $1/2$-inch-long leaves. Few other animals consume the plant.

The common name alludes to the shrub's dark color after rainstorms. *Coleogyne* refers to the sheath (*koleos*) that surrounds the ovary (*gyne*). *Ramosissima* comes from the Greek for many branched. Blackbrush has opposite branches, unlike the alternate branches of the similar-looking curlleaf mountain mahogany (*Cercocarpus ledifolius*).

Piñon-Juniper Woodland

The most widespread community. Characterized by plants that grow in rocky soils or straight out of the bedrock in joints and fissures.

BIG SAGEBRUSH
Artemisia tridentata
Sunflower family (Asteraceae)
4–7 feet

To many people sagebrush evokes the arid West, scenting the air with its pungent aroma. It grows from Nebraska to California and from New Mexico to Montana, the widest distribution of any North American shrub. The aromatic plant now covers about half its historic acreage.

Sagebrush is a crucial member of the steppe lands of the arid west. In this community of short-statured plants, sagebrush functions as the overstory. It provides a protected microhabitat for seedling establishment and for many small animals ranging from sagebrush sheepmoths (black and white, $2^3/_4$- to $3^5/_8$-inch-wide wings with yellowish body, whose caterpillars only feed on sagebrush: *Hemileuca hera*) to sage grouse (*Centrocercus urophasianus*). Sagebrush destruction has helped push many of the animals that depend on it into a downward population trend, and some may be proposed for inclusion on the federal list of Endangered and Threatened Wildlife.

FRÉMONT'S MAHONIA
Mahonia fremontii
Barberry family (Berberidaceae)
4–10 feet

Frémont's mahonia flowers produce a scent of intoxicating proportions. The yellow flowers have a confusing structure, with different parts variously interpreted as petal-like sepals and petal-like stamens. Furthermore, the pattern is based on a series of whorls consisting of three floral parts, which is unusual for a dicotyledonous plant (dicot). Edible, tangy berries appear after the spring flowering ends. Like other members of the barberry family, the leaves are spine-tipped.

Mahonia seeds can germinate over a wide range of temperatures, including temperatures below those that are tolerated by many other shrubs. This allows the plant's seeds to germinate in late winter and early spring, when soil moisture is highest. It gives Frémont's mahonia seedlings an advantage over other plants that germinate in mid- to late spring.

Bernard M'Mahon was an American horticulturist. Thomas Jefferson gave a large proportion of seeds from Lewis and Clark's expedition to M'Mahon, which he sold as novelties. Many plants in the West bear John C. Frémont's name, an indication of his widespread exploration and collecting in the 1840s.

Galls

One of the best ways to survive in the desert is to remain out of the sun, surrounded by a protective cover. This works quite well especially if someone else goes to the effort of creating your home and providing your food, which is essentially what happens in insect plant galls. Galls are tumerous growths on stems, flowers, fruits, and leaves. They result from an insect injecting eggs into the plant. Galls can be fuzzy and white, scaled like a mini artichoke, shaped like peppercorns, round like a ping-pong ball, flattened like a pancake, or even more bizarre shapes. Each one is or was home to an insect larvae.

Most gall-forming insects are midges (Family Cecidomyiidae), fruit flies (Family Tephritidae), and wasps (Family Cynipae [more than 800 species]), generally less than ¼ inch long, each of which exploits a specific plant species or even subspecies. Galls start to grow after a female deposits an egg. Upon hatching, the larvae begins to feed on its host, which reacts to the invader by altering its growth pattern to try to isolate and wall off the insect. Researchers believe that saliva secreted by the larvae triggers the plants' defensive reactions and growth of the gall. Larvae often overwinter on the plant before pupating into an adult and chewing an exit hole out of the gall.

Galls generally do not cause significant damage to a plant. Some are valuable to humans, including certain oak galls, often called oak apples, which historically were used to manufacture ink. Native peoples have used rabbitbrush galls for toothaches and stomach problems and smoked creosote galls. Still other galls and their larvae may serve as home or food to even smaller insects, as well as birds.

In canyon country, rabbitbrush, big sagebrush, oaks, saltbush, and junipers often feature a variety of galls. At least twenty-one insect species form galls on rabbitbrush, including twelve fruit flies and nine midges, which also attack sagebrush.

Sample Galls

Wooly stem gall midge (*Asphondylia floccosa*)—Produce large, white, cottony galls on shadscale.

Sagebrush plum gall midge (*Rhopalmyia calvipomum*)—Reddish, smooth, globular galls on bigleaf sage.

Juniper gall midge (*Walshomyia* sp.)—Pineapple cone-like, with green bracts below and silvery gray in the center on junipers.

Oak gall wasp (*Andricus* sp.)—Round galls may be smooth, rough, singular, clustered, tan, red, or spotted depending on which cynipid wasp is responsible.

UTAH JUNIPER
Juniperus osteosperma
Cypress family (Cupressaceae)
Up to 35 feet

OAK
Quercus species
Beech family (Fagaceae)
Up to 30 feet

Two species of juniper, Utah and one-seed (*J. monosperma*), grow throughout the 4,500- to 7,000-foot range. They are not easy to tell apart, but one-seed berries usually are smaller (pea versus gumball) and the plants are shrubbier with multiple branches growing from the base. The light blue berries are not true berries but modified cones wrapped in a drought-resistant waxy coating. Berries from the common juniper (*J. communis*), which grows throughout the Western Hemisphere and at higher elevations in canyon country, are used for flavoring gin.

The tree's most characteristic feature—gnarled, dead-looking limbs—reveals one of juniper's adaptations to arid living. In times of drought, the plant can shut off water to some of its branches. Those limbs will eventually die, but the rest of the plant will continue to grow and produce seeds. The Utah juniper and piñon pine make up the most prevalent plant community, the piñon-juniper woodland, across the Southwest.

Oaks are a notoriously promiscuous group of plants with numerous species interbreeding. This creates a conundrum for botanists attempting to ascertain which species is which. In the field, location often provides the best indicator. Three species occur in Utah. Shinnery oak (*Q. havardii*) generally grows in sand dune areas, where it stabilizes wind-blown soil. Gambel's oak (*Q. gambelii*), the most widespread species in the Southwest, is found in higher and cooler spots, forming a belt in the Colorado Plateau laccolithic mountains between 6,500 and 9,500 feet. Both species are deciduous and reproduce clonally. The one evergreen species, shrub live-oak (*Q. turbinella*), mostly occurs south of this area.

Oak's edible seeds and leaves act as a magnet attracting many animals. Deer, porcupines, and caterpillars forage on the leaves. Woodpeckers, scrub jays, and chipmunks store the fatty acorns for winter use. Many other birds come for the abundant insect populations.

Quercus is a Latin term for "beautiful tree." Valery Havard traveled in Texas as a botanist with the US Army in the late 1800s. See longnose leopard lizard (pg. 161) for information on William Gambel.

PIÑON PINE
Pinus edulis
Pine family (Pinaceae)
Up to 35 feet

UTAH SERVICEBERRY
Amelanchier utahensis
Rose family (Rosaceae)
6–15 feet

Along with junipers, piñon pine forms the dominant ecosystem across much of the Colorado Plateau at elevations between 5,000 and 7,500 feet. This community is known as the p-j woodland or pygmy forest. Piñons, which are more drought intolerant, generally grow in the higher portion of the zone. Both species rarely exceed 20 feet in height and may take 150 years to reach that point. Piñons are easy to recognize by their rounded crown and irregular shape. The short needles occur in clusters of two.

The specific epithet, *edulis,* refers to the edible nuts, which contain over 3,000 calories per pound. Trees do not produce cones each year; a bumper crop occurs only every 3 to 7 years. Like many other conifers, piñon pines have "mast" years of high seed production followed by years of minimal seed output. Masting is a defense against predation; most seeds are not eaten during masting, although many may be cached.

Because masting does not occur regularly, animals cannot adapt and plan to have larger broods to take advantage of the extra food. Or, if they are rapid reproducers, their population will crash in the years following a mast, when food resources are slim.

Utah serviceberry is another inconspicuous shrub until spring when its white, five-petaled flowers open. A sweet-smelling fragrance helps attract numerous pollinators. The upper surfaces of the toothed leaves are hairy and have prominent veins. The leaves emerge after the flowers.

The purple berries ripen in fall. Lewis and Clark, along with many who later crossed America, mixed the ground fruit of this species, or one of its relatives, with buffalo meat and fat to make pemmican. Meriwether Lewis supposedly mistook serviceberry for mountain ash. His corruption of the generic name of the ash, *Sorbus,* led to a common pronunciation "sarvisberry."

MOUNTAIN MAHOGANY
Cercocarpus species
Rose family (Rosaceae)
1$\frac{1}{2}$–7 feet

Alderleaf Mountain Mahogany

Littleleaf Mountain Mahogany

Three species of mountain mahogany grow in southern Utah. Alderleaf mountain mahogany (*C. montanus*) has wedge-shaped, deciduous leaves that are toothed at the end and sparingly gray silky above. Curlleaf mountain mahogany (*C. ledifolius*) resembles littleleaf mountain mahogany (*C. intricatus*) but has longer (greater than $\frac{1}{2}$ inch) leaves and is much larger overall. Both species are good winter browse for deer and elk.

Littleleaf mountain mahogany usually occurs in isolated patches on warm, dry rocky ridges or slopes. It grows amongst piñon and juniper and is often mistaken for blackbrush. Both plants have short (less than $\frac{1}{2}$ inch), dark green, slightly curled leaves, but mountain mahogany leaves are shinier, its branches are alternate instead of opposite, and it can be a much larger plant.

Like the tropical mahoganies (*Swietenia* sp.), southwestern mountain mahoganies have extremely hard wood.

CLIFFROSE

Purshia mexicana
Rose family (Rosaceae)
1¹/₂–8 feet

During the vernal months cliffrose is one of the noisiest plants in canyon country; its strikingly aromatic flowers attract numerous bees. One can even detect the odor while driving by in a car. Flowering begins in April with branches closest to the ground blossoming first. A secondary blooming season may occur after spring or summer thunderstorms. Each cream-colored flower is ¹/₂ to ³/₄ inch wide and produces five to ten plumed seeds.

Cliffrose may be confused with Apache plume (_Fallugia paradoxa_), which generally has a more southerly distribution but does grow in the area. Cliffrose has smaller flowers, fewer plumes, and dotted leaves. (_Fallugia_ honors seventeenth-century Italian botanist Abbot V. Fallugi.)

The world of botanical nomenclature can tax even the mellowest botanist. Consider the naming of cliffrose. Variations include _Cowania mexicana_ var. _stansburiana, Cowania stansburiana,_ and _Purshia stansburiana._ The type specimen came from Captain Howard Stansbury's Great Salt Lake Expedition. (See side-blotched lizard, page 163, for more information on Stansbury.) Frederick Pursh (1774–1820) was a German-trained botanist who produced the first plant book to cover America north of Mexico, _Flora Americae Septentrionalis._

WILDFLOWERS AND GRASSES

The evolution of flowering plants (angiosperms) 120 million years ago was one of the great events in the history of our planet. They soon became the dominant plant form, supplanting the gymnosperms (e.g., conifers, cycads, and ginkgos), and now compose 90 percent of all plant species on earth. One key to the success of flowering plants was their pollination method. Gymnosperms depend on wind pollination, which requires producing a tremendous quantity of pollen that is small, light, and easily transportable by air currents. This method is haphazard because it is completely dependent upon the vagaries of the wind. Angiosperms rely primarily on insect pollination, a much better method because insects are like traveling salesbugs going from plant to plant carrying their valuable commodity, pollen, to a willing recipient.

The following diagram shows a typical flower, which consists of an outer series of parts, sepals, that surround the base of the flower. Sepals are usually green but can be colorful, as in the lilies. The group of sepals is called the calyx. Petals grow within the calyx. They are generally colorful and are the most important attractor of insects. The group of petals makes up the corolla.

The next layer within, stamens, produces the plant's pollen, which is released from the anther, a clublike appendage found at the end of the stamen. The female part of the flower is the pistil. It is topped by the stigma, which rests atop the style, which in turn connects to the ovary. Plants can have either both male and female parts on the same plant (monoecious) or on separate plants (dioecious).

The desert's most common plant family, sunflowers or composites (Asteraceae), has evolved another variation on general flower architecture. Composite refers to the two types of flowers present in the inflorescence: ray and disk. Asteraceae used to be known as Compositae, but recent nomenclature rule changes have decreed that all family names end in -"aceae"; therefore, the change. The flower head, which looks like a single flower, actually consists of a few to several hundred minute flowers. The rays make up the outer whorl of the head and consist of a corolla, fused at the base into a tube, but flattened at the top, surrounding a ring of five stamens. The interior disk flowers consist of narrow, tubular five-lobed corollas. This disk, in turn, surrounds a tinier tube of five fused stamens.

Flowers are merely a plant's billboard with a simple, provocative message: "Hey, pollinator! Come see me and I'll give you a nice reward!" The reward is nectar, a watery, sugar-rich substance, relished by many animals. The action begins soon after the billboard is in place. A pollinator, maybe a beetle, bat, bee, or bird, arrives and seeks out the nectar. While reaching for the nectar, which is usually deep within the flower, the animal rubs against the anther and unknowingly picks up a load of pollen. The pollinator then flies or crawls to the next flower where the pollen is deposited onto the stigma and pollination takes place.

Color and odor help flowers advertise. Many white flowers have a strong scent because they are pollinated at night. Most pollination, though, occurs during the day, so color and shape are important for attracting visitors.

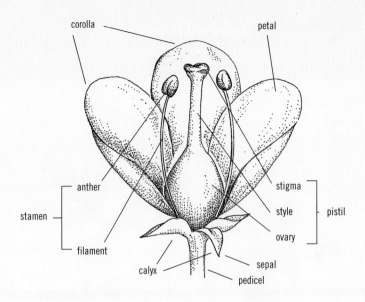

Typical Flower Parts

The relationship between flowers and their pollinators has led to the great diversity of plant and animal life on the planet. Unfortunately, habitat degradation has led to a loss of pollinators, especially insects.

Scientific names in this section conform to the USDA Plants Database (http://plants .usda.gov/java/) and family names conform to Angiosperm Phylogeny Database (www .mobot.org/mobot/research/apweb/welcome.html).

SWEETROOT SPRING PARSLEY
Cymopterus newberryi
Carrot family (Apiaceae)

The glossy, dark green leaves of spring parsley push up through the soil sometimes as early as January. They rise a few inches above the ground, followed by small, yellow flowers that grow in a compound umbel at the end of a short, leafless stem. Like other species in the genus, the plants have a fleshy, edible taproot, although the local species is generally hard to dig out of its gravelly soil. The generic name, *Cymopterus,* Greek for wavy wing, relates to the fruit.

John Strong Newberry was a member of the first US government survey into southeastern Utah in 1855.

CANYONLANDS BISCUITROOT
Lomatium latilobum
Carrot family (Apiaceae)

Canyonlands Biscuitroot

Parry's Lomatium

A perennial member of the carrot family, canyonlands biscuitroot reproduces by seed and cloning. An individual biscuitroot clump includes many clones. Once the clump reaches a critical size, flowering can begin, with yellow flowers producing between 20 and 60 seeds per inflorescence. They bloom in March and April and set seed before hot weather begins.

Canyonlands biscuitroot exemplifies the link between plants and rocks. The plants grow only in the narrow eroded canyons between the fins of the Entrada Sandstone (see page 9 for more information). This restricts biscuitroot to Grand and San Juan Counties in Utah and Mesa County in Colorado. Areas of abundance include the Fiery Furnace and Devils Garden in Arches National Park.

The closely related Parry's lomatium (*Lomatium parryi*) has a wider distribution and carrotlike, finely dissected leaves. Canyonlands biscuitroot has aromatic, pinnately compound leaves. Dried white leaves may persist through summer and into the next season of growth. The generic name *Loma* comes from the Greek for border, in reference to the winged fruit. Parry honors Charles Christopher Parry, a nineteenth-century botanist who explored Colorado and the Mexico-US boundary.

HOPI BLANKETFLOWER
Gaillardia pinnatifida
Sunflower family (Asteraceae)

COMMON SUNFLOWER
Helianthus annuus
Sunflower family (Asteraceae)

Many people know *Gaillardia* as a common garden plant. All blanketflowers have broad heads with wedge-shaped, yellow, three-lobed ray flowers. Most garden varieties have red and yellow ray flowers. *G. pinnatifida* disk flowers color as they mature, and yellow buds may be present with purple-brown, opened flowers.

The predominantly basal leaves are hairy and pinnate. Each stem bears a single flower head with 7 to 13 rays; the plants range in size from 3 to 25 inches tall. Hopi blanketflower commonly occurs on roadsides and is widespread between elevations of 3,500 and 7,000 feet. *Gaillardia* honors Antoine René Gaillard de Charentonneau, an eighteenth-century French magistrate and patron of botany.

During the summer, yellow sunflowers infuse the desert with golden light. They grow along roads and in other disturbed sites, often covering extensive areas. One of the tallest annuals, commonly up to 6 feet or taller, they also have large (up to 8 inches long), ovate to heart-shaped leaves. Short hairs cover the leaves, giving them a rough feel. Each flower head consists of purple-brown disk flowers and bright yellow ray flowers.

Common sunflower grows throughout the Southwest and into the Great Plains. It is the Kansas state flower and thus sometimes called Kansas sunflower. The seeds were and are important to both people and animals. *H. annuus* commonly hybridizes with the smaller prairie sunflower, *H. petiolaris,* and distinguishing between the two is difficult. The generic name comes from the Greek for sun (*helio*) and flower (*anthus*).

HYALINEHERB
Hymenopappus filifolius
Sunflower family (Asteraceae)

STEMLESS WOOLLYBASE
Tetraneuris acaulis
Sunflower family (Asteraceae)

Numerous subspecies of *Hymenopappus fili-folius* grow throughout the Rocky Mountains and Great Basin with one, and possibly three, found in canyon country. Our subspecies has yellow flowers in solitary heads of more than 30 disks per head. The plants have basal leaves (up to 8 inches long) that grow on the stem.

This great number of subspecies represents a single species adapting to climatic and geologic changes over a broad area. Paleontologists believe the ancestor of *Hymenopappus* moved into the Rockies during the Oligocene epoch (34 to 23 million years ago) with the greatest radiation of subspecies occurring in the last 7 million years.

At present these subspecies can interbreed, producing viable offspring, but the stage is set. If the subspecies remain geographically isolated, they will continue to adapt and evolve, eventually forming new species.

Short tufts of hair growing around the leaves at the plant's base give this daisy its common name. Hairs also cover the leaves and flower stalk. A single flower head, which flourishes at the end of an 8- to 10-inch-long stalk, has yellow disk and ray flowers. The five to nine ray flowers end in toothed tips.

Most flowers in the *Tetraneuris* genus have a narrow distribution. Stemless woollybase is unusual, growing from New Mexico to Canada in a wide range of soil types and sometimes forming extensive roadside displays. *T. acaulis* also has a great variety of subspecies with variations in leaf shape, plant size, and density of hairs.

Some books refer to this plant as stemless four-nerve daisy. That name comes from the four (*tetra*) nerves (*neuron*), or veins, on the ray floret of the corolla.

DESERT DANDELION
Malacothrix sonchoides
Sunflower family (Asteraceae)

LOBELEAF GROUNDSEL
Packera multilobata
Sunflower family (Asteraceae)

Dandelions, the common bane of gardens and yards, also grow in canyon country, but the desert variety is in a different genus, found only in western North America. The native species closely resembles the alien variety with a yellow flower head, no disk flowers, and wavy, lobed leaves. Desert dandelions are widespread, growing in dry areas up to 6,000 feet in elevation and reaching heights of up to 14 inches.

Dandelion is an anglicized version of the French term *dent de lion*—tooth of the lion—a reference to the toothlike edges of the leaves. The garden variety, *Taraxacum officinale,* is an invader from Europe and occurs throughout the region. Two other native dandelion species are woolbearing dandelion (*Taraxacum ceratophorum*) and harp dandelion (*T. scopulorum*), both widely distributed throughout Utah's alpine and subalpine areas. *Malacothrix* is a combination of the Greek *malacos* and *tricos,* or soft hairs, in reference to the feathery hairs that cover the fruit and aid in its dispersal by acting as a parachute.

As the species name implies, lobeleaf groundsel has leaves with many lobes. The dark green, shiny leaves are 1 to 5 inches long and cluster at the base of the plant. Flowering stalks produce a panoply of bright yellow flower heads. A single row of green bracts surrounds each $1/2$- to $3/4$-inch-wide head. This makes them easy to distinguish from daisies, which have more than one row of bracts surrounding the flower head.

Lobeleaf groundsel grows throughout canyon country. In dry years, when many annuals do not bloom, the perennial groundsel forms a distinctive part of the late spring and early summer flora. Recently it was moved out of the genus *Senecio,* a name derived from a Latin term for "old man," in reference to the whitish hairs on the seeds of some species. This is also the origin of the word "senescent."

ROUGH MULE'S EAR
Scabrethia scabra
Sunflower family (Asteraceae)

YELLOW CRYPTANTHA
Cryptantha flava
Borage family (Boraginaceae)

Grabbing a leaf of mule's ear feels like grabbing a piece of sandpaper, rough and scratchy. Short hairs cover the leaves, protecting the plant from desiccation by reflecting sunlight. The long, narrow leaves give the plant its common name. The basal leaves may be absent, reduced, or the same size as the 1- to 7-inch-long stem leaves.

Mule's ear grows in sand dunes forming clumps several feet wide and high. The clumps are well-suited to dune growth because organic detritus collects under the plants, providing valuable nutrients as the detritus decays. Like many dune plants, the adventitious roots of mule's ear, which tap underground moisture, arise from thick tuberous roots. In spring the plants produce 2- to 4-inch-wide flowers that resemble sunflowers. When hot weather hits, the flowers quickly wilt.

Recently moved out of the genus *Wyethia, Scabrethia* comes from the Latin for "rough," as in the word "scab."

Although yellow cryptanthas do not possess a large flower, they are conspicuous by their sheer numbers. The plant flourishes in sandy soil, which is common throughout the Colorado Plateau. Each inflorescence contains 45 to 55 fused yellow flowers. One plant can produce several flower clusters. The inflorescence arises from a leaf rosette consisting of nearly vertical, hirsute leaves that grow from a branched woody base.

This plant may also be called Brenda's yellow cryptantha. Brenda Casper did her dissertation on *C. flava* at the University of Utah. Evidently no one had studied the plant, and a later botanist honored her work by using her name.

The genus *Cryptantha* contains over 15 species in southern Utah including annuals, perennials, and biennials. Most are short plants (less than 18 inches) covered in stiff, almost spiny hairs. All have small yellow or white flowers, or a combination of white with a yellow eye, similar to the closely related forget-me-nots (*Myosotis* sp.). Roughseed cryptantha (*C. flavoculata*) is particularly noticeable with a deep yellow throat surrounded by white.

PUCCOON
Lithospermum incisum
Borage family (Boraginaceae)

PINNATE TANSY MUSTARD
Descurainia pinnata
Mustard family (Brassicaceae)

Puccoons produce showy yellow flowers. As in other members of the Borage family, the petals are united to form a trumpet-shaped tube. Puccoon flowers are $1^1/_2$ to 2 inches long, and the five lobes have fringed margins. Their aroma is so delectable that one park ranger encourages visitors "to get down on their knees and sniff."

Puccoons rarely cross-fertilize; instead, late in the season after an initial showy flowering, small, inconspicuous flowers produce seeds. Self-pollination provides insurance for years when pollinator populations are low. Without gene mixing, though, plants cannot adapt as well to changing environmental conditions. (See plateau striped whiptail, page 166.) The generic name, *Lithospermum,* refers to the plant's rock-hard seeds. The common name puccoon comes from an Algonquian name for another species of *Lithospermum.*

Tansy mustard appears early in spring, regularly growing on roadsides. Often labeled as a weed due to its proclivity for disturbed sites, *Descurainia pinnata* is native to this area and has been used since prehistoric times as a human food resource. Dense hairs cover the finely dissected, 1- to 2-inch-long leaves. Like prince's plume, seedpods and flowers of tansy mustard will grow on the same plant.

During the 1950s uranium boom, botanists found that *Descurainia* ranked first in absorption of uranium and vanadium and thus indicated soils rich in these minerals. (See Close-Up on page 70 for more information.) François Dèscourain (1658–1740) was a French botanist and apothecary.

WESTERN WALLFLOWER
Erysimum asperum
Mustard family (Brassicaceae)

TWINPOD
Physaria sp.
Mustard family (Brassicaceae)

Wallflower has the most evident flowers of the mustard family in canyon country. The four-petaled, ³/₄-inch-wide, bright yellow flowers mostly grow at the top of a 6- to 36-inch-long stem. Narrow, linear leaves are concentrated at the base with a few leaves ascending the stem.

Wallflower grows in numerous habitats, including sandy soils, along the base of walls, and under the protective foliage of shrubs. They range from Saskatchewan to Washington and south to New Mexico and Arizona. Western wallflower's elevation range, from 2,490 to 12,467 feet, is the broadest among plants in Utah.

The emergence of twinpod is a clarion call signaling that spring will soon arrive in canyon country. Spatulate leaves, which form a basal rosette, appear as soon as early season temperatures start to rise. Fine hairs give the leaves a gray hue. Numerous small flowers grow at the end of a short upright stem and the four yellow petals have the typical mustard family cruciform shape. Twinpods usually set seed, two paired balloon-shaped pods, which give the plant its common name, before most plants in the region begin to flower. *Physaria* hybridize easily throughout their range. The most common species are *P. newberryi* (Newberry's twinpod) and *P. acutifolia* (sharpleaf twinpod). Identification requires an analysis of the seeds.

PRINCE'S PLUME
Stanleya pinnata
Mustard family (Brassicaceae)

Prince's plume is the largest and most showy mustard plant in the area with flower-covered stems (the plume) growing up to 4 feet tall. Stalks hold on to the dried seed-pods until the following growing season. At first glance, the yellow flowers do not look like a typical mustard, but close inspection exposes the characteristic four-petaled corolla. They open from the bottom of the plant up, and it is not unusual to find a plant with this season's seeds, open flowers, and unopened flower buds.

Prince's plume grows in a wide variety of soil types but is usually an indicator of selenium-rich soils. Selenium substitutes for sulfur in the plant's amino acids and does not appear to affect the plant's growth habits. Experiments with high amounts of uranium-rich carnotite, however, produced stems of imperfect flowers lacking petals and stamens.

British ornithologist Edward Stanley, earl of Derby (1773–1849), was a president of the Linnaean and Zoological Societies in London.

PLAINS PRICKLY PEAR
Opuntia polyacantha
Cactus family (Cactaceae)

YELLOW SPIDERFLOWER
Peritoma lutea
Cleome family (Cleomaceae)

Prickly pears employ many successful adaptations to desert environments. The spines, which are modified leaves, provide shade, slow drying desert winds, and protect the plant. The shallow root system that spreads out from the plant can obtain water from even light rainstorms. Succulent pads expand to store water for later use during times of drought.

Each spring, yellow and/or pink flowers burst forth from the areole, an organ found only on cacti. They bloom for only a few days. The 1½-inch-wide flower may be pollinated by bees or moths, some species of which have coevolved to pollinate only one particular species of cactus.

Although plains prickly pear has one of the widest distributions of any cactus, growing from southern Canada to Texas, they also have expanded their natural distribution, moving into disturbed and overgrazed sites. Plains prickly pear are unusual in the cacti world; unlike most cactus species they can withstand temperatures near or below freezing, an important limiting factor in cacti distribution.

Yellow spiderflower shares physical attributes with several other plants in the region. Like lupines, spiderflowers have palmate leaves and, like mustard plants, they have flowers with four petals and sepals. Spiderflowers, however, have six protruding stamens.

During summer months this annual grows in sandy areas, along roads, and in other disturbed areas, reaching to 5 feet in height. Flowers bloom at the end of a single, many-branched stem. Overstuffed seedpods (up to 1½ inches long) hang from a short stalk, known as a stipe. This is also known as yellow beeplant.

DESERT BLAZING STAR
Mentzelia multiflora
Stickleaf family (Loasaceae)

Pointed petals and numerous long stamens give blazing star one of its common names. The other common name, stickleaf, comes from the barbed hairs that cover the leaves, seeds, and stems, giving the plant a sandpaper-like texture. When animals brush up against the plant, they carry away seeds that have latched on with barbed hairs. Along with these characteristics, the plants are easy to recognize by their branched white stems and green, narrow, many-lobed leaves.

Blazing star has an unusual floral structure. Half the petals are shorter and narrower than the other half. Furthermore, five of the stamens have a petal-like shape so the plants appear to have fifteen yellow petals. Blazing star often grows along roadsides or in other disturbed fine-grained soil. Linnaeus named the genus in honor of Christian Mentzel (1622–1701), a German botanist and lexicographer.

DESERT TRUMPET
Eriogonum inflatum
Buckwheat family (Polygonaceae)

On April 24, 1844, while crossing the Mojave Desert, John C. Frémont wrote "a new and remarkable species of *Eriogonum* made its first appearance." The inflated stems provide structural support for the plant, and tall desert trumpets may have several levels, giving the impression that someone has stacked the plants atop each other. The dried stems may persist for many years, dotting the landscape with their remarkable appearance. Spring rains trigger the basal growth of shiny, dark green leaves. Stems appear several weeks later, followed by tiny yellow flowers that grow on needle-thin stalks.

Close-up

Controversy Over a Plant Condo

A small controversy about the desert trumpet's inflated stem results from the classic 1941 field guide *Desert Wild Flowers*. Naturalist Edmund C. Jaeger wrote that wasps in the genus *Onyerus* drilled a hole into the plant's inflated stem, filled it with minute pebbles, stuffed in a bunch of insect larvae or nymphs, laid eggs, which will feed on the insect, and added more grains of sand. Unfortunately, no such genus exists. As it turns out, Jaeger's book contains a typo, which still creeps into books and articles about this plant. The correct spelling is *Odynerus,* although they are generally ground nesting wasps and may or may not have been the insect seen by Jaeger.

Numerous wasps and bees do take advantage of the inflated stem, says Frank Parker, former head of the USDA bee lab in Logan, Utah. Through the years he has found at least ten different species nesting in the pods, including *Solierella blaisdelli* and *S. similis, Lomachaeta variegata,* and *Hedychridium solierellae,* which range in size from the head of a pin to a honeybee. In some cases, after one wasp has built her nest, as Jaeger described, another wasp will come along and parasitize the egg and eat the nymph. Others will parasitize the wasp larva. Parker says that he will often break off the top of the old *Eriogonum* stems to provide more habitats. "One problem contributing to the population decline of wasps and bees is reduced nesting habitat," says Parker. After breaking off the stems, Parker "generally found that someone has moved in."

To try to determine what or who caused the inflation, two researchers in the 1970s conducted an extensive study of *Eriogonum inflatum* and concluded that minute larvae of two insects, a moth (family Pyralidae) and a beetle (family Mordellidae), triggered the inflation of the stem. Stem inflation depended upon time of initial insect damage and duration of larval inhabitation.

In contrast, scientists in the 1980s determined that the inflated stems are an adaptation to allow the plant to continue photosynthesizing when otherwise it might be too dry to do so. Basically the inflated stem acts as a storage unit, holding CO_2 produced by the plant during the night. Then during the day, the plant uses the CO_2 for photosynthesis, which reduces water loss because the plant does not need to open its stomata to take up CO_2. Opening the stomata leads to water loss.

Intriguingly, the concentrations of CO_2 in the stem are high enough to kill any insect larvae though some larvae escape this death. When their parent laid the egg in the stem, she drilled a hole in the stem, which allows CO_2 to escape.

White Flowers

NARROWLEAF YUCCA
Yucca angustissima
Asparagus family (Asparagaceae)

> Despite its fierce defenses, or perhaps because of them, the yucca is as beautiful as it is strange.
>
> —Edward Abbey, *Desert Solitaire*

Unlike the closely related agaves, which flower once and die, yuccas can produce a new flower stalk each spring. Cream-colored flowers bloom on stalks that can reach up to 5 feet tall. After the yucca flowers, a unique relationship begins between the plant and its pollinator. Female *Tegeticula altiplanella* moths gather pollen, form it into a ball, stuff it into one of another yucca's stigmas, and then lay their eggs in the plant's ovaries. The yucca moth larvae eat some of the seeds but leave enough so that some will mature. Most species of yucca have their own species of pollinating moth, although some moths, like *T. altiplanella*, can pollinate a variety of species. No other plants and animals in the desert have such a mutualistic relationship. (For more information, see page 187.)

Yucca might be described as the precursor of the corner market in the Southwest. Saponin-rich plant roots make an effective soap and shampoo. Fibers extracted from the long, straight leaves were used in belts, straps, sandals, ladders, and baskets. During World War I, over eight million pounds of burlap and bagging material were made from yucca fibers. Fruits from the datil yucca (*Y. baccata*) can be either eaten raw or cooked and saved for winter use.

In 1593 the English botanist John Gerard applied the term "yucca" to plants that he mistakenly thought were related to cassava, which the native Haitians called *iucca*.

SILVERY TOWNSENDIA
Townsendia incana
Sunflower family (Asteraceae)

TEXTILE ONION
Allium textile
Amaryllis family (Amaryllidaceae)

Townsendia exemplifies the flowering pattern of the sunflower, or composite, family. This family, worldwide in occurrence with between 15,000 and 20,000 species, is the second largest family and most common one outside of the tropics.

Cutting open a townsendia head reveals numerous separate flowers. The outer, petal-like parts, known as ray flowers, consist of a corolla, fused at the base into a tube but flattened at the outside edges, surrounding a ring of five stamens. The interior parts, called disk flowers, consist of narrow, tubular five-lobed corollas. This disk, in turn, surrounds a tinier tube of five fused stamens.

Within this basic pattern variation exists. Dandelions, for example, only have ray flowers; in this group the rays are bisexual. Thistle flower heads, on the other hand, consist only of disk flowers. Most composites have both rays and disks.

The great English botanist William Jackson Hooker named this genus for Pennsylvania botanist David Townsend (1787–1858), writing that he had "imbibed the most ardent love of Botany."

Several species of onion occur in this region and share many traits, the most obvious of which is the plant's distinct odor. All have grasslike leaves and a leafless stem topped by an umbel of small, white to pink flowers. Like other members in the Amaryllis family, the flowers consist of three sepals and three petals. Textile onion flowers are white to pinkish with purple nectar guides.

Allium bulbs are edible, though the taste may be too strong for some. A fibrous sheath surrounds the bulb. Exercise caution when eating them because the closely related death camas (*Toxicoscordion paniculatum*) resembles onion plants and is toxic to humans.

MOUNTAIN PEPPERWEED
Lepidium montanum
Mustard family (Brassicaceae)

SEGO LILY
Calochortus nuttallii
Lily family (Liliaceae)

Numerous slender branches grow from a woody base and give the plant a shrubby appearance. Numerous small white flowers grow at the end of each of these branches. Pepperweed generally has a spring blooming season, but some subspecies flower in late summer and early fall. Although the petals are minute, the plants form a prominent part of the piñon-juniper ecosystem floral display due to their great abundance. True to its name, the edible seeds have a peppery taste. The flowers and the ¹/₈-inch-wide seeds may be on the plant at the same time.

Sego lilies differ from typical lilies, in that the petals are larger and more ornate than the sepals. One to four white flowers grow at the end of a leafless stalk. Like most lilies, sego lilies have three sepals, three petals, and six stamens.

In April, stiff grasslike leaves begin to grow in sandy, dry soil amongst piñon, juniper, and sagebrush. One would not expect such a beautiful flower as the sego lily to emerge from these innocuous, basal leaves. The Greek-derived generic name refers to the leaf shape, *kalo* (beautiful) and *chorta* (grass).

Like garlic and onion, sego lily bulbs are edible. Following the long, cold winter of 1848 to 1849, Mormon pioneers in the Salt Lake Valley depended on "sago roots" as a primary food source until their crops produced. The Utah legislature made sego lily the state flower to honor its place in the state's early history.

This plant is named in honor of English ornithologist and botanist Thomas Nuttall (1786–1859), who collected the first cactus specimens west of the Mississippi.

SAND VERBENA
Abronia fragrans
Four O'Clock family (Nyctaginaceae)

To be overcome by the fragrance of
flowers is a delectable form of defeat.
—Beverly Nichols, English writer,
1898–1983

Many night-blooming flowers have a sweet
smell, but none more intoxicating than sand
verbena. These small plants begin to grace
sand dunes in early spring with $3/8$- to 3-inch-
long elliptical leaves. During the day, numerous (more than 25 individuals) blossoms are
tightly enclosed in drooping flower balls.
At dusk these heads open, revealing $1/8$- to
$1/4$-inch-wide white flowers. Sweet nectar
attracts hawk moths.

Soft hairs cover the plant, slowing
water evaporation by reflecting sunlight.
The hairs are often hard to see because
sand verbena plants secrete a sticky substance, which acts like flypaper catching
sand grains. *Abros,* from the Greek for "delicate," refers to the flowers.

DWARF EVENING PRIMROSE
Oenothera cespitosa
Evening Primrose family (Onagraceae)

In certain years the abundance of dwarf evening primrose gives the impression that a
box of white tissues has opened and blown
about the desert. The 2- to 3-inch-wide white
flowers, which usually appear in April, can
flourish in dense accumulations in sandy
areas and along roadsides. Each flower grows
on a couple-inch-long floral tube directly
from the plant's base. Blossoms open in early
evening and close in the morning, avoiding
water loss during the hottest part of the day.
If they open a second night, the flowers are
pink and evening primroses often have both
colored flowers on one plant.

Linnaeus named the genus *Oenothera,*
a Greek word meaning "wine pursuing" or
"imbibing." In early times it was said that eating the roots of an evening primrose would
incite a desire for wine.

PALE EVENING PRIMROSE
Oenothera pallida
Evening Primrose family (Onagraceae)

Sphinx Moth

Pale Evening Primrose

Pale evening primrose grows on partially stabilized dunes and other sandy areas. They have smaller flowers (1 to 1¹/₂ inches wide) and narrow and shorter leaves, and are much taller (up to 18 inches) than the closely related *O. cespitosa*.

Evening primroses have a quasi-parasitic/symbiotic relationship with their principal pollinator, sphinx moths (*Hyles* sp.). The moth's larval stage, the green horn-worm, eats the plant, but in return, after metamorphosis, the sphinx moth ensures the survival of its host by carrying pollen from plant to plant, keeping the cycle going.

Close-up

Can You Hear It?

When the flowers of evening primroses open at dusk, they slowly unfurl in a 20-minute display that ends with a final burst of the petals flinging open. This action led the poet John Keats to write in 1817: "A tuft of evening primroses / O'er which the mind may hover till it doses / O'er which it well might take a pleasant sleep / But that 'tis ever startled by the leap / Of buds into ripe flowers."

I once read that you could actually hear an audible pop when the flowers opened, so one evening I went up near Moab's fine dump with four other curious, botanically inclined individuals to seek out audible *Oenothera*. We found a plant with flowers that appeared to be getting ready to open and gathered around like we had never seen this plant before. In a way we hadn't.

None of us had ever taken the time to sit and watch the petals unfurl. In describing this moment, one of the people on this little expedition has written: "This night gave me a greater appreciation for flowers; having considered the amount of energy expended to produce one flower, I rarely pick flowers anymore. The event also encouraged me to 'experience' these plants to a greater depth, to go beyond the nomenclature and really look at a plant in all its complexity. To get down on my knees in the soft dirt or the rough gravel . . . To search for pollinators . . . To just sit and watch and wait for nature to unravel itself in the simple, yet elegant form of a desert wildflower."

We did not hear the pop that night, but I have heard a pop on subsequent *Oenothera* adventures. Watching this simple, yet elegant act is one of my fondest memories of living in the desert.

BASTARD TOADFLAX
Comandra umbellata
Sandalwood family (Santalaceae)

Toadflax reproduces by both sexual and vegetative reproduction and grows in partly to completely open dry sites. The small white flowers, which bloom in the spring, lack petals; instead, the five sepals are white. The erect stems grow to 1 foot in height.

As a parasite, bastard toadflax depends upon other plants for survival. Within 2 weeks of toadflax seed germination, subterranean connections, known as haustoria, attach themselves to nearby vegetation to obtain nutrients and water. *Comandra* can parasitize over 200 woody and herbaceous species, the most diverse and largest natural range of any parasitic plant. Although bastard toadflax is always parasitic, it can also make its own food through photosynthesis.

The common epithet, bastard toadflax, while colorful, may mislead; neither the flower nor leaves resemble a flax or a toadflax. Toadflax, a common name given to several plants in the snapdragon family, received its name because the flowers "be yellow, having a mouth unto a frog's mouth," according to John Gerard's 1597 *Herbal*. Sixty years later another English botanist, William Coles, in his *Adam in Eden, Nature's Paradise*, claimed the name arose "because Toads will sometimes shelter themselves amongst the branches of it." Bastard means false or of unusual shape or size.

DATURA
Datura wrightii
Potato family (Solanaceae)

Datura produces the largest flowers in canyon country—5- to 7-inch-long, funnel-shaped white blooms. The fragrant corollas, which open at dusk and close in early morning, are commonly pollinated by moths, as well as beetles and wasps. In *Cannery Row*, John Steinbeck wrote that "the flowers smelled of love and excitement, an incredibly sweet and moving odor." The dark green, shiny leaves, on the other hand, are often described as "smelling like a wet dog." The plants sprout at the base of cliffs in protected spots and can grow to 4 or 5 feet across with tens of blossoms.

Like many plants in the potato family, the leaves and flowers of datura are poisonous, containing the toxic alkaloids atropine, scopolamine, and hyoscyamine (a nerve toxin). Some people use the plant to induce hallucinations in religious ceremonies. Humans and animals, however, have been killed by eating datura.

Datura is also called jimsonweed, a corruption of Jamestown, Virginia, where soldiers in 1676, during Bacon's Rebellion, boiled the leaves of another datura species and spent many days in "frantick condition." Charles Wright (1811–1885) collected plants extensively during the US-Mexican Boundary Survey of the 1850s.

SHOWY MILKWEED
Asclepias speciosa
Dogbane family (Apocynaceae)

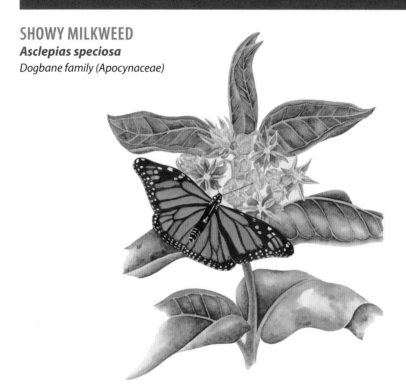

Showy milkweed has oval, dark green, opposite leaves covered in soft hairs. The thick leaves can be as wide as 6 inches and as long as 8. Erect stems may grow up to 5 feet tall topped by an umbel of pinkish flowers. Plants reproduce by underground rootstocks or via windblown seeds that burst out of 4-inch-long seedpods late in the summer.

Several species of milkweed occur in canyon country and share many characteristics. All are poisonous to livestock due to glycosides, a cardiac compound found in the milky sap. Monarch butterflies and their caterpillar larvae, however, can tolerate the toxin, becoming toxic themselves. Monarchs, in fact, depend upon milkweed for survival. This relationship is so strong that the introduction of milkweed in Hawaii, New Zealand, and Australia led to colonization by monarch butterflies.

Milkweeds have an unusual pollination method that sometimes leads to the death of visiting insects. The plant's pollen is contained in saddlebag-shaped packets, known as pollinia. When a pollinator lands on a milkweed, hooks on the pollinia attach to the visitor's legs and unhook when the insect reaches another milkweed. Small bees and insects, though, may get caught by the hooks and become unable to fly away.

Linnaeus established this genus in reference to the Greek god of medicine, because of the many remedies made from members of the genus.

ARIZONA THISTLE
Cirsium arizonicum
Sunflower family (Asteraceae)

Thistle flower heads are often showy and lack ray flowers. They may be pink, red, purple, or whitish and generally rise above the plant on stout stems. The locally abundant Arizona thistle (*C. arizonicum*) has pink to bluish pink flowers. *C. undulatum,* which grows from British Columbia to Minnesota and south to Arizona, has creamy white flowers. Another species, New Mexico thistle (*C. neomexicanum*), has creamy white heads and dried flower stalks that may persist for several years. Upon maturity, winds disperse the umbrella-shaped seeds.

Both native and alien (generally Old World) thistles occur in southern Utah. Most of the aliens grow on cultivated and disturbed lands. Natives may have a narrow distribution, such as the hanging garden endemic, Rydberg's thistle (*C. rydbergii*), or broad distribution, like the widespread wavyleaf thistle (*C. undulatum*). All species have large, toothed- or wavy-margined leaves. Sharp spines on the leaves, stems, and flower bracts protect the edible plant.

Legend holds that when Norse invaders attacked Scotland in the thirteenth century, they attempted a sneak, barefoot attack, so they wouldn't be heard, but one soldier stepped on thistle and yelled, revealing the presence of the army. Because of this, the thistle is Scotland's national emblem.

UTAH FLEABANE
Erigeron utahensis
Sunflower family (Asteraceae)

SMALL WIRELETTUCE
Stephanomeria exigua
Sunflower family (Asteraceae)

Utah fleabane's basal leaves wither and disappear before the flowers open. The 10 to 40 ray flowers may be pink, purple, blue, or, less commonly, yellow or white, and bloom for several weeks. The 8- to 12-inch-tall plant can form large clumps with many flowering stems.

The wide array of daisies and fleabanes growing in the Southwest creates a taxonomically difficult genus. Some only occur in seeps (*E. kachinensis*) or on mountains (*E. mancus*). Others have a wide distribution. The Utah fleabane grows in slickrock areas. To add to the confusion, another group of composites, the asters, resembles fleabanes. Asters, though, usually bloom in midsummer, as opposed to the generally spring-blooming *Erigeron*, which have more heads per stalk, fewer and wider rays, and more definitively layered bracts.

Erigeron comes from the Greek for "early old man," an allusion to the hairs that appear on the seeds early in the year. Geriatric and gerontology share the same root. Apparently, the smoke of burning plants drove away fleas, hence the common name.

Like most desert annuals, wirelettuce flowering depends directly upon winter and early spring moisture. Abundant precipitation produces larger plants, with sizes ranging from 4 to 15 inches. The thin stems branch often, producing abundant and delicate pink to purplish flower heads. Wirelettuce is an unusual composite in that it does not have disk flowers. Each $1/2$- to $3/4$-inch-long ray flower has a toothed tip.

Wirelettuce is widespread across the western United States. It ranges from California to New Mexico and grows on dry plains and slopes in sandy to clayey soil. The lettucelike leaves reveal that it is related to cultivated lettuce. Another composite, showy rushpink (*Lygodesmia grandiflora*), looks like a steroid-supplemented *S. exigua* with 1- to 2-inch-wide flower heads.

BEAUTIFUL ROCKCRESS
Boechera pulchra
Mustard family (Brassicaceae)

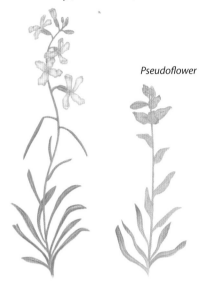

Pseudoflower

CRESCENT MILKVETCH
Astragalus amphioxys
Pea family (Fabaceae)

Two species of rockcress bloom in early spring. Their subtle colors and small flowers make them an inconspicuous part of the desert community, and they are hard to tell apart. *B. pulchra* has pale pinkish to white flowers with 2 1/2-inch-long linear fruits that are hairy and pendulous. Common rockcress (*B. perennans*) often grows intermixed with desert shrubs and uses them for support. It has darker purple, smaller flowers than *B. pulchra*. Rockcress was formerly a member of the genus *Arabis*.

In July and August fungus spores, carried by winds, may invade rockcress plants, producing a botanical invasion of the body snatchers. Over the winter these rusts, as they are also known, infect the mustard's growth tissue. The infection will influence any future development, usually creating a plant with more leaves and leaf rosettes. The infected mustard also produces a stem topped by leaves coated in a bright yellow sugary material, the rust's spermatial fluid. Botanists refer to these plants as pseudoflowers. They begin to appear early in the year during the first warm days of spring, usually about a month before uninfected mustards flower.

Crescent milkvetches have short stems and grow low to the ground, commonly along roadsides, where extra moisture and warmer temperatures facilitate early season blooming. Flowers range in size from 1/2 to 1 inch long and in color from pinkish to purple. The key to identification is the crescent-shaped seedpod. Dense, short hairs cover the red-splotched pods.

More than 350 species of *Astragalus* grow in the United States. Utah has more than 100 species, so determining which species is which challenges most beginning, and some experienced, botanists. Looking at the flower is just the beginning; most identification keys require seedpods, number and shape of leaflets, and type of hairs covering the plant.

WOOLLY MILKVETCH
Astragalus mollismus
Pea family (Fabaceae)

Woolly milkvetch is one of the few relatively easy milkvetches to identify in canyon country; no other *Astragalus* is as densely covered in hairs. Pinnately compound leaves start to push up along roadsides often as early as February. They may be as tall as 10 inches with numerous flowers growing on long flower stalks. The plants often have a gray appearance because of the abundance of hairs.

Woolly milkvetch is also known as locoweed because of its toxicity to livestock. Unlike other *Astragalus,* this species does not concentrate selenium; the dominant alkaloid is known as locoine. Although locoweed is considered unpalatable, some animals, especially horses, may become addicted. Symptoms include hallucinations, delirium, slowness of gait, and lusterless hair. In sheep, locoweed consumption leads to difficulty in being herded.

Close-up

Of Plants and Uranium

During the 1950s when uranium fever spread across the Colorado Plateau, prospectors developed many ways to find radioactive materials. Most methods used Geiger counters to detect the minerals' radiation. Botanists working with the US Geological Survey, however, started researching the possibility of using plants as indicators of mineral deposits. They knew that many plant species concentrated uranium, vanadium, selenium, and other trace elements in their roots and stems and hypothesized that both wildflowers and woody plants might lead to ore deposits.

Researchers showed that carnotite, a uranium-rich mineral, increased a plant's ability to absorb sulfur and selenium and that these two elements increased the absorption potential of uranium and vanadium in plants. Indicator plants revealed mineralized ground accurately to within 50 feet of the surface. The botanists found five bodies of ore near Moab, Utah, solely based on plant data. Two members of the pea family, *Astragalus pattersoni* and *A. preussi,* were the most effective concentrators of radioactive materials.

Other useful species included Prince's plume and tansy mustard. Junipers provided the best deep-deposit information. Their long roots could tap into buried ore deposits and "bring" the information to the surface.

DWARF LUPINE
Lupinus pusillus
Pea family (Fabaceae)

SCORPIONWEED
Phacelia crenulata
Waterleaf family (Hydrophyllaceae)

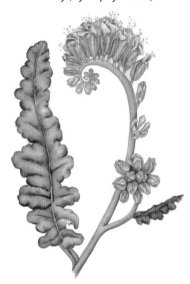

Lupines are easy plants for beginners to identify; all species have leaves that consist of leaflets spreading like fingers from a central point. The dwarf lupine (up to 9 inches high) grows in sandy to gravelly soils, with bright bluish purple flowers blooming throughout the cooler vernal months. Like many plants they cannot withstand hot summer temperatures.

The great botanist Asa Gray wrote that the generic name came from the Latin term for wolf, *lupus,* because lupines "were thought to devour the fertility of the soil," to which Thoreau responded, "This is scurrilous." All members of the pea family improve soil quality by fixing nitrogen, a process by which bacteria attached to the plant's roots convert atmospheric nitrogen into a form useable by plants.

The purple flowers of scorpionweed grow on only one side of a curling stem. This resemblance to a scorpion's tail gives the plants their common name. Two- to 3-inch-long lobed, basal leaves emerge in spring and emit a pungent aroma. Gray hairs, which some people are allergic to, cover the leaves.

Most annual species on the Colorado Plateau depend upon winter precipitation for soil moisture recharge. During winter months, precipitation generally exceeds potential evaporation; therefore, moisture remains in the soil for use by plants. If snow or rain does not fall, then seeds will not germinate in the spring. Scorpionweed is no exception to this generalization; its abundance directly relates to winter precipitation.

COLORADO FOUR O'CLOCK
Mirabilis multiflora
Four O'Clock family (Nyctaginaceae)

ANDERSON'S LARKSPUR
Delphinium andersonii
Buttercup family (Ranunculaceae)

As the name implies, Colorado four o'clock opens late in the afternoon, remaining open until the following morning. Unlike many night-blooming species, which have white flowers, magenta to purple flowers adorn these plants. Hawk moths pollinate them. *Mirabilis* blossoms are deceptive though. Purple sepals, not petals, form the flower. To add to the confusion, green bracts that look like sepals form a bell-shaped structure from which the flowers emerge.

When not in bloom, four o'clock's vegetation and growth habits aid in identification. Heart-shaped, opposite, dark green leaves cover the sprawling plant. They grow on rocky slopes among piñon and juniper and can have stems up to 3 feet long. During wet years four o'clocks can be a conspicuous part of the desert flora.

Larkspur flowers have an unusual floral structure—the two lower petals are short, wide, and purple, and the upper two petals are spurred, white, and narrow. Five purple sepals form an elongated spur, giving the flower a vaguely dolphin-like profile. *Delphinium* is the Greek word for dolphin. Larkspurs grow in sandy soils, rising above nearby plants on 2-foot-tall flower stalks.

All parts of the plant contain toxic alkaloids. Although generally not poisonous to sheep and horses, larkspur ingestion can kill cows, which has led to calls by ranchers for larkspur eradication. The use of herbicides may backfire because some herbicides enhance the plant's palatability. Charles Lewis Anderson (1827–1910) was a doctor who botanized extensively in Nevada.

CLARET CUP
Echinocereus triglochidiatus
Cactus family (Cactaceae)

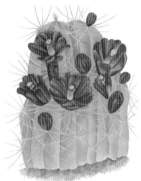

SCARLET GLOBEMALLOW
Sphaeralcea coccinea
Mallow family (Malvaceae)

During a short period in April and May, claret cup cacti produce some of the most striking flowers in canyon country. Brilliant scarlet flowers bloom on a dense mound of many stems; large groupings can consist of more than 50 individual plants. The cylindrical, ribbed stems are 4 to 6 inches high and covered in short, straight spines. Unlike most cacti, these are pollinated by hummingbirds instead of insects. They grow on rocky or gravelly slopes, often among piñon and juniper.

Another barrel-shaped cactus also blooms during spring in this area: whipple fishhook (*Sclerocactus whipplei*). Several lavender flowers top the 5- to 8-inch-tall solitary cactus. They grow in sandy areas and seem to thrive in biological soil crust gardens. One-inch-long spines that resemble fishhooks protect the plant.

Unfortunately, cactus enthusiasts like to collect these two species, and in some places their populations are declining. Uprooted cacti, though, rarely survive in captivity. In some states it is illegal to collect certain species of cactus.

Globemallow grows in sandy areas and on roadsides. A single plant consists of 1- to 2-foot-tall stems extending from a woody base. Star-shaped hairs cover the leaves, giving plants a grayish hue. These fine hairs are also a skin irritant. Several species occur in this region. *S. coccinea* generally has deeply divided, fine-lobed leaves, whereas small-flower globemallow (*S. parvifolia*) has leaves that are more triangular with less-divided lobes, and scaly globemallow (*S. leptophylla*) has narrow-lobed leaves that resemble a bird's foot.

Like many plants, globemallows are pollinated by bees, but globemallows extend this relationship by providing a nighttime home for some of the bees. The principal *Sphaeralcea* pollinators are small bees (less than $1/3$ inch) in the genus *Diadasia*. Female *Diadasia* bees form aggregations of 10 to 50 individual nests, which they build on hard-packed soils away from vegetation. Males, on the other hand, do not construct nests. Instead, they spend the night in the bowl-shaped globemallow flowers curled around the anthers and stamens.

COMMON PAINTBRUSH
Castilleja chromosa
Broomrape family (Orobanchaceae)

Common paintbrush is a deceptive plant—the brilliant colors come not from the flower but from the bracts and calyx. The inconspicuous green corolla forms a narrow tube ($^3/_4$ to 1 inch long) that protrudes out from between the colorful bracts. The bracts emerge early in spring, adding a spark of color to the landscape. Paintbrush range in size from several inches to a foot or more in diameter and are usually covered in fine hairs.

Plants in the *Castilleja* genus are partially parasitic. Although they can survive on their own, paintbrush are healthier when obtaining water and other nutrients from a host. The underground portion of the plant has special conducting tubes, known as haustoria, that attach to the roots of other plants (often sagebrush or buckwheat). This relationship does not appear to harm the host.

Three *Castilleja* species grow in this area. Common paintbrush (*C. chromosa*) and rough paintbrush (*C. scabrida*), early season bloomers, share many characteristics, making identification a challenge. In general, *C. chromosa* is larger, more upright, and has a shorter corolla. Wyoming paintbrush (*C. linariifolia*), a larger, summer blooming species, is the state flower of Wyoming. *Castilleja* is named for Domingo Castillejo, an eighteenth-century Spanish botanist. Plants in the genus *Castilleja* were formerly in the figwort family (*Scrophulariaceae*), but new genetic evidence led scientists to place them in the broomrape family, of which many are parasitic.

EATON'S PENSTEMON
Penstemon eatonii
Plantain family (Plantagnaceae)

Eaton's Penstemon

Utah Penstemon

Unlike many penstemons, Eaton's penstemon corolla tubes do not flare at the mouth. Instead the fused petals form a tight tube. They blossom in early spring and grow in well-drained gravelly and sandy soils. Eaton's penstemon may be recognized by its opposite, shiny, spear-point-shaped leaves that clasp the flower stalk. Longer, basal leaves persist throughout the winter.

Although penstemon plants derive their name from the Latin for five stamens, most penstemon possess only four fertile stamens. The fifth stamen is sterile and often covered in dense hairs, leading to the common moniker "beardtongue" for many penstemon species. This hairy stamen, or staminode, serves two purposes: It repels small insects seeking nectar, and it acts as a guide for bees seeking nectar.

The shape and color of a penstemon flower also influences pollinators. The stigma and stamens, advantageously located to receive and transmit pollen from pollinators, hang down from the top of the floral tube. Most penstemons flare open at the lower lip of the corolla, providing a landing pad for pollinators. In a nonflaring species (e.g., Eaton's), access is restricted to pollinators that can hover, which translates to hummingbirds and butterflies. Red flowers generally lack odor; therefore, they are pollinated by birds, which tend to have poorly developed olfactory abilities. Insects, on the other hand, often use odor as a key for finding flowers.

More than 250 species of penstemon grow in the United States with more than 65 species occurring in Utah. In 1939, Richardson Wright wrote in *The Gardener's Bed-Book,* "Next year, sans faut, I shall go exploring into the hinterlands of the Penstemon world…. I've no illusions about all of the Penstemons being beauties, yet the experience will be worth the trouble." In southern Utah penstemon range in color from blue (blue penstemon, *P. cyanocaulis*) to deep red (Utah penstemon, *P. utahensis*) to lavender (Palmer's penstemon, *P. palmeri*).

Daniel Cady Eaton was a nineteenth-century Yale botanist who collected in Utah. Edward Palmer collected more than 100,000 plant specimens, which he sold to museums across the United States.

SCARLET GILIA
Ipomopsis aggregata
Phlox family (Polemoniaceae)

During a scarlet gilia's first year, the plant develops a rosette of finely divided leaves. In subsequent years, a single 10- to 32-inch-long stem develops, followed by flowering, reproduction, and death. This process takes between 1 and 8 years. Gilia are sometimes mistaken for Eaton's or Utah penstemon, two other red tubular flowers. However, penstemon does not produce pointed-tipped flowers, and has three fused petals on the bottom and two on the top of the flower, unlike the radially symmetrical gilia.

One ecologist described scarlet gilia as "the wiliest wildflower in the West" because of its dynamic ability to adapt to changes in its environment. Unlike many plants, scarlet gilias thrive when mule deer eat them. After being browsed, the plants produce new flowering stalks that grow faster and yield more flowers and fruits than ungrazed plants.

Scarlet gilia also adapts to seasonal changes in pollinators. Early in the year when hummingbirds are more common, its flowers are red, the color preferred by the small birds. Later in the summer, most gilias are pink to white. By then, hummingbirds have migrated out of the region, and a pollinator that prefers lighter-colored flowers, the sphinx moth, has become dominant.

The common name honors Italian astronomer and botanist Felipo Gilli (1756–1821).

Grasses and Inconspicuous Flowers

HALOGETON
Halogeton glomeratus
Amaranth family (Amaranthaceae)

In the January 15, 1951, *Life* magazine, the article titled "Sheep-Killing Weed" described a deadly scourge threatening "more than a third of US flocks." The toxic plant, *Halogeton glomeratus,* had driven one rancher out of business when 1,620 of his 1,700 sheep had eaten the plant and died. Oxalic acid in the leaves had combined with calcium in the blood and killed the animals within hours.

Native to eastern Russia and northern China, *Halogeton* was first collected in the United States on June 20, 1934, near Wells, Nevada. Not until 1942 did ranchers discover its toxicity, which has now been found to be worse for cattle than sheep. The short shrubs thrive in disturbed soils and saline soils, where they can grow in dense stands. They have 0.5-inch long, fleshy leaves shaped like a sausage and tipped with a short spine. Although the flowers are inconspicuous on the red stems, they produce abundant seeds, which can remain viable for more than a decade. The plants resemble tumbleweeds when young. *Halogeton* comes from the Greek for "salty neighbor."

RICEGRASS
Achnatherum hymenoides
Grass family (Poaceae)

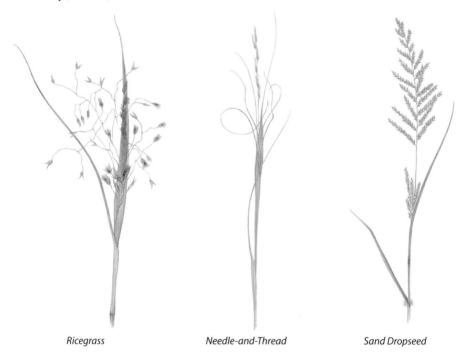

Ricegrass   Needle-and-Thread   Sand Dropseed

Many desert grasses grow in clumps or bunches in contrast to the familiar sod formers found in people's yards. Ricegrass is a classic desert grass, growing in bunches up to 2 feet tall. In spring or early summer, it sets relatively large seeds (about half the size of a grain of rice), which are black and protein rich. In fall, when the seeds have dropped, the two papery bracts that surrounded the seed remain on the plant. Ricegrass seeds were a prominent part of the diet of the hunter-gatherer cultures that lived throughout the Southwest.

Bunch grasses are an important part of the desert community and can cover extensive areas. They are well adapted to dry, hot summers and cold, relatively wet winters. Most are perennial, living for many years. During the long summer drought season, the grasses become dormant and only turn green again with the return of spring rains.

A closely related bunch grass often found growing with ricegrass in sandy areas is needle-and-thread (*Hesperostipa comata*). The common name refers to the seed, which has a needle-sharp head with a thread extending out from it. These seeds will corkscrew into the ground.

Sand dropseed (*Sporobolus cryptandrus*) is another tall bunch grass. It is relatively easy to seed and is commonly used to reseed damaged areas.

CHEATGRASS
Bromus tectorum
Grass family (Poaceae)

GALLETA GRASS
Hilaria jamesii
Grass family (Poaceae)

Cheatgrass is an annual with 2- to 6-inch-long seed heads. The tallest plants can be 30 inches high, although most cheatgrass is shorter.

Cheatgrass invaded the western United States between 1889 and 1894, probably from European wheat brought with settlers. It quickly established itself across a vast region, "cheating" farmers out of their normal wheat crop. Cheatgrass moved into areas damaged by overgrazing and cultivation, eventually outcompeting the native grasses.

Several factors combined to produce the successful invasion. Cheatgrass was pre-adapted to the West: It required wet, cold winters and dry, hot summers. Increased land use by livestock permitted the alien grass to colonize disturbed areas. In areas where fire altered the land, cheatgrass outcompeted native grasses and shrubs by being more effi-cient at using the available subsurface water.

One ecologist summed up the effects of cheatgrass: "Seldom in the recent transfor-mation of the Earth's vegetation by mobile Occidental man and his plants has the vegeta-tion of such a large area been transformed so swiftly and (apparently) permanently."

Because galleta grass withstands heavy grazing, it is an important range species. This 15-inch-tall grass often grows in asso-ciation with blue grama (*Bouteloua gracilis*) in sagebrush plains. The seed head of a blue grama looks like eyelashes. These two spe-cies do not form clumps, but they do form sod. They spread by runners or creeping underground stems, known as rhizomes. Both species are perennials.

Blue grama

COMMON REED
Phragmites australis
Grass family (Poaceae)

CANAIGRE
Rumex hymenosepalus
Buckwheat family (Polygonaceae)

The common reed, usually just referred to by its generic name *Phragmites,* flowers and produces seeds between July and September. Vegetative reproduction, however, accounts for most new growth. Plants reach heights of 10 feet or more crowned with a foot-long plume of flowers. A fence-like growth habit gives the common reed its generic name, *Phragmites*. *Phragma* is Greek for "fence."

Phragmites has one of the largest distributions of any plant, occurring naturally on six continents. It grows in freshwater, brackish, acidic, and alkaline wetlands and is typically the dominant species, often forming dense, monotypic stands.

Phragmites also colonizes disturbed areas and can become invasive. During the winter, when the plants die and dry out, the potential fire hazard may increase. Furthermore, large stands may negatively affect wildlife habitat and water flow regimes. Distinguishing natural populations from invasive populations is often challenging, but if this information is known, control and management are feasible.

A cluster of nonshowy flowers grows on top of stout 2- to 4-foot-long reddish stems. The edible stem gives canaigre its other common name, wild rhubarb. Some people also call it dock, an Old English term. White to pink three-winged fruits replace the flowers, producing a more visible display.

Canaigre (Spanish: *cana agria,* white/gray hair + sour) looks out of place in a desert environment with its 3-inch-wide, 9-inch-long leaves. A deep tuberous root provides the moisture to sustain the fleshy leaves. To prevent desiccation, canaigre starts growing early in spring before the temperatures become too hot; by summer the lush foliage has withered away.

Also, look for the roots, which are high in tannin and can closely resemble a dried-up poop when broken off from the plant.

MOSSES

Mosses are members of the bryophytes, which include liverworts and hornworts. ("Wort" comes from the Old English *wryt* for plant.) All lack fruits, flowers, and well-defined vascular tissues, the parts of a plant that transport water. Most liverworts and all mosses do have leaves; hornworts and some liverworts instead grow via a thallus, a flattened structure that looks like a leaf. Typical growth habitat is a packed mat or cushion. When they reproduce, plants send up stalked capsules, their fruiting body.

All bryophytes reproduce by spores and not by seeds, which gives them a fundamentally different lifestyle than vascular plants. Spores develop in a capsule that grows on the end of a seta, or stalk. Within the capsule, the spores are held by toothlike structures, which swell and contract in relation to the amount of moisture in the air. The teeth open in drier conditions, releasing the spores into the wind. Mosses can also reproduce asexually.

Mosses are remarkable organisms, able to go from "mummies to active plants" in seconds, as one ecologist told me. Despite the lack of a well-developed vascular system, mosses can trap and store water. In addition, although they lack true roots, they have rootlike holdfasts called rhizoides, which enable them to anchor to atypical places for plants, such as bare rock, and some mosses have pigments that protect them from solar radiation. These adaptations, along with their ability to survive for years in a completely desiccated state, have allowed a wide variety of mosses to adapt to southwestern deserts.

Desert mosses grow best in the shade when the temperature is between 60°F and 70°F. In the desert, this means that mosses often grow on north-facing slopes and at the base of rocks and shrubs. They require moisture for photosynthesis and at least 24 hours to produce food for growth.

One of the amazing abilities of mosses is their seeming ability to resurrect themselves, that is to spring back to life, even after years of dormancy, when watered. Watering a moss with a water bottle, however, can be very damaging to the moss, particularly if done on a hot summer day. In this situation, the moss colony can dry out very quickly, which can severely damage shoots and leaves adapted to slow changes.

Walking on desert mosses can further damage the plants. If the damage is excessive, the mosses could take decades to recover, but if very limited, foot traffic could aid a colony by dispersing fragments to new habitat.

Although we felt it was important to include mosses, we chose not to illustrate them because of the difficulties inherent in identifying individual species.

SILVER-TIPPED MOSS

Bryum argenteum

Bryaceae family

One of the few bryophytes found on all the continents, often occupying disturbed habitat, including golf courses and city parks. In Utah, silver-tipped moss grows in full sun and partial shade, on rocks, soils, tree bark, and cement. This is the largest moss genus in the moss world, with its distinctive white to silver color. Two species, however, found on the Colorado Plateau, *B. kunzei* and *B. caespiticium,* are dull yellowish green when dry. When wet they turn more golden yellow. *B. caespiticium* has a red stem.

ONION MOSS

Pterygoneurum ovatum

Pottiaceae family

The common name refers to the growth habit, which resembles bulbous, miniature cabbages or onions. They can form dense cushions, dominated by the whitish, tufted awns that extend out from the yellowish to brown leaves. The leaves may not be visible, such that the cushion looks like a fuzz patch. They commonly grow with *Syntrichia caninervis.*

SHORT TWISTED MOSS

Syntrichia caninervis

Pottiaceae family

When dry, plants are black above and brown below. They can form extensive ground cover in areas of blackbrush, though curiously they are almost always female populations with just a rare male or two. Short twisted mosses typically do not reproduce sexually or, if they attempt it, a lack of moisture and nitrogen will lead to aborted fertilizations. So few males exist because it takes so much energy to produce sperm, no matter whether they are successful at mating or not. Egg production, on the other hand, is relatively low cost, because females don't have to nurture offspring, and females can devote more energy to survival and growth, which allows them to become dominant in deserts.

TWISTED MOSS

Syntrichia ruralis

Pottiaceae family

When dry, plants are dull to black above and reddish below. They turn bright green when moist. The white awns that protrude above act as a sort of umbrella, allowing only the densest rains to soak the moss. This prevents plants from receiving too little moisture, which can lead to rapid desiccation and not enough time for complete photosynthesis. Awns may also help reduce the amount of sunlight reaching the plant. The stems can grow up to several centimeters high. Like *S. caninervis,* they grow on soils, although *S. ruralis* is more cosmopolitan.

Close-up

Why Names Change

Every few years a number of revisions to plant and animal names occur. Some families had historic names that no longer reflect modern requirements. For example, all plant families must end with *-aceae,* so that the legumes, formerly *Leguminae,* are now *Fabaceae.* Another reason for change may simply be due to an original misspelling of the name or due to someone realizing that an earlier name was correct and needed to be restored. Some common names change in part because of fashion or political correctness.

The more substantial changes are due to modern techniques with DNA. With DNA studies, scientists have been able to tease out deeper and more fundamental details, particularly on an evolutionary scale, where research shows different relationships between plants. For example, the DNA might show that morphological characters are an artificial relationship not backed up by molecular data. This could lead either to splitting or lumping of species.

A similar situation occurs with the geological timescale. Better techniques, due to better understanding of radiometric dating and better machines, have allowed geologists to more precisely date rocks. In addition, all time periods are based on a specifically defined rock layer, and sometimes geologists realize that a specific layer did not accurately reflect worldwide changes.

No matter why dates and names change, you can expect them to continue to evolve for the foreseeable future.

LICHENS

One of the marvels of the natural world—neither plant nor animal—lichens have been described as more like an ecosystem than an individual organism. They grow through a symbiotic relationship between fungi and algae or cyanobacteria (called photobionts), both of which can photosynthesize and produce sugars and other carbohydrates. In a lichen, fungi feed off the nutrients produced by the photosynthesizers.

Approximately 14,000 lichen species grow worldwide from the deserts to temperate rain forests to the frozen Arctic. One study estimated that lichens form the dominant vegetation on 8 percent of Earth's land surface. They can live on bark, wood, rock, soil, leaves, and even animals. For instance, lichens growing on a lacewing larvae help camouflage the immature insect. Often growing less than a millimeter per year, lichens can live for several thousand years, and can withstand months of drought and temperatures ranging from well below freezing to almost boiling.

Lichens range from white to black to yellow to red to green and can vary within species depending upon age, substrate, and exposure to sunlight. All of these colors occur in canyon country lichens. The vivid colors may help protect the algae from solar radiation.

Lichens are often pioneer species, colonizing bare rock. They propagate via broken fragments and fungal spores, as well as through reproductive bundles that consist of hyphae (branching, threadlike structures of fungus responsible for feeding, growing, and reproduction) and photobiont cells. As they grow, lichens help break down the rock, as hyphae penetrate into the rock. They also set the stage for vascular plants by trapping dust and seeds, and by dying, which provides organic material for soil development.

Unlike vascular plants, lichens lack true roots, leaves, and stems. They do have a body, known as a thallus (plural thalli). Thalli come primarily in three varieties. Most common are flattened crustose lichens, so tightly attached to their substrate that they cannot be pried up without destroying them. Foliose lichens look a bit more lettucelike with a leafy body that protrudes beyond the substrate. Fructose lichens grow as shrubby, branching bodies or dangle in long strands. In the four corners region, more than half the species are crustose. Foliose species make up 38 percent and fructose 4 percent.

HOARY COBBLESTONE LICHEN
Acarospora strigata
Acarosporaceae family

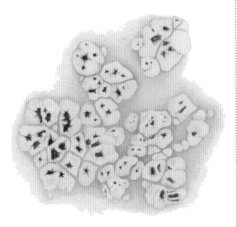

VARYING RIM-LICHEN
Lecanora argopholis
Lecanoraceae family

These yellow-green to gray lichens grow primarily on non-calcareous rocks but may also occur on mosses or plant remains. Sagebrush rim-lichen (*L. garovaglii*) has a light green, sagebrush color with folded lobes. This is also common on sandstone.

Most members of this genus are covered in pruina, or a thin layer of dead hyphae or calcium oxalate crystals. In other words, the lichen has a gray to white surface coating that looks a bit like flour or frost. Some lichenologists propose that the pruinose veneer blocks solar radiation, some that it concentrates light for cells that photosynthesize. Others think that it provides moisture via the water entrapped in the calcium oxalate crystals. Underneath the pruina, this species is dark brown, which is often visible in the center of the white coating, such that the thalli look like tiny dabs of marshmallow dotted with black eyes.

BROWN ROCK POSY
Rhizoplaca peltata
Lecanoraceae family

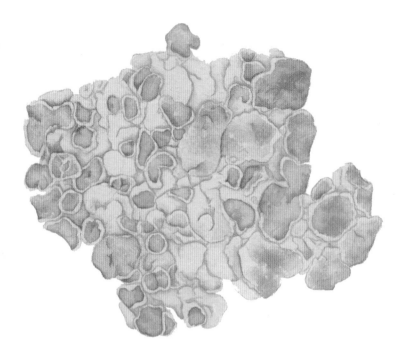

The common name refers to the superficial resemblance to flowers with some lobes flaring out above the surrounding structure. In profile, the fruiting bodies have a wineglass-like shape, with a yellow-green rim and tan center. Thalli can be more than 2 inches wide. Unlike other members of this genus, *R. peltata* lacks a pruinose coating on the fruiting bodies. One of many saxicolous, or rock-dwelling, species of lichens, they grow primarily on calcareous rocks.

PLITT'S ROCK SHIELD
Xanthoparmelia plittii
Parmeliaceae family

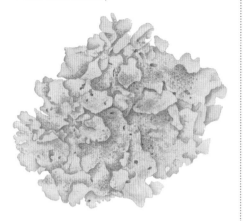

DESERT FIREDOT LICHEN
Caloplaca trachyphylla
Teloschistaceae family

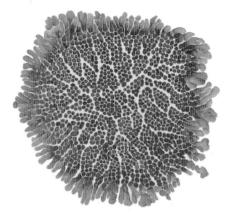

A classic-looking, light green lichen with leafy lobes, Plitt's rock shield is one of many *Xanthopermelia* species growing across the Colorado Plateau. Most are hard to distinguish but *X. chlorochroa,* or tumbleweed shield lichen, is somewhat unusual with branching light green lobes that look like tiny antlers. The lobes curl inward. This lichen is further unusual because it grows loose on soil—hence the tumbleweed moniker—and because it may be toxic to cattle, sheep, and elk. Researchers attributed the death of 400 to 500 elk in Wyoming in 2004 to lichen intoxication. In contrast, pronghorn eat tumbleweed shield lichen without any issues.

This striking orange, crustose lichen grows on calcium-rich rocks, primarily sandstone, where it can form roundish bodies, several inches wide. The spreading lobes look like miniature orange mudflows fingering their way across rock. Not terribly fast growers, they spread at less than $3/_{50}$ inch per year. Other species of *Caloplaca* are also orange to yellow, though a few varieties are also gray. Another species of lichen, the whitish *Acarospora stapfiana* (no common name), often invades and parasitizes its more vibrantly colored cousin.

Hanging Gardens

Despite the desert's appearance, water is abundant; the only problem is that much of it is held within the porous sandstone. During a rainstorm most water runs off the barren surface, but some soaks into the rock and slowly percolates down. When the water encounters a less-porous rock unit, such as shale, it flows downslope until it emerges at the surface as a spring or a seep.

On vertical surfaces, the water weakens and eventually collapses the rock, forming an overhang that provides a prime microhabitat for plants to exploit—a constant supply of water that is often shaded. Animals exploit this water, too, and it is common to see a wide array of mammal tracks near these ecosystems.

Within a hanging garden environment, three different growing areas develop. One group of plants grows directly at the seep layer, where water is abundant and soil minimal. A second group of plants, generally algae, flourishes on the vertical wall below the seep. Here soil is essentially nonexistent and water constant, but less plentiful than above. The third, largest, and most diverse area forms where the vertical wall changes to a sloped wall. The water supply at this lowest level is generally good and the soil most abundant.

Recent studies have shown that hanging garden systems are extremely fragile. The main source of soil for the lowest, most accessible area comes from the collapsing walls; therefore, soil develops slowly and any damage is long lasting.

Many of the plants growing in hanging gardens are endemic to the Colorado Plateau and are only found in these moist habitats.

One of the first people to study hanging gardens was botanist Alice Eastwood, a Denver schoolteacher. She made her first studies near Bluff, Utah, in 1895. She eventually headed the California Academy of Sciences, gaining fame for saving numerous botanical specimens during the San Francisco earthquake of 1906.

Cave-dwelling primrose (*Primula specuicola*) is one of several plants that she discovered in the hanging garden environment. The small plant roots into the algal mat on the rock surface or within flaking rock layers. Several small lavender, five-petaled flowers grow at the end of a short stem. They bloom early in the year, giving the plant its other common name, Easter primrose. The generic epithet also refers to this early blooming habit; *Primula* is derived from the Latin for first, *primus*.

A brilliant red flower, Eastwood's monkey-flower (*Mimulus eastwoodiae*), honors Eastwood's botanical contributions. This perennial bears elliptical, dark green leaves. The 1-inch-long flowers appear in late spring and bloom into summer. Corollas flare open with three lobes hanging down and two pointing up.

Alcove columbine (*Aquilegia micrantha*), a relative of the better-known state flower of Colorado, grows in the lowest level of the hanging garden. The white flowers bloom throughout the summer. Columbines are generally the largest flowering plant in this environment.

Other hanging garden endemics include maidenhair fern (*Adiantum capillus-veneris*), alcove bog orchid (*Plantanthera zothecina*), and sheathed deathcamas (*Anticlea vaginata*).

1. Water runoff and seepage in hanging garden environment
2. Cave (Easter) Primrose
3. Maidenhair Fern
4. Monkey-flower
5. Alcove Columbine
6. Alcove Bog Orchid
7. Sheathed Deathcamus

MAMMALS

We are mammals. We have key universal features: hair and mammary glands. Although hair only provides limited protection for humans, it is the primary insulator for many mammals. It also aids in camouflage; most mammal hair is a muted color, such as buff, gray, brown, or black, that helps the animal blend into its surroundings. Blotches or spots provide additional camouflage. While we only have two mammary glands, which in females produce milk for our young, other species, such as small rodents, may have eight to ten nipples to supply their large brood.

Baby mammals come in two varieties. Altricial young are born naked, blind, deaf, and unable to walk. Many rodents, bats, and shrews give birth to altricial young. Precocial young, on the other hand, are born with full coats of hair and can see, hear, and move around, at least somewhat. Deer, humans, porcupines, and jackrabbits produce this type of young.

Mammals are "warm-blooded," which means that we regulate our body temperatures internally. Warm-blooded animals are known as endotherms, as opposed to ectotherms, whose body temperatures respond directly to the temperature of the surrounding environment. Birds are other endotherms, while reptiles and amphibians are ectotherms.

One unusual, but not universal, mammalian characteristic is the ability to produce a horn or antler. Horns are made of sheaths of keratin, like fingernails, that grow over a bony core. Unlike antlers, which consist entirely of bone, fall off in winter, are generally branched, and are limited to the deer family, horns grow continuously throughout their bearer's life and are not shed.

Torpor is another common, but not universal, mammalian activity. Torpor consists of a considerably reduced metabolic rate with subsequent slow breathing and heart rate. The body temperature drops down near the ambient temperature and the animal goes to sleep, living off its accumulated fat. An animal may go torpid daily, as in the case of bats. Seasonal torpor is known as hibernation (winter) or estivation (summer).

The first mammals appeared about 220 million years ago, having evolved from the therapsids, or mammal-like reptiles. The earliest ones were mouse-size and primitive with a small brain. Dinosaurs were the dominant life form for over 100 million years of our predecessors' evolution. The early mammals would have to wait until the end of the Cretaceous period and the extinction of the non-avian dinosaurs before they had their chance to radiate into myriad sizes and shapes. Most modern mammal genera had evolved by 25 million years ago. Common and scientific names are based on *Mammal Species of the World*, Third Edition, except for canyon bat, a name that changed after the publication of that book.

Please note: Do not feed any mammals. Feeding animals is against the law in national parks. A study of deer in the Grand Canyon revealed many deer that had consumed human food were starving to death because the animals also ate plastic bags, which blocked their stomachs and prevented them from absorbing food. In addition, some mammals carry diseases that can be transmitted to you when you are feeding them.

Bats, Rabbits, and Rodents

CANYON BAT
Parastrellus hesperus
Order Chiroptera, Vespertilionidae family
Length 2³/₄–3³/₄ in., wingspan 7 in., ashen
gray above and below

As the summer sun sets, one of the most conspicuous mammals in canyon country appears, the canyon bat, known until 2006 as the western pipistrelle. They fly near lights, consuming numerous small insects such as leafhoppers, mosquitoes, and small moths. These tiny bats (they weigh less than a nickel) emerge from rocky crevices and start foraging just after sundown, remaining aloft for a few hours before returning to night roosts. Canyon bats are one of the few species of bat that may be seen during the day.

The bats' activity is temperature dependent. They have a relatively large surface area in proportion to their mass, which leads to thermoregulatory problems. If the temperature drops too low or rises too high, they must become dormant. During winter, bats hibernate communally in caves and abandoned mines or singly in cracks and tree trunks, or they migrate south. Be careful not to disturb them if you encounter bats in winter, as you may force them to come out of hibernation, which uses up their stored food reserves.

Parastrellus comes from the Greek, *para*, meaning beside or aside, in reference to its previous scientific name, *Pipistrellus,* from the Italian word for bat, *pipistrello.*

Bat Habitat

Bats have an undeserved reputation as rabies-spreading, blood-sucking beasts. Most studies show that the chance of contracting rabies from a bat is slim. Bats are extremely beneficial animals, consuming enormous numbers of insects (including such agricultural pests as potato beetles, corn-borers, and cutworm moths) and pollinating many flowers. Only three species of bat, none of which occur in this region, depend upon blood for nourishment.

Although habitat destruction has contributed to the decline of many bat populations throughout the West, one human change to the landscape has benefited bats: mines. In the search for minerals, tens of thousands of mines were dug over the last 150 years. Several species of bats now exploit this newly created habitat. All of the bat species in this region use mines, and several may depend upon mines as their primary roosting or maternity sites.

Many mines are deep and/or unstable, and entering them is hazardous. Groups throughout the country are beginning to inventory and protect bat-filled mines. Gates built across a mine entrance allow the bats to move freely in and out, while prohibiting human entrance.

At this point, white nose syndrome, a fungal disease that has killed millions of bats in the northeastern United States, has not reached canyon country or Utah.

BIG BROWN BAT
Eptesicus fuscus
Order Chiroptera, Vespertilionidae family
Length 4¹/₈–5 in., wingspan 16¹/₂ in., brown fur, short eared

Big brown bats occur throughout the lower 48 states and live in a wide variety of habitats. They commonly roost in attics, barns, and other man-made structures; thus, they may be the most commonly seen American bat. These small insectivores consume flying insects, especially beetles. Because big browns are found in association with humans, they often eat insects we don't like. When big browns emerge at night, they fly 20 to 30 feet above the ground in a predictable, straight flight, often feeding in the same locality for several weeks.

Like most canyon country bats, big browns mate in fall before winter hibernation. Ovulation and fertilization occur in the spring. Usually two blind, deaf, and nearly helpless young are born 2 to 3 months later. They begin to fly well in 4 to 6 weeks. Summer maternity colonies of females and their young may include more than 300 individuals. None of the common bats in this region form large colonies like the millions of Brazilian free-tailed bats (*Tadarida brasiliensis*) at Carlsbad Caverns National Park in New Mexico.

PALLID BAT
Antrozous pallidus
Order Chiroptera, Vespertilionidae family
Length 4^1/$_4$–5^3/$_8$ in., wingspan 14 in., smoky white, with large ears

DESERT COTTONTAIL
Sylvilagus audubonii
Order Lagomorpha, Leporidae family
Length 13^3/$_4$–16^1/$_2$ in., tail 1^3/$_4$–2^3/$_8$ in., ears 2^1/$_4$–2^3/$_4$ in., pale gray with a yellowish tinge, paler sides, white beneath

In contrast to most bats, pallid bats forage primarily on the ground and are relatively good walkers. They consume large insects, lizards, scorpions, and small mice. They also incidentally ingest the seeds and fruits of cactus while catching juice-seeking moths. Ground feeding has its costs though. Pallid bats may rip a wing membrane, have their skin pierced by thorns and spines, or be eaten by snakes or owls. Pallid bats have a strong odor, particularly noticeable when they are alarmed.

Bats locate their prey, maneuver in the roost, and navigate by transmitting calls and receiving echoes, a process known as echolocation. Bats emit sounds through their mouths, usually at frequencies too high for humans to hear. The echo that returns from an object provides information on size, speed, shape, and direction of movement.

Pallid bats also use vocalizations for communication as well as navigation and hunting. One study found five different types of signals: intimidation, squabbling, contentment, plaintive, and directional. (See prairie dogs, page 97, and coyotes, page 107, for other mammal vocalizations.)

The widespread desert cottontail is active eating plants in the evening and at dawn and dusk. It does not tolerate high temperatures and spends the day in abandoned badger or coyote burrows or under vegetation. Cottontails often leave their hiding spot when approached. This characteristic and their general abundance made cottontails an important food source for the early inhabitants of the Southwest. They still constitute one of the most important North American game mammals.

Cottontails reach sexual maturity at 4 months of age. After a 4-week gestation period, they give birth to two to three altricial young (unlike jackrabbit young, which have open eyes and are fully furred). The young leave the protective nest in a couple of weeks and usually breed during their first season. Without predators, rabbit populations would go unchecked, creating boom-bust cycles. Their average life span is less than a year.

Desert cottontails might be confused with the less abundant Nuttall's, or mountain, cottontail (*S. nuttalli*). Nuttall's cottontails usually live at higher elevations and have shorter, black-tipped ears. See Sego lily, page 62, for information on Thomas Nuttall.

BLACK-TAILED JACKRABBIT
Lepus californicus
Order Lagomorpha, Leporidae family
Length 18¹/₄–24³/₄ in., tail 2–4³/₈ in., ears
3⁷/₈–7 in., black-tipped ears, black tail

HOPI CHIPMUNK
Tamias rufus
Order Rodentia, Sciuridae family
Total 7³/₄–9⁵/₈ in., tail 3¹/₈–4 ¹/₄ in., white facial
stripes, central dark stripe on back

In contrast to many North American mammals, black-tailed jackrabbits have increased their range because of human changes to the landscape. Decreases in predator populations, increases in cultivation, and overgrazing have created conditions ideal for this hare to exploit. They prefer open areas that offer grasses and forbs to eat and scattered shrubs to hide under. Open country also offers ideal escape terrain; when pursued, they can sprint up to 35 miles per hour interspersed with 20-foot leaps. Predators include coyotes, foxes, raptors, and larger snakes.

Jacks spend the day in forms, shallow depressions dug under shrubs or near clumps of grass. They cope with high temperatures by dissipating heat through their large ears; ear vein dilation releases a third of their body heat. Feeding occurs at dawn and dusk. Like other lagomorphs, jackrabbits excrete two types of feces, hard and soft. The soft material is reingested, which provides the hare with vitamins and aids in digestion, a process known as coprophagy. They obtain most of their water from their food.

A seasonally dependent diet and need for free water dictates the Hopi chipmunk's habitat requirements. Their food consists of ricegrass seeds in early summer; ricegrass, juniper berries, and cliffrose and skunkbush seeds in late summer; and Russian thistle, piñon nuts, and acorns in the fall. They live in piñon-juniper woodlands or in the ecotone between the piñon-juniper and sandy ricegrass flats. Because they do not metabolize water from seeds, Hopi chipmunks usually build their nests in rocky areas where rainwater can collect in shallow depressions.

Hopi chipmunks are one of the most commonly seen mammals in canyon country. They are often confused with the white-tailed antelope squirrel. Chipmunks are smaller, have white facial stripes, and do not carry their tails over their heads when running.

The closely related and similar-looking least chipmunk (*T. minimus*) also occurs in the region. They are more common in the western part of the state and are smaller and lighter colored than the Hopi chipmunk.

MARMOT
Marmota flaviventris
Order Rodentia, Sciuridae family
Length 19–28 in., tail 6–7¹/₂ in.,
yellowish brown

WHITE-TAILED ANTELOPE SQUIRREL
Ammospermophilus leucurus
Order Rodentia, Sciuridae family
Total 7⁵/₈–8³/₈ in., tail 2¹/₈–3 in., reddish back, two white stripes on side of back, white eye ring, no facial stripes

Marmots may be encountered throughout the higher plateaus of southern Utah, although they are more common in mountainous regions. They usually inhabit rocky places on mountain slopes and meadows. Nearby rocks serve as a sort of deck for sunning and observation. When alarmed, marmots shriek and waddle into their rocky home. Like their close relative, the woodchuck, marmots dig underground burrows for nursing areas and hibernation. They can hibernate from September to May.

The specific epithet refers to the yellow (*flavo*) belly (*ventris*). The tail is long and bushy. The marmot is the largest member of the squirrel family.

Few small canyon country mammals are diurnal; the white-tailed antelope squirrel is one exception. During the day they scurry from shady spot to shady spot, stopping and standing often to survey the surroundings. When running, they hold their bushy tails over their backs, exposing the white undersurface. They cope with the heat by allowing their body temperature to climb above 106°F. Antelope squirrels cool themselves by spreading saliva on their faces, and if the temperature gets too hot, they remain in their burrows.

These squirrels are not choosy feeders. Seeds and fruits make up about 50 percent of their diet. As spring approaches they turn to succulent greens. Late summer food includes grasshoppers, beetles, and Jerusalem crickets. Other items on their seasonal menu include lizards and rodent carrion. Antelope squirrels are frequently encountered sitting atop shrubs, eating fresh greens. Visitors often mistake these perching squirrels for bushy-tailed birds. When alarmed, the squirrel produces a loud, birdlike call.

ROCK SQUIRREL
Spermophilus variegatus
Order Rodentia, Sciuridae family
Total 16⁷/₈–20³/₄ in., tail 6³/₄–9⁷/₈ in., gray with black and white flecks, reddish rump

Rock Squirrel

Abert's Squirrel

Golden-mantled
Ground Squirrel

Most animal names tell a story, and in the case of the rock squirrel, the common and scientific names provide good information. These are ground-dwelling animals that prefer rocky terrain on slopes or in canyons, though like most squirrels, they will climb trees for food. *Spermophilus* means seed lover, a reference to their diet, which also includes fruits, blooms, foliage, and occasionally insects and carrion. The specific epithet refers to the variegated coloring of black and white flecks on a grayish background with a reddish rump. They have long bushy tails.

Rock squirrels build burrows under and around boulders, or, if near humans, under woodpiles or junk cars. They may be seen near their burrows sunning on rocks. Hibernation ranges from 1 to 6 months, but they are "light sleepers" and usually emerge from their den once a week. Rock squirrels are not territorial, although they may defend a small personal space. When alarmed, they deliver a high-pitched whistle-like cry or chirp.

Two other members of the squirrel family inhabit the region: the Abert's squirrel (*Sciurus aberti*) and the golden-mantled ground squirrel (*S. lateralis*). The Abert's, which is tree-based, lives exclusively in ponderosa pine forests. Its splendid tail is black and white above and pure white below. Samuel Woodhouse collected the first Abert's specimens in Arizona's San Francisco mountains and named them in 1853 in honor of John James Abert of the Corps of Topographical Engineers. The golden-mantled, a ground dweller, is a denizen of moist conifer forests. They may be confused with chipmunks, but they lack facial striping and have no middorsal black stripe.

WHITE-TAILED PRAIRIE DOG
Cynomys leucurus
Order Rodentia, Sciuridae family
Length 13³/₈–14⁵/₈ in., tail 1⁵/₈–2³/₈ in., white-tipped tail

GUNNISON'S PRAIRIE DOG
Cynomys gunnisoni
Order Rodentia, Sciuridae family
Length 12–14 in., tail 1¹/₂–2⁵/₈ in., gray-tipped tail

White-tailed Prairie Dog

John Ordway, a member of the Lewis and Clark Expedition, called these rodents prairie dogs because their vocalizations sound like a dog's bark. (Clark liked "ground rats" while Lewis preferred "barking squirrels.") Prairie dogs have a wide range of calls, including a repetitive warning bark (often used when golden eagles and other raptors fly overhead), a threatening snarl or growl, and a distress scream. This allows the animals to communicate throughout the colony, or town. Unlike the black-tailed prairie dog *(C. ludovicianus)*, which inhabits grasslands, the two canyon country species do not build large towns. Separate colonies of as few as three or four or as many as a hundred individuals, though, may be close enough together to give the impression of one large town.

In the past, ranchers and farmers systematically destroyed towns, believing these animals contributed to deterioration of rangeland. More recently, though, ecologists have started to show that prairie dogs actually benefit rangelands and do negligible damage to range plants and animals. As one ecologist noted, "If the prairie dog were overwhelmingly destructive . . . it is not likely they would have flourished for the million or so years they [inhabited] the prairie."

Both species in this area are strictly diurnal and eat mostly grasses, forbs, and sedges, but will eat insects when necessary. Badgers, coyotes, and golden eagles prey upon both species. Prairie dogs occur in open grassy or shrubby areas, seeming to prefer areas of shale-derived soils.

White-tailed prairie dogs are the larger of the two species, have a shorter and whiter tail, and are more yellowish than cinnamon colored. They are found north and west of the Colorado River. White-tailed prairie dogs hibernate.

Gunnison's remain underground during colder months, but it is not known if they hibernate. Gunnison's burrows are shallow and the entrance mound is simply a small pile of dirt excavated from the burrow tunnel. They strictly occur south and east of the Colorado River. The closely related Utah prairie dog *(C. parvidens)* is the only prairie dog found in the far western part of Utah.

John Gunnison (1812–1853) was on a Corps of Topographical Engineers expedition near Utah's Sevier River when he was killed. The Gunnison River in Colorado and Gunnison's prairie dog are two reminders of his explorations in this region.

NORTHERN POCKET GOPHER
Thomomys talpoides
Order Rodentia, Geomyidae family
Total 6³/₄–9¹/₂ in., tail 1³/₄–3 in., grayish, hairless tail

PLAINS POCKET MOUSE
Perognathus flavescens
Order Rodentia, Heteromyidae family
Total 4³/₈–5¹/₈ in., tail 1⁷/₈–2³/₈ in., pale buff with blackish coloring above, lighter below, tiny ears

Northern pocket gophers are rarely seen, but they do live across the region, generally emerging at night to forage on forbs, tubers, and bulbs. The word gopher comes from the French *gaufre,* meaning honeycomb, a reference to the animal's extensive underground burrow system. A tunnel network may stretch up to 500 feet and include numerous entrances. The most common gopher sign is a 3- to 5-inch-high mound of dirt.

Plains pocket mice are primarily seed eaters and, like several other desert species, they get water from the fat of seeds they consume. During the spring they may also eat insects. These small, soft-furred animals, sometimes called silky pocket mice, live in sandy areas with mixed vegetation. Studies in Canyonlands National Park found that pocket mice seem to prefer degraded rangeland. They are nocturnal and plug their burrow entrances to keep the internal humidity high.

ORD'S KANGAROO RAT
Dipodomys ordii
Order Rodentia, Heteromyidae family
Total 8$^{1}/_{8}$–11$^{1}/_{8}$ in., tail 3$^{7}/_{8}$–6$^{3}/_{8}$ in., long hind feet, large cheek pouches

The kangaroo rat is often called the quintessential desert mammal. Kangaroo rats avoid the desert heat by foraging only at night, spending the day in an underground burrow, plugged to keep it cool and moist. These rats further conserve water by using their elongated nasal passages to cool and recapture outgoing breath. They efficiently reduce waste by producing extremely concentrated urine and feces. Probably their best-known adaptation, shared with many desert denizens, is their ability to survive without drinking water; they metabolize water from seeds they eat.

Ord's kangaroo rat has the widest range of the six species of kangaroo rats that inhabit the Southwest. They live in a variety of habitats but require sandy substrates for cleaning, open areas for escape routes, and plants with abundant seeds. Their oily fur becomes matted unless they periodically bathe in sand. All species of *Dipodomys* have large hind limbs that allow them to move quickly in a kangaroo-like fashion. When pursued they bound away unpredictably; their long tails act as balances, enabling them to maintain control when moving erratically. While foraging, they stuff their cheek pouches full of plant seeds as diverse as evening primrose, cliffrose, and pepperweed.

Adults are antisocial and antagonistic except during breeding season, which varies widely over their geographic range. In canyon country, mating occurs from January to March and late August to October. They produce two to three altricial young. After leaving the nest, kangaroo rats either build their own burrow or inhabit an abandoned one. The elaborate multiroom complex usually opens under a shrub or clump of grass. An adult lives alone in its burrow.

This species is named for George Ord (1781–1866), who described and named several mammals and birds from the Lewis and Clark Expedition, including the grizzly bear and pronghorn.

BEAVER
Castor canadensis
Order Rodentia, Castoridae family
Total 35–46 in., tail 12–17 in.; sleek, brown
fur; webbed hind feet; broad, flat tail;
up to 50 lb.

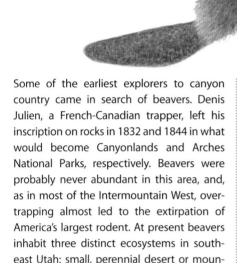

Some of the earliest explorers to canyon country came in search of beavers. Denis Julien, a French-Canadian trapper, left his inscription on rocks in 1832 and 1844 in what would become Canyonlands and Arches National Parks, respectively. Beavers were probably never abundant in this area, and, as in most of the Intermountain West, over-trapping almost led to the extirpation of America's largest rodent. At present beavers inhabit three distinct ecosystems in southeast Utah: small, perennial desert or mountain streams; the Colorado and Green Rivers; and wetlands along the Colorado River.

Beaver building practices vary distinctly with habitat. On large rivers, they live in dens built into banks. The opening is below the water line and leads back to a den platform, which is above the water line. Along the Colorado River, dens are usually associated with willows along sections of river wider than 80 yards. Low water may expose the round, 18- to 20-inch-wide den entrance.

On tributary streams and in wetlands, canyon country beavers build the classic dam and lodge combination. Look for characteristic tooth marks on willows and cottonwoods. The mud-and-stick dam serves to regulate stream flow (reducing the effects of high runoff), protect the lodge, and facilitate movement of food and supplies. The lodge has an underwater entrance that leads to an above-water living chamber. This home provides good protection against most predators, who can neither break through the sticks nor enter from underwater. Land predators include coyotes, mountain lions, and eagles.

In all habitats beaver life revolves around the family group or colony. The colony consists of an archetypal "nuclear family" of a male, female (who selects the colony site), yearlings, and kits. Midwinter mating is followed by a 107-day pregnancy. The monogamous female gives birth to 1 to 6 young, known as kits. Beavers reach sexual maturity as two-year-olds, when they leave to form a new family unit. Adults continue growing for several years and may live more than fifteen years.

The generic name, *Castor,* refers to castoreum, the musky secretions of the castor gland, which is situated in the beaver's groin. Castor oil comes from a member of the euphorb family (*Ricinus communis*) native to the tropics. *Ricinus* comes from the Latin for tick because Linnaeus thought the seeds resembled ticks.

WESTERN HARVEST MOUSE
Reithrodontomys megalotis
Order Rodentia, Cricetidae family
Total 4^1/$_2$–6^3/$_4$ in., tail 2–3^7/$_8$ in., grayish brown above, pale below, bicolored and sparsely haired tail

NORTH AMERICAN DEER MOUSE
Peromyscus maniculatus
Order Rodentia, Cricetidae family
Total 4^3/$_4$–8^3/$_4$ in., tail 1^3/$_4$–4^3/$_4$ in., sharply bicolored with dark brown above and pale below

These small, nocturnal mice usually inhabit moist, vegetation-rich areas such as washes, streams, or irrigation ditches. These grassy areas provide the best locale for cover and nesting materials. Harvest mice are not burrowers; instead they construct softball-size nests of woven plant materials, lined with the soft fibers of cottonwood and milkweed seeds. Nests are hidden in dense vegetation or under logs or rocks. Several mice may huddle together inside, helping to keep each other warm.

Like most mice, western harvest mice have a high rate of reproduction. Fecund females give birth from spring to fall with an average of five young per litter. Gestation takes 23 days and young mice can reproduce at the age of 4 weeks. Most young do not live long; their small bodies provide a good meal for any carnivore large enough to eat them. They probably have a complete population turnover each year.

As the name implies, these deer mice are widespread and common across North America. In canyon country they are more abundant in piñons, junipers, shrubs, and grasslands than in riparian habitats. They may build their own home, but more commonly borrow a burrow and make a small ball-shaped nest of fur and shredded plant material. Deer mice primarily subsist on seeds but will also eat insects and larvae when they become available in the warmer months.

During years with plentiful food, deer mice populations can explode. Females can breed year-round, but give birth more often in spring and fall. On average four young, known as pinkies, are born in each litter with as many as five litters in a single season. Breeding can occur at 7 weeks of age.

In 1993, after a particularly wet spring and winter, a mysterious respiratory disease began to kill people in the Four Corners states. Scientists identified the disease as a strain of hantavirus, carried and spread by a burgeoning population of deer mice. The disease is spread by contact with mice or their excrement.

CANYON DEER MOUSE
Peromyscus crinitus
Order Rodentia, Cricetidae family
Total 6¹/₄–7⁵/₈ in., tail 3¹/₄–4³/₄ in., pale-reddish above, buff below, smallish ears, bicolored and conspicuously tufted tail

BRUSH DEER MOUSE
Peromyscus boylii
Order Rodentia, Cricetidae family
Total 7¹/₈–9³/₄ in., tail 3⁵/₈–4³/₄ in., brown above and white below

A canyon deer mouse's fur color varies depending upon environment, ranging from black in lava-rich areas to gray in granitic regions to reddish in canyon country. In southeast Utah, canyon deer mice are the most brightly colored *Peromyscus*. Like deer mice, canyon deer mice have smallish ears, but their tail is longer than their body, unlike deer mice.

Canyon deer mice seldom venture into brushy or tree-covered areas, but move easily through rocky terrain, running with their long, tufted tail arched over their back. Canyon deer mice have adapted to slickrock so well that they were the only mammals found on an isolated butte in Canyonlands National Park, accessible to people only by helicopter. They were seven times more abundant on the butte than in the surrounding area. Lack of competition seems to have allowed the canyon mouse population to explode and dominate the butte. They depend mostly upon seeds in their omnivorous diet.

Brush deer mice inhabit rocky, brushy habitat, usually in piñon-juniper woodlands or oak groves. Their long tails aid in a partially arboreal lifestyle by providing a counterbalance when climbing. One study found that longer-tailed individuals spent more time in trees than shorter-tailed brush mice. They also may use their long tail as lizards do, as a defensive mechanism, allowing a predator to get the tail but not the body.

Brush deer mice have a diversified diet that includes arthropods, juniper berries, cactus fruit, acorns, and mistletoe. They are active throughout the year and do not store food. Females can give birth to several litters of three to four young in a year. Gestation lasts about 3 weeks.

The four most common species of *Peromyscus* (white-footed deer mice) in the area have several distinct differences. North American deer mice have shorter tails, piñon mice have larger ears, and canyon deer mice have smaller ears.

PIÑON DEER MOUSE
Peromyscus truei
Order Rodentia, Cricetidae family
Total 6³/₄–9 in., tail 3–4³/₄ in., upper parts cinnamon buff, body and tail white below, ears up to 1 inch long

Piñon deer mice are abundant and conspicuous. They have the largest ears (up to 1 inch long) of any *Peromyscus* in the area. This small mammal inhabits primarily the piñon-juniper ecosystem, using juniper bark for nests, abandoned trees for storage and nesting sites, and juniper berries and piñon nuts as major food sources. Telltale signs of a piñon mouse are a tree base or crotch covered by cracked-open seeds and rice-shaped droppings. Like other species of white-footed deer mice, they are nocturnal.

All species of *Peromyscus* give birth to hairless, helpless young. Birth usually occurs during the warmer months after a 22- to 28-day gestation period. Hair starts to grow in several days, and pinkies can hear and see in about 3 weeks. They are fully grown in 3 to 4 months and start reproducing soon after this.

This species was named for Frederick True (1858–1914), curator of mammals at the National Museum. Ironically, True studied large marine mammals because he had poor eyesight.

NORTHERN GRASSHOPPER MOUSE
Onychomys leucogaster
Order Rodentia, Cricetidae family
Total 5¹/₈–7¹/₂ in., tail 1¹/₈–2³/₈ in., grayish above and white below, whitish tail, stockier than deer mouse

Onychomys means "clawed mouse" and is a fitting name for this voracious predator. Northern grasshopper mice specialize in eating invertebrates, including scorpions, which they kill by immobilizing the tail and then eating head first. They will also attack other rodents, using their long claws and rapier-sharp teeth to bite through the head. Males mark their territory and will quickly kill other males that intrude, unless a dominant-subordinate relationship is established more quickly.

Grasshopper mice have several wolf-like features. Males help rear the young and bring food back to the nest. Like dogs, grasshopper mice emit territorial calls. When calling, they rear up on their hind legs, point their head upward, and emit a high-pitched howl, which is sometimes audible to humans.

They inhabit grasslands and shrubby areas with sandy soils, which they require for dust bathing (see Ord's kangaroo rat, page 99). Northern grasshopper mice may also live in overgrazed rangeland.

WHITE-THROATED WOOD RAT
Neotoma albigula
Order Rodentia, Cricetidae family
Total 11$^5/_8$–15$^3/_4$ in., tail 3–7$^3/_4$ in., most distinguishing characteristic is white throat

White-throated wood rats have a close relationship with prickly pear cacti. These rodents often build their elaborate homes around the cacti and use the spines for "decoration" and defense. Seemingly able to elude the spines, they move quickly through, around, and over prickly pear. White-throated wood rats also obtain most of their food from cactus pads. Because the pads contain abundant water, this small rat may not need free water for survival.

Close-up
Middens

Four species of wood rat, or pack rats as they are more commonly known, inhabit canyon country. They are collectors, dragging or carrying items back to their home. An "item" may include cow dung, bones, rocks, sticks, car keys, nuts, and seeds—anything close by and portable. These items are used for construction, "decoration," and protection of a house, or midden. Wood rats usually build nests in rock cracks, beneath overhangs, or under vegetation.

This habit of collecting and assembling goods has provided a treasure chest of materials for paleoecologists trying to reconstruct past environments. Because middens are rich in organic material, scientists can use carbon-dating techniques to establish the age of a midden. The wood rat's limited foraging range means that any material found in a midden came from within a few hundred feet of its current location. Ecologists have used pack rat middens to reconstruct the past 40,000 years of Southwestern ecological history.

BUSHY-TAILED WOOD RAT
Neotoma cinerea
Order Rodentia, Cricetidae family
Total 11$^1/_2$–18$^1/_2$ in., tail 4$^3/_4$–9$^1/_4$ in., brownish above and pale below, relatively long whiskers, bushy tail

Bushy-tailed wood rats are the only wood rats in canyon country that consistently deposit feces and urine in a single location. The tarlike excrement and whitish urine help cement a wood rat's house together. Building materials include sticks, cactus pads, and small stones aligned to form a protective entryway into the rocky crevices where they like to build.

Bushy-tailed wood rats are distinguishable from the other three species of wood rat in canyon country by their bushy tail and large size. They are commonly called trade rats due to their propensity to drop whatever they are carrying when they come across a more enticing object.

DESERT WOOD RAT

Neotoma lepida

Order Rodentia, Cricetidae family

Total 8³/₄–15¹/₈ in., tail 3³/₄–7³/₈ in., yellowish brown above and grayish below, white hind feet

Desert wood rats are not common east of the Colorado River in Utah, but they are abundant throughout areas of rocky rubble and slickrock. They build their homes under rocks and in the crotches of juniper trees. One study found that desert wood rats took 7 to 10 days to build a nest; during the first five nights they added more than 200 bits of material per night. The desert wood rat's preferred foods include piñon nuts, juniper berries, and fresh foliage.

MEXICAN WOOD RAT

Neotoma mexicana

Order Rodentia, Cricetidae family

Total 11³/₈–16⁵/₈ in., tail 4¹/₈–8¹/₈ in., tail sharply dark above and light below

Mexican wood rats feed on nearly any kind of vegetation, but prefer foliage over flowers or fruit. A well-stocked larder includes juniper, sagebrush, pepperweed, or Mormon tea. Mexican wood rats seem not to be picky about their houses. They may build their own, renovate an existing structure, or move into an abandoned wood rat house.

NORTH AMERICAN PORCUPINE
Erethizon dorsata
Order Rodentia, Erethizontidae family
Total 25–36 in., tail 6–12 in., weight up to
25 lb., bushy, spiny body

When you look at a porcupine, possibly the first questions that come to mind are "How do they mate?" and "How are they born?" "Carefully," would be the flip answer. Porcupine babies have soft quills that harden within an hour of birth, and the undersides of porcupines are soft, providing an area for mating and nursing.

The tender underbelly is their only vulnerable point, and several predators, including mountain lions, are adept at flipping porcupines over, thus avoiding the quills. The hollow quills are modified hairs, loosely attached to the body. Porcupines cannot shoot their quills; when harassed, they swing their tail about, driving the spirally barbed points into an adversary. The best method for removing quills is to cut them in two and slowly twist and pull out the barb.

Porcupines are nocturnal, or crepuscular, vegetarians, active throughout the year. During the day they sit in the crotch of a tree or retreat to a den in a cave or hollow of a tree. Young porcupines can climb soon after birth. In the winter, when they often spend most of their time near one feeding tree, large volumes of scat, which resemble deer feces, accumulate in the entryway to the den site. Their primary habitat is the piñon-juniper belt, but they will also forage in riparian woodlands.

Although they prefer leaves, roots, flowers, and berries, porcupines will eat the soft, inner bark of piñon pines and cottonwoods. Porcupines are also attracted to salt and have been known to eat packstraps, bike helmet padding, and boots.

COYOTE
Canis latrans
Order Carnivora, Canidae family
Total 41–52 in., tail 12–15 in.,
shoulder height 23–26 in.,
grayish buff body,
off-white belly

Despite humanity's best (or worst) efforts to eradicate them, coyotes have persistently remained in, and even slowly expanded, their geographic range. Originally found only in grasslands and open country, they now occur almost everywhere, from tundra to deserts. Success is tied to intelligence; coyotes are clever and resourceful, able to adapt to changing conditions, and to take advantage of the extirpation of their cousin, the wolf. Coyotes have taken over this predator's former range: Old-timers called coyotes "prairie wolves" to distinguish them from "timber wolves."

It has been estimated that several million coyotes have been killed by hunters, ranchers, fur trappers, and government agents, and yet coyotes are the most abundant carnivore in the Southwest. They eat rabbits (which they can outsprint), rodents, and mammalian carrion. If their main prey is absent, coyotes will eat domesticated animals, deer, pronghorns, bighorn sheep, and even grasshoppers or fruit.

No one has conclusively proven that coyotes do extensive damage to livestock; an individual may go on a killing rampage, but as a species coyotes are not significant predators of sheep or cows. In reality, their consumption of jackrabbits and rodents may help improve the range.

Females go into heat once a year for 2 to 5 days, usually between January and March. Prey abundance affects breeding success, with lower birth rates and fewer breeding females in years of low prey, particularly low jackrabbit populations. After a 9-week gestation, an average of six pups are born in an underground den. They are weaned within 6 weeks and disperse in 6 to 9 months. Although they are not as social as wolves, both the female and male help raise the young; yearlings may sometimes aid in feeding the next generation, too.

Coyotes communicate through both olfactory and auditory methods. They leave distinctive feces (usually fur and bone-filled, but they may contain porcupine quills or surveyor's tape) in prominent locations on rocks or logs, at trail intersections, or high points, providing much information for the next coyote that ambles by. Their scientific name refers to their vocal ability (*latrans* means barking). Along with barking, coyotes growl, yip, whine, and howl. The distinctive, soul-piercing coyote howl communicates location within a group or family.

KIT FOX

Vulpes macrotis

Order Carnivora, Canidae family

Total 28–33 in., tail 10–13 in., shoulder height 12 in., weight under 4½ lb., black-tipped tail, large ears

Kit foxes resemble a cartoon animal with their oversize ears and long tail that's roughly a third of their total length. Although they are the only true desert fox, kits are uncommon in this region. They dig their dens in the sandy areas of grasslands and desert scrub. Scat, food remnants, and tracks often surround the small openings, usually three to four per den. The entrance is a little higher than wide and too narrow for a coyote. A female with young will move the pups often from den to den, perhaps to avoid parasites or to find better feeding grounds.

Jackrabbits and kangaroo rats constitute their major prey, but kit foxes also eat reptiles, ground-nesting birds, and insects. Although they may eat marshmallows, white bread, chips, and other such delectables found in campgrounds, kit foxes, like all mammals, should not be given access to human food. Coyotes and eagles prey upon kit foxes, but humans are their major killer. Because of their curiosity, kit foxes often die in traps set for other animals.

Like other canids, kit foxes produce extensive vocalizations. They may bark to alert other foxes, growl to intimidate, or yelp in fear.

The closely related red fox (*V. vulpes*) is also found across the region with reproductive populations in Capitol Reef, Canyonlands, Mesa Verde, and Zion National Parks.

GRAY FOX

Urocyon cinereoargenteus

Order Carnivora, Canidae family

Total 31–44 in., tail 9–17 in., shoulder height 14 in., weight between 5½ and 15 lb., salt-and-pepper coloring on back, black ridge of hair running down tail

Unlike other canids, gray foxes readily climb trees, where they forage, rest, or hide. In canyon country they live in open areas with shrubs and trees. Dens are constructed under boulders, in cliff crevices, tree hollows, or even mineshafts. Gray foxes are crepuscular, or nocturnal, and have a seasonally dependent diet. Fruit dominates from September to February, with arthropods and grasses becoming more important the rest of the year. Rodents, lizards, and carrion supplement these items.

Abundant fruit in their diet produces dark, seed-rich fecal material. Gray foxes use their scat and urine to mark rocks, logs, or trail intersections, indicating a family's home range. A family consists of a monogamous pair and their young. An average of four kits is born in March, and the young can hunt on their own in about 4 months.

RINGTAIL
Bassariscus astutus
Order Carnivora, Procyonidae family
Total 24–32 in., tail 12–17 in., white almost encircles eyes, six or seven black rings on tail, grayish brown

If one were to design a climbing animal to exploit this region of cracks, ledges, and vertical cliffs, the ringtail might be it. Its considerable tail provides balance for negotiating narrow ledges and limbs, even allowing it to reverse directions by performing a cartwheel. The animal can rotate its hind feet 180 degrees, giving purchase for rapidly descending cliffs or trees. Furthermore, ringtails can ascend narrow passages by stemming (pressing all feet on one wall and their back against the other or pressing both right feet on one wall and both left feet on the other), and wider cracks or openings by ricocheting between the walls.

As would be expected, ringtails prefer rough, rocky habitat, usually not too far from water. They make dens in tree hollows, under rocks, in cracks, or even abandoned buildings. Like most members of the order Carnivora, these nocturnal hunters eat a wide variety of food. Favorite foods include mice, wood rats, squirrels, and rabbits. If these aren't available, carrion, lizards, insects, snakes, fruit, and birds will suffice.

Ringtails have several other names. Although they are not related to cats, people have referred to them as miner's cats, civet cats, and cacomistles (a Nahuatl term meaning half mountain lion). Ringtails are members of the raccoon family.

AMERICAN BADGER
Taxidea taxus
Order Carnivora, Mustelidae family
Total 20–34 in., tail 4–6 in., weight up to 24 lb., black legs, white stripe extends from nose and may continue down entire length of back

Badgers are formidable diggers and will quickly ransack a rodent's den in pursuit of a meal. Short legs with long claws in front and flattened claws in back provide good tools for excavating and shoveling soil. Their elliptically shaped burrow entrances often have a large mound of dirt in front. Badgers may move into the den whose former owner they just ate.

The badger's diet includes kangaroo rats, pocket gophers, and ground squirrels. They occur wherever their prey base lives; thus, badgers are found in open grasslands and deserts. Hunting takes place at night and during twilight hours. Badgers are solitary except during fall mating season. Two to three altricial young are born in late spring and leave the birth den in summer.

An early study on Utah mammals included this musing: "How anyone acquainted with this animal's habits should desire to kill it, is beyond comprehension; yet some farmers will actually shoot badgers and at the same time complain that they will have to give up their farms if something is not done with the ground squirrels."

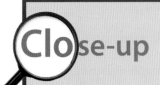

Close-up

The Night Shift

While many of us head indoors in the dark, many animals start their "day" when the sun sets. They rely on the cover of darkness to forage and to avoid predators. They move from place to place and, in the case of birds, may migrate hundreds to thousands of miles in the dark. During the day they will sleep in a den or burrow, or some other protected place out of the heat.

To survive in the dark, these animals rely on different senses than we generally do. Bats echolocate. Owls have large eyes for light gathering, and snakes rely on taste. When flicking out their tongue, snakes absorb taste and odor molecules, which they send to a pair of sensory chambers (Jacobson's organ). This organ connects, via nerves, to the brain, where the chemical information is processed.

Nighttime can be a good time to go out and see these nocturnal animals. Scorpions are one group easy to locate. Under ultraviolet, or black light, their exoskeleton will fluoresce, or glow. Older scorpions glow better than younger ones. Bats can also be seen by using a bat detector, a machine that picks up the calls of bats and plays them back at frequency that we can hear. If you don't have any equipment, no worries, just be patient. Your eyes and ears will adjust, and you will start to discover the animals on the night shift.

Because of the importance of the dark for so many animals, and for astronomy, a movement has begun to educate people about the downside of too much light at night. In 2007, Natural Bridges National Monument became the world's first International Dark Sky Park. Park employees shielded outdoor lights and reduced the wattage, relying on fluorescent bulbs. The changes have saved money and made it safer for animals and more enjoyable for visitors to see one of the darkest night skies in the United States.

WESTERN SPOTTED SKUNK
Spilogale gracilis
Order Carnivora, Mustelidae family
Total 13–18 in., tail 4–7 in., four to six whitish stripes broken into spots on sides, jet black fur

Western Spotted Skunk   Striped Skunk

Neither of the two species of skunk in the area is common. The western spotted skunk is more commonly associated with drier areas, often in foothills or canyons. They primarily forage at night, seeking out rodents, insects, eggs, carrion, or fruit. During the day they rest in dens in brush piles, tree hollows, or abandoned burrows of other animals. Unlike other skunks, this agile animal climbs trees.

Skunks are well known for their defensive tactics. When harassed they will first attempt to retreat, followed by a warning of stomping with their forefeet. Spotted skunks follow up this action by standing on their forefeet, raising their rear end, and shooting a distressingly strong spray. Most animals quickly learn to leave skunks alone, but a few, like the great horned owl, are successful predators.

Mating occurs in autumn and, like several other mammals, including river otters and badgers, egg implantation does not occur until the following season. On average four young are born in May. The blind, helpless young are weaned in 2 months and full grown in 3.

The closely related striped skunk (*Mephitis mephitis*) also occurs in this region. It is larger (total 20 to 31 inches), occasionally forages during the day, usually lives closer to water, and has a winter dormancy period. Striped skunks do not raise their hindquarters when spraying, and the discharge is less pungent than a spotted skunk's. The name *mephitis* comes from the Latin for bad odor, *mephitis*.

NORTH AMERICAN RIVER OTTER

Lontra canadensis

Order Carnivora, Mustelidae family
Total 35–51 in., tail 12–20 in., weight 10–30 lb., dark brown fur, silvery gray on throat, webbed feet

At one time river otters occurred in most of the major rivers of Utah. Although they have been legally protected in Utah since 1899, otter sightings have been rare until the last decade. Water pollution, habitat loss, and unregulated trapping all contributed to the otter's decline. Improved water quality and restoration are now helping a dramatic comeback of this sleek weasel. Habitat is characterized by densely wooded cover along the water's edge, abundant prey, and year-round open water.

Otters are principally animals of the water, swimming gracefully about in a slow, undulatory motion. They can stay submerged for several minutes. Because their small eyes are located high on their head, otters can move about with only the top of their head above the water. Sensitive facial whiskers help otters to locate prey in sediment-filled water. River otters are omnivorous, consuming fish (especially slow ones like suckers and carp), crayfish, toads, and juvenile muskrats and beavers.

You will more often see signs of otters than the animals themselves. They have 2- to 3-inch-wide tracks with a stride of 15 to 22 inches. Otters often leave slide marks on snow or ice; it's easier to travel by sliding than walking. Because otters have large home ranges (up to 50 miles), they use numerous den sites, which can be abandoned beaver lodges and bank dens or log or rock piles. Another distinctive sign is their scat, which consists of the hard, bony remains of their diet.

COUGAR
Puma concolor
Order Carnivora, Felidae family
Total 59–108 in., tail 21–36 in., shoulder height 26–30 in., weight of average male 154 lb., average female 92 lb., reddish buff above, white belly

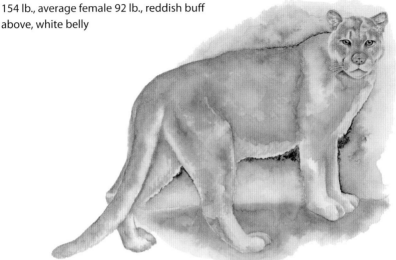

Cougars range from Argentina to Canada (the most extensive of any North American mammal), and at one time inhabited all 48 contiguous states. With such a large range they have received many names: puma and cougar (from South America), catamount, mountain lion, and panther (of English origin). Like all large predators, they have been hunted and poisoned by humans, almost to the point of extinction in the United States. However, they do not eat carrion, and thus escaped this method of killing (death by poisoned carrion). At present, the best place to see a mountain lion is in the desert Southwest.

Cougars kill quickly and efficiently. They roam far and wide to locate prey, most often mule deer, but also livestock, pronghorns, porcupines, and rabbits. These large cats pounce on or chase down their victims (outrunning deer for up to 150 feet) and kill with a bite to the back of the neck, severing the spinal cord. They devour several pounds of meat and then cover their prey with sticks, leaves, and soil, returning over the next several days, until the meat spoils. Males kill about once every ten days; females with young about once a week.

Adults are solitary except during the breeding season or while females raise young. Females can breed throughout the year and give birth to an average of two to three altricial young, who remain with her for up to 2 years. Females reach sexual maturity in their third year, but do not breed until they establish their own territory. Males do not help in raising the young and will even kill them if possible.

Cougars will follow hikers, usually more out of curiosity than hunger. Still, you should exercise caution and learn about how to behave in lion country. If approached by a lion, do not run. Stand your ground, make plenty of noise, and make yourself appear as tall as possible: Raise your arms, raise a stick, and step up on a rock if possible.

BOBCAT

Lynx rufus

Order Carnivora, Felidae family
Total 28–49 in., tail 4–7 in., shoulder height
20–23 in., weight 16–23 lb., reddish buff
coloring, two to four tail stripes, prominent
ears with dark ear tufts

Bobcats move stealthily through the landscape, seldom seen by people. They are most active at night and spend the day in rock shelters. Bobcats occur throughout the area, preferring broken woodlands with cliffs and rocky outcrops. They wait patiently next to a game trail for their prey to pass by and then attack with a quick leap and a flurry of claws and teeth. Although lagomorphs constitute the majority of the diet, bobcats also eat rodents and small nesting birds. Their only enemies are mountain lions, and humans who want their pelts.

Bobcats share many attributes with domestic cats. They growl, hiss, and purr, in louder and deeper tones. Bobcats cover their scat, although they may make only a slight effort, leaving scratch marks near the deposit. Bobcats also sometimes use trees as scratching posts.

Unlike animals in the dog family, felids retract their claws when wandering. Bobcat tracks are much smaller (2 inches wide) than those of a mountain lion (3$\frac{1}{2}$ inches wide) and have two lobes at the front end of each pad. A domestic cat's pad, on the other hand, has a single lobe.

Close-up

Scat

As the classic children's book informs us, everybody poops. In doing so, animals provide a wonderful sign of their presence, even when we do not see them. For example, at high points or on elevated rocks in trails, you may find the poop of coyotes and foxes, who defecate at prominent spots to mark their territory. Look for sausage-shaped, often fur-rich scat with a tapered end. If there are several sausages, usually just one is tapered. A fox's scat is usually smaller than a coyote's.

Not only does poop tell who was there but also what they ate. Look for fur, bones, insect remains, teeth, or possibly non-food objects in a carnivore's droppings, though the presence of the remains of another animal does not mean that the defecator killed it; it may have scavenged its meal. Some droppings may also be resplendent with colorful fruits during berry season. Herbivore feces, in contrast, are often small, rounded, and copious due to containing less accessible nutrients, which results in less digestion and greater production.

Less obvious, unless you are a member of the species who pooped, is that some mammals discharge a redolent secretion in their poop during the height of mating season, which lets other members of their species know they are sexually receptive. Also on a chemical level, an animal's health can be detected by measuring different hormones in scat.

Often overlooked but often easy to find, insect feces, or frass, is another sign of those who went before. The droppings are usually brown to black cylinders, less than ⅛ inch long, and may have grooves or not. In one butterfly family, the skippers, the larvae will actually shoot their poop, up to 3 feet. In contrast, some keep their frass closer to home, utilizing it as a defensive mechanism. Butterfly larvae of the Weidemeyer's admiral and the Arizona sister (*Adelpha eulalia*) bind silk and droppings together into a frass chain, which they build as a safe haven off the end of a leaf. The chain keeps the larvae away from predators such as ants that prowl the leaf's surface. Leaf and tortoise beetle larvae (subfamilies Cassidinae and Cryptocephalinae) take a different approach by fashioning a shield of feces, which incorporates poisonous compounds ingested from plants, including mint and *Solanum* sp. Held over the backs of the larvae, the toxic turds discourage most predators.

Scat is not to be confused with bird pellets, the undigested remains of meals. For example, owls, which swallow their food whole, will regurgitate a pellet of bones, fur, and feathers. Hawks, flycatchers, and corvids also eject indigestibles. Such pellets usually are found singly and are usually easy to distinguish by the abundance of body parts. Good places to locate them are below cliffs or other perching spots.

Because scat carries the potential for bacteria and disease, you should not handle it with bare hands.

Ungulates

MULE DEER
Odocoileus hemionus
Order Artiodactyla, Cervidae family
Total 44–78 in., shoulder height 36–42 in., weight average male 264 lb., average female 143 lb.

During the early fall, after fawns begin moving, mule deer are one of the most conspicuous mammals in the national parks, especially around the campgrounds. This was not always the case. Most, if not all, early travelers in this region did not mention seeing mule deer, and at the turn of the century, after 50 years of expanded settlement, increased domestic herds, and unrestricted hunting, mule deer were near the point of extinction in some parts of Utah. Now that humans have eliminated most of the deer's predators, mule deer numbers have skyrocketed.

Mule deer feed on woody vegetation and forbs. During the spring they eat new, succulent growth, and during the winter they consume more woody plants. Although they may forage at any time, mule deer are most active at dawn and dusk. They are not shy animals and will become habituated to human food, even to the point of stealing it. In some areas, deer become problematic and must be removed. In one case, an autopsy found that deer were starving to death because they had consumed too much plastic, which was prohibiting digestion. **It is illegal to feed any animal in a national park.**

In late fall the rut begins. Males have rubbed off the velvet, blood-rich tissue that provides nutrients for growing antlers, and are preparing to fight for dominance and breeding rights. Antlers are dropped after the rut and begin to regrow in springtime. Harems do not exist, but one male may mate with several females. Does usually give birth to twins 200 to 208 days later. A lack of detectable odor and spotted coloring are a fawn's only protection during the first few weeks of life. By late fall they are mobile, following their mothers to forage.

Mule deer occur throughout this region, migrating to higher country during the summer. They move gracefully, but almost comically, by bounding like a spring (all four legs leave the ground simultaneously, known as stotting) instead of running. They will run short distances, but stot when alarmed. Stotting may have evolved to allow quick and easy movement through varied, ledgy terrain. No other North American deer moves in this manner.

PRONGHORN

Antilocapra americana

Order Artiodactyla, Antilocapridae family
Total 48–56 in., tail 2³/₈–6³/₄ in., shoulder height 35–41 in., weight average male 125 lb., average female 90 lb., tan back, white belly and rump

Swift as an arrow and as graceful as Hyperion, the antelope is truly the Ladas of the plains, the fleetest animal of the wilds. Elegance, too, is its natural attribute, for its delicate shape is second only to its wondrously beauteous eyes.

—Claude T. Barnes,
Mammals of Utah, 1922

Along with bison, pronghorns were the dominant animals that pioneers encountered on their westward migration. Pronghorns encountered the same fate as bison; in 1805, when Lewis and Clark first saw them, more than 35 million pronghorns roamed North America, but by 1900 only 13,000 remained. Protection and stricter hunting regulations have contributed to a resurgent population, now estimated at about 750,000.

Pronghorns require large, wide-open spaces without human or physical barriers. One study found that they can jump barriers up to 8 feet high, but rarely leapt over fences more than 32 inches high. They will be mobile or remain in an area, depending upon water and forage availability. Shrubs, such as sagebrush and cliffrose, are their principal food throughout the year. In the spring they feed on forbs and occasionally new grasses. Pronghorns can survive without water if plant moisture exceeds 75 percent. Otherwise, water requirements may reach three quarts a day.

When distressed, pronghorns erect the hairs on their white rump, effectively alerting neighbors of potential trouble; however, as adults, pronghorns have few predators; no animal can outrun them. Top speed is 65 miles per hour, and they can run for several miles at a speed of 30 to 35 miles per hour. Young pronghorns may be eaten by coyotes, bobcats, and eagles, though. Hard winters and drought also contribute to population control.

In spring and summer, bachelor males remain together in small herds. As breeding season approaches, they fight for dominance, and once a territory is established, bucks will form harems of up to twenty does. Females and young also form herds, which range through these territories. Twins, literally dropped to the ground, are born after a 230- to 250-day pregnancy. Females ingest the young's urine and feces, eliminating odors and preventing predators from detecting them.

Pronghorns are often called antelope, which is a misnomer. True antelope exist only in the Old World. Pioneers also referred to pronghorns as goats or mountain goats.

BIGHORN SHEEP
Ovis canadensis
Order Artiodactyla, Bovidae family
Total 52–72 in., tail 3¹/₂–6 in., shoulder
height 30–42 in., pale tan body, rump and
belly whitish

Like deer and pronghorns, bighorn sheep were once on the verge of being extirpated from canyon country. Hunting, disease, and competition from domestic sheep contributed to a critically low bighorn sheep population. The formation of Canyonlands National Park, though, helped push the numbers back up to the point where bighorn sheep from the Island in the Sky district have been transplanted to Capitol Reef and Arches National Parks.

Bighorn sheep inhabit rocky slopes, where they can use their excellent climbing skills to escape from predators. The best time to see the sheep is during the late fall to winter rut, when males, ewes, and lambs congregate. Males often butt heads at this time, fighting to establish their dominance.

They charge each other at more than 20 miles per hour; the loud crack can be heard for miles. Males and females live separately through the rest of the year.

Females give birth to one precocial lamb in the spring. The mothers and young form nursery bands and move to traditional feeding zones. A typical bighorn diet consists of about equal amounts of shrubs and grasses, with blackbrush and galleta grass predominating. They usually live near water but also obtain moisture from their diet.

Bighorn sheep are well known for their magnificent, curled horns. Although both sexes grow horns, only the males' curl back around on themselves. The horns grow longer each year and can be used to determine the sheep's age.

Animal Tracks

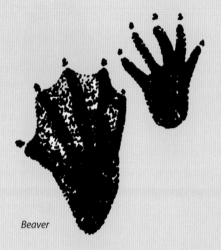

Beaver

North American River Otter

Striped Skunk

Western Spotted Skunk

Animal Tracks

Bighorn Sheep

Mule Deer

Cougar

Marmot

American Badger

Coyote

North American Porcupine

Kit Fox

Northern Pocket Gopher

Ringtail

BIRDS

Defining a bird is easy to do. They have wings and feathers. They are warm-blooded and have backbones. They are dinosaurs. In fact, many paleontologists refer to the non-avian dinosaurs (the dinosaurs we know and love) and the avian dinosaurs (birds), recognizing their close relationship.

Birds in southeastern Utah range in size from a hummingbird with a 3-inch wingspan to the recently reintroduced California condor with a wingspan of 9 feet. Some are strictly vegetarian. Others eat only carrion. Almost anything is possible in the world of birds.

Unlike most mammals, male and female birds of the same species often look different. Adult males tend to have more brightly colored plumage, especially during breeding season when they need to attract a mate. The drab colors of females and juveniles are protective and allow them to blend into the scenery better. This is particularly important when the female and unfledged young are on the nest and susceptible to predators.

Another difference between the sexes is that males sing and females rarely do. Ornithologists divide calls and songs by length and complexity of vocalization. A male sings either to attract a mate or to defend his territory. Songs are generally learned. A call, on the other hand, is generally innate. Both sexes call. Common reasons include warning and communication between mates.

Birds are the most frequently encountered animal in canyon country. They are out flying around every day of the year. They are also the most diverse class of the vertebrates. Dinosaur National Monument lists more than 215 species. Glen Canyon National Recreation Area lists 269 and Canyonlands National Park, 273 species. This book describes 57 of the most common or intriguing species found across southern Utah.

The birds are divided into four groups based on habitat. Obviously this is somewhat arbitrary because birds don't stay in one place and can easily cross these boundaries. The categories include birds most likely to be found in a particular habitat. The first and largest group of birds is in the riparian and wetlands, which is the smallest habitat. This clearly shows the importance of water in the desert.

The next largest group of birds is found in the grasslands and open terrain. This group contains some of the most vocal birds, which can be heard great distances across the wide open landscape. The birds of cliffs and debris slopes include some of the premier fliers of canyon country. Their nests and whitewash are often a conspicuous feature of vertical walls. The fewest number of birds listed in the book inhabit the piñon-juniper woodlands.

Common and scientific names conform to the *American Ornithologists' Union Checklist of North American Birds,* Seventh Edition, fifty-second supplement.

Riparian and Wetlands

GREAT BLUE HERON
Ardea herodias
Heron family (Ardeidae)
Length 42 in., wingspan 72 in.

BALD EAGLE
Haliaeetus leucocephalus
Hawk family (Accipitridae)
Length 31 in., wingspan 80 in.

Great blue herons are the tallest birds in canyon country. With their thin neck outstretched, they top out at about 4 feet tall. Despite this great height, great blue herons efficiently hunt fish, their preferred meal, and other water dwellers like crayfish and toads. During the hunt, they stand motionless in shallow water, waiting for a meal to swim by, and then quickly grab it with their long bills. Meals are swallowed whole.

In spring, the birds return to nesting colonies, known as rookeries, which they use year after year. Great blues build their elaborate stick nests in crowns of trees, usually in wetlands or near rivers or ponds. Both sexes help in nest building.

Look for them along the Green, Colorado, and San Juan Rivers throughout the year. Great blue herons have a distinctive flight silhouette with their neck and head tucked against their massive chest and their long skinny legs trailing behind.

Despite the fierce image of bald eagles with their sharp talons and beak, they usually use these assets to scavenge and steal from other birds. A preferred tactic is to dive-bomb another bird of prey, forcing it to drop its food, which the bald eagle will try to grab before it hits the ground. Bald eagles may harass ospreys but will also attack red-tailed hawks.

Approximately ten pairs of bald eagles are known to nest in the state of Utah, with several found on the Colorado River near the Colorado-Utah boundary. Winter is the best time to see bald eagles, when some migrate along the major waterways of the region. They also prowl nonriparian areas searching for jackrabbits.

Bald eagles do not develop their well-known white head and tail until their fourth or fifth year. Immature birds are brown with darkly mottled, white blotchy underwings and tail. Immature golden eagles have similar coloring, but it is more sharply defined. Bald eagles also have a shorter tail and proportionally longer head than golden eagles.

SHARP-SHINNED HAWK
Accipiter striatus
Hawk family (Accipitridae)
Female length 12 in., wingspan 25 in.; male length 10 in., wingspan 21 in.

COOPER'S HAWK
Accipiter cooperii
Hawk family (Accipitridae)
Female length 18 in., wingspan 33 in.; male length 15 in., wingspan 29 in.

GOSHAWK
Accipiter gentilis
Hawk family (Accipitridae)
Female length 23 in., wingspan 43 in.; male length 19 in., wingspan 39 in.

Sharp-shinned Hawk

Cooper's Hawk

Goshawk

Goshawk illustration © Todd Telander

Three species of accipiters or "true hawks" inhabit the Colorado Plateau. All three have gray-and-white striped underwings, a brownish gray back, and a dark head, a good camouflage scheme in their forested or wooded habitat. The undersides of the smaller Cooper's and "sharpies" are rufous colored. Short, wide wings and long tails facilitate quick bursts of speed and excellent maneuverability. This is especially important when hunting birds or small mammals in dense vegetation. All three hawks fly with a series of quick wing beats followed by a short glide, which they repeat throughout their flight.

Size is the main difference among the species, thus each exploits a different size of prey. Within each species, males and females, which display the greatest amount of sexual dimorphism of any bird of prey, also hunt different-size animals. Researchers believe that sexual dimorphism evolved to broaden the range of prey of an individual species and to aid the female during breeding season. The larger female needs to protect herself from the male's talons and also to build up larger food reserves to produce eggs.

The riparian-inhabiting Cooper's hawks are the most common. During breeding season they will dive-bomb people who walk under cottonwoods in which they have built a nest. Sharp-shinned hawks inhabit the montane zone and then move to a lower elevation in winter. Goshawks also nest at higher elevations. They are rare in winter.

Cooper's hawk honors William Cooper (1798–1864), who founded the New York Lyceum of Natural History. The Cooper Ornithological Society is named for his son, also a prominent ornithologist.

RED-TAILED HAWK

Buteo jamaicensis
Hawk family (Accipitridae)
Length 19 in., wingspan 51 in.

Illustration © Todd Telander

BLACK-CHINNED HUMMINGBIRD

Archilochus alexandri
Hummingbird family (Trochilidae)
Length 3³/₄ in.

Red-tails are the most widespread and abundant large bird of prey in the United States. Their specific epithet, *jamaicensis*, refers to the location of their first discovery. The key distinguishing characteristics are the rufous tail and the dark patches on the forward side of the underwing. Like other *Buteos,* the relatively short tail and long, wide wings facilitate soaring on thermals, a common practice for this variety of hawk. Red-tailed hawks may be encountered throughout the year. If you see a large raptor in canyon country, chances are that it will be a red-tail. And if you hear a screeching *kee-eeee-arrr* in a movie, it is the call of a red-tail, no matter what the bird is supposed to be.

Because red-tailed hawks usually construct their stick nests in tall trees, they generally live near riparian areas or human habitations where large trees grow. They commonly sit on telephone poles and fence posts; most hunts start from perches. When prey is sighted, the bird glides silently down and snatches its meal with a quick thrust of its claws. Prey, carried to a feeding perch, may be swallowed whole or sectioned with beak and talons. Red-tails prefer small mammals but also are known to catch, kill, and eat rattlesnakes and gopher snakes.

Describing hummingbird flight requires a thorough aeronautic vocabulary. Their unique skeletal structure allows them to fly forward, backward, sideways, and on their backs. Hummers can hover, take off vertically, and pivot on a stationary axis. In black-chins this requires a wing beat frequency of 50 beats per second. The smaller the bird, the faster the rate. It also requires massive muscles that make up a third of their two- to three-gram body weight.

Black-chinned hummingbirds perform an elaborate breeding season courtship display. Males execute a series of U-shaped swoops where they pass close to a female at the bottom of their arcs. During the pendulum-like flight, their wings make a whirling or whistling sound. If successful, the female builds a minute nest woven together from spider webs, down from plant seeds, and leaf hairs. Nests are built low in the canopy and upright on any structure from a limb to a telephone wire.

The black-chin is metallic green on the upper part of the wings and back. Good light reveals the purple patch just below the black chin.

The specific name honors a Dr. Alexandre, who discovered the species in the Sierra Madre of Mexico and sent it to France. Nothing else is known of this man.

BROAD-TAILED HUMMINGBIRD
Selasphorus platycercus
Hummingbird family (Trochilidae)
Length 4 in.

HAIRY WOODPECKER
Picoides villosus
Woodpecker family (Picidae)
Length 9¹/₄ in.

DOWNY WOODPECKER
Picoides pubescens
Woodpecker family (Picidae)
Length 6³/₄ in.

Hummingbirds demand huge amounts of food to replenish the energy used in flight; therefore, they seek out flowers rich in sweet nectar. Although many flowers meet this nectar requirement, hummers prefer tubular flowers that either hang down or stick out horizontally. These features discourage bees and other insects, which neither hover nor have long tongues or proboscises. In addition, hummingbirds consume spiders and insects for their protein.

To survive in the colder, mountainous environments where they live, broad-tails enter a state of torpor, where they lower their body temperature by roughly 30°, and drop their pulse from 250 to 50 beats per minute. Torpidity reduces daily energy expenditure dramatically, allows birds to survive cold snaps, and extends their breeding season.

Broad-tailed hummingbirds inhabit mountain meadows and forested areas. Their lichen-covered nests are well camouflaged in shrubs or trees. When they are flying, broad-tails produce a distinct and loud trilling whistle. Their red throat and their broad tail with rufous patches distinguish them from black-chinned hummingbirds.

Hairy woodpeckers generally live in riparian areas and the upper piñon-juniper woodlands. Their longer bill and greater length distinguish them from downy woodpeckers. Both have a white back and a red spot on the nape of the head.

Most woodpeckers hunt for insects and larvae by listening for their movements and then probing, prying, and excavating bark. The hairy woodpecker is no exception. To feed, it ascends a tree via a series of hops. Once an insect is found, the bird snatches a meal with its barbed tongue. Sticky saliva helps secure the morsel.

A woodpecker's typical rat-a-tat drumming consists of about a dozen rapid beats, often repeated multiple times. Both males and females drum for territorial purposes. They may also drum to announce intruders or locate a mate. A thick skull, jaw muscles that act as shock absorbers, and a bill structure that spreads out the pounding force combine to protect against "headaches."

WILLOW FLYCATCHER
Empidonax traillii
Tyrant flycatcher family (Tyrannidae)
Length 5³/₄ in.

GRAY FLYCATCHER
Empidonax wrightii
Tyrant flycatcher family (Tyrannidae)
Length 5³/₄ in.

Willow Flycatcher

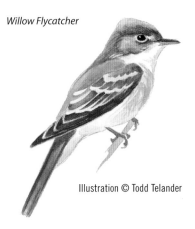

Gray Flycatcher

Illustration © Todd Telander

Illustration © Todd Telander

Several species of flycatcher live in the Southwest. Known by some birders as "LGBs," or little gray birds, all are small and drab, with white wing bars and a light-colored ring around the eye. All share traits found throughout the tyrant flycatcher family: aggression toward other birds and aerial insect catching. These small birds, though, are less aggressive than the related kingbirds.

Birders generally distinguish *Empidonax* species by habitat and song. Willow flycatcher's song is *fitz-bew,* as opposed to the gray flycatcher's *chi-bit.* As their name implies, willow flycatchers dwell in willows near water.

They construct nests, which have dangling material, in low clumps of ferns or shrubs.

The closely related gray flycatcher is found away from riparian environments in piñon-juniper woodlands. Like willow flycatchers, grays hunt insects close to the ground. They often perch on the top of piñons or sagebrush.

Thomas Traill (1781–1862) was a Scottish physician and friend of John James Audubon. Charles Wright (1811–1885), an American botanist, may have collected the first specimen of the gray flycatcher.

PLUMBEOUS VIREO
Vireo plumbeus
Vireo family (Vireonidae)
Length 5½ in.

Ornithologists recently split the solitary vireo into two separate species: plumbeous and solitary. The new name, plumbeous, refers to the bird's lead gray coloring. (Early plumb bobs were made of lead.) This vireo also lacks yellow-green sides and flanks, a feature found in the West Coast and eastern varieties of solitary vireos. *Vireo* is from Latin for green. Like many other vireos, the plumbeous has a distinct white eye line and eye ring.

This common songster builds an elaborate nest suspended by branches in riparian areas up through the piñon-juniper woodlands and into montane forests. During their summer residency, they may be found in any of these habitats but are most common in the riparian zone. Their song consists of two six-note phrases. Plumbeous vireos move slowly through higher levels of trees and shrubs, gleaning insects.

BLACK-BILLED MAGPIE
Pica hudsonia
Crow family (Corvidae)
Length 19 in.

With their long tail, white wing bars, and white and black body, magpies are an arresting western sight. Their common and scientific names refer to this highly visible pattern. Pie alludes to their pied (black and white) coloration and *pica* is Latin for pied or piebald. Magpies complement their visibility with a penchant for noisy, raucous calling. They are also known to gather in groups of up to 40 at "funerals" when another magpie dies. No one knows why.

Males and females mate for life. They also build their nest together. Magpies generally build a new nest each year. The 2- to 4-foot-tall stick structure has a mud floor, a domed roof, and a door on the side. Audubon once described a magpie nest as a "formidable fortress." The structures may persist for several years. Subsequent inhabitants include mallards, owls, kestrels, or raccoons. Magpies eat mostly insects, but they are also opportunists and consume carrion, eggs, and the young of many animals.

In *Macbeth,* Shakespeare referred to the European species as "magot-pies," a reference to these birds perching on the backs of cattle and eating insects or maggots. English ornithologist Edward Sabine originally named these birds *Corvus hudsonius,* from birds collected near Hudson Bay, Canada, on John Franklin's journey between 1819 and 1822.

BLACK-CAPPED CHICKADEE
Poecile atricapillus
Titmouse family (Paridae)
Length 5¹/₄ in.

MOUNTAIN CHICKADEE
Poecile gambeli
Titmouse family (Paridae)
Length 5¹/₄ in.

Black-capped Chickadee

Both of these species of chickadee have a black cap and bib, but the mountain chickadee also has a white eyebrow and gray sides. They are common in winter, flitting about the piñon-juniper woodlands. Mountain chickadees also reside in higher-elevation conifer and aspen forests, while black-caps may be found in the riparian zone. They glean spiders and spider eggs, as well as insects, from branches. Black-caps generally excavate their nest cavities, whereas the mountain species moves into natural cavities or abandoned woodpecker holes. Black-capped chickadees are easily recognized by their call, a slow *chick-a-dee-dee-dee.*

Chickadees often group together to harass, or mob, a predator. This mobbing behavior may serve to educate young birds about potential predators or merely to encourage the larger bird to move along.

YELLOW-RUMPED WARBLER
Setophaga coronata
Wood warbler family (Parulidae)
Length 5¹/₂ in.

Yellow-rumped warblers generally breed in the mountainous areas of southern Utah. They forage in the tops of conifers and have a conspicuous habit of circling the crown of a tree while hawking insects. They supplement their mostly insect diet with fruits and berries. In winter, they migrate down in elevation to forage in cottonwoods.

Like many bird species, the yellow-rumped male is the more colorful of the sexes, especially during breeding season. A yellow rump, side patch, and crown stand out amidst the dark green foliage of their coniferous ecosystem.

Several other warblers, including Virginia's (*Oreothlypis virginiae*), Wilson's (*Cardellina pusilla*), and MacGillivray's (*Geothlypis tolmiei*), migrate through the region in spring and fall. Virginia's warblers honor Virginia Anderson, wife of the species' first scientific collector, William Wallace Anderson. Alexander Wilson has been called the father of American ornithology. Scottish ornithologist William MacGillivray was a friend of John James Audubon.

COMMON YELLOWTHROAT
Geothlypis trichas
Wood warbler family (Parulidae)
Length 5 in.

Marshy land does not occur commonly across southern Utah, but where it does, one is likely to encounter common yellowthroats, especially in association with cattails and willows. Yellowthroats also nest in grassy fields, irrigation ditches, and riparian areas. Look for them foraging for insects low to the ground; they rarely spend time above the level of low vegetation, and finding one can be rather frustrating. Common yellowthroats sing a distinct *witchity-witchity-witchity* song and a raspy cheek call note.

Both sexes have a yellow throat and breast. Males also wear a distinct black facial mask bordered above by white. Southwestern varieties are the brightest yellow of this continent-wide bird.

YELLOW-BREASTED CHAT
Icteria virens
Wood warbler family (Parulidae)
Length 7½ in.

This is another summer resident that nests and forages in the riparian zone. Yellow-breasted chats forage in the densest jungle of streamside vegetation and are more often heard than seen. The monumental *Life Histories of the Wood Warblers* described the male's vocalization: "[He] laughs dryly, gurgles derisively, whistles triumphantly, chatters provokingly, and chuckles complacently, all in one breath." The chat's behavior elicited a similar response in A. C. Bent, the author of *Life Histories,* who called the birds "eccentric," "ludicrous," and the "buffoon of the briar patch."

At up to 7½ inches long, including tail, the yellow-breasted chat is the largest North American warbler. Unlike other warblers, they often hold their food with a foot and have a relatively thick bill. Their common name aptly describes their coloration. A thin white line running around the eyes and across the face gives the appearance of a pair of spectacles.

BLUE GROSBEAK
Passerina caerulea
Cardinal family (Cardinalidae)
Length 6³/₄ in.

SPOTTED TOWHEE
Pipilo maculatus
Warbler family (Embrezidae)
Length 8¹/₂ in.

Blue grosbeaks nest near the ground in shrubby thickets and brushy roadside areas. In low-light situations they may be confused with brown-headed cowbirds, because their brilliant blue plumage is only evident in full light. Female grosbeaks lack the blue coloration but share the species habit of tail twitching.

Because birds use their forelimbs for flight, they have had to adapt other body parts to substitute for the functions normally performed by these appendages. The principal organ of replacement is the beak, which may be used for digging, prying, clasping, or fighting. Beaks are usually good indicators of what and how a bird eats. Consider the rapier-sharp beak of a raptor for ripping flesh, or the fine, curved bill of a hummingbird for obtaining nectar. Cracking nuts and other seeds, on the other hand, requires a stout, or gross, beak. Oddly though, blue grosbeaks prefer insects and grubs, but the beak does serve them well in cracking piñon shells.

The life of a spotted towhee centers on the ground, nesting and foraging on it or close to it. They are more often heard than seen. Foraging towhees scratch the ground, effectively stirring up invertebrates, nuts, and seeds. This scratching sounds like a fox or other small mammal moving through the brush. Their distinctive *drink-your-tea* call is another good indicator of spotted towhees. In flight the bird's white wing patches and white-cornered tail are conspicuous. Both sexes also have reddish sides and a spotted underside. On the ground, if flushed from the nest, females run like a small mammal.

Spotted towhees were formerly known as rufous-sided towhees, a name which no longer exists. The eastern species is now called the eastern towhee.

WHITE-CROWNED SPARROW
Zonotrichia leucophrys
Warbler family (Embrezidae)
Length 7 in.

DARK-EYED JUNCO
Junco hyemalis
Warbler family (Embrezidae)
Length 6¹/₄ in.

RED-WINGED BLACKBIRD
Agelaius phoeniceus
Blackbird family (Icteridae)
Length 8³/₄ in.

White-crowned Sparrow

Unlike most of the human visitors to canyon country, white-crowned sparrows and dark-eyed juncos migrate here during the winter months. The sparrow's trip is not far as they generally breed in the mountains during the summer. With their arresting white-and-black head stripes, they are easy to distinguish from other riparian zone birds. They form gregarious flocks that include another common winter migrant, dark-eyed juncos.

Juncos often travel in groups to bird feeders seeking seeds. In winter, outside of towns, they forage in riparian areas. During the breeding season they nest and forage at higher elevations. Their distinctive black head gives juncos the appearance of an avian executioner wearing a black hood.

Chattering cacophonies mark the return of red-winged blackbirds. Males produce a rolling song described as either *conqueree* or *konk-la-ree*. Males arrive en masse in late winter, usually returning to the same territory as the previous year. They then begin to vigorously defend their small patch of the wetland. Red-wings nest off the ground in cattails, trees, or bushes.

Red-winged blackbird is an apt appellation for these noisy animals. Males have a prominent red wing bar, or epaulet, which they display during territorial battles and mating. Studies have shown the importance of the red epaulet; if it is covered, the bird loses all its territorial status.

Dark-eyed Junco

BROWN-HEADED COWBIRD
Molothrus ater
Blackbird family (Icteridae)
Length 7¹/₂ in.

HOUSE FINCH
Carpodacus mexicanus
Finch family (Fringillidae)
Length 6 in.

Illustration © Todd Telander

Once relatively rare, brown-headed cowbirds have increased their range with the expansion of grazing. Originally known as "buffalo birds" because they followed bison, eating insects stirred up by trampling, the birds gained the cowbird designation by following cattle as both species spread across the continent.

Cowbirds do not build their own nest; instead, they lay their eggs in other birds' nests, a practice known as brood parasitism. The generic epithet *Molothrus* is a corruption of the Greek *molobros* for a glutton or greedy beggar and refers to the bird's parasitic nature. More than 200 species may become hosts, ranging from gnatcatchers to meadowlarks. After removing one or two host eggs, a cowbird lays a single egg in the nest. If the host does not remove or destroy the cowbird egg, the young cowbird will be raised by its host. Yellow warblers combat cowbirds by building a new nest on top of their old nest if the cowbird egg is there—sometimes up to four levels stacked on top of each other.

Brood parasitism can be detrimental to the host species in several ways. Host eggs are removed. Cowbird eggs may be larger and receive more heat from the incubating host. A cowbird may be born first or may be significantly larger, gaining additional attention and food. Brood parasitism by cowbirds has pushed Kirtland's warbler (*Dendroica kirtlandii*), a northern Michigan species, to the level of endangered species.

House finches, originally native to only the western and southwestern United States, now commonly occur throughout the eastern part of the country, too. In 1940, unscrupulous dealers on Long Island released birds that they called "Hollywood finches" into the wild. These birds have subsequently colonized the eastern seaboard.

Their abundance, coupled with the male's reddish throat, head, and rump, make house finches a commonly seen visitor to backyard bird feeders. Outside of towns in the West, they are best known as residents of riparian areas. House finches may nest in the fork of an upright tree limb, in a cavity or projection of a building, or in a shrub. Male house finches may sing throughout the year. Their rambling, lively song is another indicator of this common bird.

GOLDEN EAGLE
Aquila chrysaetos
Hawk family (Accipitridae)
Length 30 in., wingspan 79 in.

Illustration © Todd Telander

With their 6-foot wingspan and effortless soaring flight, golden eagles are one of the most impressive and beautiful sights in canyon country. The wide-open terrain and wealth of nesting locations on cliffs provide ideal habitat. Sitting on a ledge, catching thermals, or perched on a utility pole, these large raptors can survey the terrain for prey ranging from reptiles to coyotes. Some national park employees even tell apocryphal stories of golden eagles swooping down on free-roaming dogs. Jackrabbits, cottontails, and carrion make up the base of their diet.

Golden eagles construct stick nests on cliff ledges and in alcoves. A pair mates for life and annually returns to the same nesting territory, which often contains several nests. Over the years, nests may grow up to 4 to 6 feet in diameter and 5 feet deep. Females do most of the incubating of the two-egg clutch.

The adult's light golden head gives the birds their common name. The underside of the wings is solid brown in adults and has well-defined white patches near the outer tips. Juvenile bald eagles, sometimes mistaken for goldens, have more splotchy white underwing patches, a larger head, and a shorter tail.

Like many avian predators, golden eagles have been consistently harassed by humans, who blame the birds for lost lambs and calves. They have been federally protected since 1962.

AMERICAN KESTREL
Falco sparverius
Falcon family (Falconidae)
Length 10 in., wingspan 21 in.

BURROWING OWL
Athene cunicularia
Owl family (Strigidae)
Length 9¼ in.

Illustration © Todd Telander

American kestrels are the most commonly seen diurnal bird of prey in canyon country. At just 10 inches long, they nest in small natural cavities in trees or cliffs. Although this small hunter uses telephone wires as a favored perch site, kestrels most often hunt by hovering. In a wind hover, as ornithologists refer to this behavior, the bird stays in place by flying into the wind at a speed equal to that of the wind. From a height of 15 to 20 feet, a kestrel can silently descend to its meal. They primarily eat grasshoppers but may indulge in mice, reptiles, or smaller birds.

Kestrels have white cheeks graced by two black bars, or mustaches, a trait shared by all falcons. Their rufous tail and back make them one of the more colorful raptors. Females, which are larger, lack the rufous back. Like other falcons, kestrels have long, pointed wings and a long tail. Kestrel comes from the French for "little bell-ringer," in reference to the bird's repeated high-pitched *killy-killy* call.

Burrowing owls inhabit open desert grasslands, although their numbers have dropped dramatically due to systematic elimination of prairie dogs. They defy many owl stereotypes by living underground in abandoned prairie dog burrows and by commonly appearing aboveground during daylight hours, although they feed primarily at night or during the crepuscular hours. One study of burrowing owl pellets—the regurgitated, undigested bones, teeth, feathers, and fur of their previous meal—indicates that they prefer kangaroo rats and voles, along with grasshoppers, crickets, and lizards. The young may imitate a rattlesnake buzz when alarmed. Their long legs help distinguish burrowing owls from other owl species.

COMMON NIGHTHAWK
Chordeiles minor
Nightjar family (Caprimulgidae)
Length 9$^{1}/_{2}$ in.

COMMON POORWILL
Phalaenoptilus nuttallii
Nightjar family (Caprimulgidae)
Length 7$^{3}/_{4}$ in.

Common Nighthawk

Illustration © Todd Telander

NORTHERN FLICKER
Colaptes auratus
Woodpecker family (Picidae)
Length 12$^{1}/_{2}$ in.

Despite their common name, nighthawks are neither nocturnal nor closely related to hawks. They feed mostly at dusk, flying in an erratic pattern chasing insects, which they scoop out of the air with their large mouths. Sensitive bristlelike feathers surrounding the bill help nighthawks locate food. Flying also reveals a distinguishing characteristic: white epaulets on the underside of the wings. Be cautious when driving at dusk, as nighthawks occasionally crash into car windows while chasing insects.

Both sexes have loud nasal *peent* calls. While they dive and climb during courtship, wind moving across their wing feathers produces a "booming" sound. This has led to another common name: bullblasts.

Another member of this family, which includes poorwills and goatsuckers, is the common poorwill. The distinctive *poor-will* call, often produced before going on a hunt at dusk, gives the bird its common name. If disturbed while sitting on its minimalist nest, it may hiss like a snake.

Northern flickers are ubiquitous across North America from Alaska to Mexico. The western variety's tail feathers have a red shaft, whereas eastern ones are generally yellow, and Texas ones, gilded. They inhabit open woodland or sagebrush areas. Their propensity for prefab housing means that flickers may end up moving into clothesline poles, or holes in houses, haystacks, fence posts, or trees.

Unlike other woodpeckers, flickers forage on the ground. Ants make up as much as 45 percent of their diet. Springtime also reveals another unusual characteristic, at least in southwestern woodpeckers. Flickers do not generally rely on drumming for communication. Instead they produce a loud, rapid *wika-wika-wika*. Their undulating flight pattern and the flash of their red shafts are good identification aids.

SAY'S PHOEBE
Sayornis saya
Tyrant flycatcher family (Tyrannidae)
Length 7¹/₂ in.

MOUNTAIN BLUEBIRD
Sialia currucoides
Thrush family (Muscicapidae)
Length 7¹/₄ in.

WESTERN BLUEBIRD
Sialia mexicana
Thrush family (Muscicapidae)
Length 7 in.

Mountain Bluebird

Say's phoebes' appearance in late February or early March indicates that spring will arrive soon. Look for a pale orangish-brown chest and their habit of perching on top of shrubs. Of all the flycatchers, these little gray birds (LGBs) dwell closest to the ground, exploiting a microclimate where warmer ground temperatures allow low-flying insects to move about sooner. Say's phoebes have adapted well to human environments and often build their grass and plant fiber nests in the eaves of buildings or under bridges. Phoebes are an efficient insectivore, eating bees, wasps, flies, and grasshoppers, which they catch from an elevated perch such as a sagebrush.

The name phoebe comes from the eastern phoebe's *fee-be* song. See Great Plains toad, page 175, for information on Thomas Say.

Western bluebird and mountain bluebird habitat has steadily decreased due to humanity's propensity to remove dead trees and cut off dead limbs, which bluebirds require for nesting. The spread of competing cavity nesters such as European starlings and house finches has also contributed to a decline in bluebird numbers across the United States. In response, people put up bluebird nest boxes to replace natural habitat.

Both species eat insects and seasonally supplement their diets with fruit and berries. One ornithologist has likened mountain bluebirds to "scaled-down kestrels" because of their unusual behavior of hovering and consuming mostly insects. Western bluebirds neither hover nor depend upon insects as much as mountain bluebirds.

Mountain bluebird males are all blue with the chest lighter than the back. Females are brownish gray with blue tinges in the wings. Both sexes of western bluebird have chestnut-colored breasts. Mountain bluebirds are common summer residents above 5,000 feet.

LOGGERHEAD SHRIKE
Lanius ludovicianus
Shrike family (Laniidae)
Length 9 in.

The generic epithet for this songbird, *Lanius,* means butcher. It is an appropriate name for these small gray birds that kill by severing the cervical vertebrae and then impaling their prey on a thorn or barbed wire. Like other perching birds, loggerhead shrikes have weak feet; therefore, they must hook or hang their prey on something that will allow the birds to use their raptoresque beak for dissection. They inhabit open areas, and typical food items include reptiles, mammals, birds, and insects.

Shrikes usually eat their meals immediately but may also leave the carcass for several days. This may serve as storage, as a mate attractant, or as a method to let poisons degrade from chemically noxious prey.

Herbicide spraying and habitat loss have contributed to a steady decline in the loggerhead shrike population. The name loggerhead refers to the bird's relatively large head. Loggerhead also means blockhead. The closely related northern shrike (*Lanius excubitor*) is a winter resident. Both are gray birds with black wings and a black eye mask. The loggerhead has a shorter bill.

NORTHERN MOCKINGBIRD
Mimus polyglottos
Mimic thrush family (Mimidae)
Length 10 in.

Mockingbirds live in open woodlands of the Southwest. They also inhabit towns where they will vigorously defend their territory against large and small, whether human, dog, or bird. When confronting a potential predator, mockingbirds often raise up their wings and flash a warning with their white wing patches. They also flash their wing patches while foraging on the ground.

The best-known behavior of mockingbirds is their ability to mimic practically any sound they hear, a fact reflected in their specific epithet. These avian synthesizers' repertoires include imitations of chickens, squeaky wheelbarrows, and pianos, as well as numerous varieties of birds. During the spring breeding season, males will sing for hours, day and night. A male may acquire 150 distinct song types throughout his life.

LARK SPARROW
Chondestes grammacus
Warbler family (Embrezidae)
Length 6¹/₂ in.

Illustration © Todd Telander

A distinct head pattern of five white stripes outlined in black, with chestnut patches in between, distinguishes lark sparrows from other birds. They are also large for a sparrow. Lark sparrows eat seeds but also consume insects with an emphasis on grasshoppers.

They are omnipresent in grassland areas, feeding and nesting on the ground. As summer progresses, small flocks increase in size, steadily becoming noisier.

BLACK-THROATED SPARROW
Amphispiza bilineata
Warbler family (Embrezidae)
Length 5¹/₂ in.

Illustration © Todd Telander

One ornithologist described black-throated sparrows as a "handsome, black-bibbed obligate of the hot, little-watered areas." This fittingly summarizes one of the most well-adapted desert animals. Black-throats survive away from water by metabolizing moisture from insects and green vegetation. To aid in water retention, they can reduce the moisture content of their excrement by one-fourth when water is not readily available. Unlike other desert-adapted animals, black-throats are active even during low-water conditions.

Black-throated sparrows are birds of the North American deserts; some people call them desert sparrows. They are found in valleys and grasslands or on mesas nesting in small shrubs. Their song begins with two to three clear notes, followed by a trill.

WESTERN MEADOWLARK
Sturnella neglecta
Blackbird family (Icteridae)
Length 9¹/₂ in.

Western meadowlarks often perch on poles, shrubs, or wires located near roads. Their brilliant yellow chest with its distinct black chevron-shaped collar makes them a conspicuous member of the southwestern bird community. Their rich, joyous song is a sure harbinger of spring.

Despite being known for perching, meadowlarks generally spend their time on the ground in grasslands. Their nests consist of grass and bark domes, which the birds enter from the side. They prefer insects such as caterpillars, beetles, and Mormon crickets, but may indulge in spiders, grass seeds, and snails. Meadowlarks have also been known to eat roadside bird carrion. Lark comes from an Anglo-Saxon term, *lawerce*, for traitor.

Cliffs and Debris Slopes

TURKEY VULTURE
Cathartes aura
American vulture family (Cathartidae)
Length 27 in. , wingspan 69 in.

Turkey vultures hold their wings in a V shape while soaring and look rocky or unbalanced while flying, unlike golden eagles, which soar gracefully. The undersides of the wings are two-toned, mostly white with black on the forward parts. They often soar in flocks.

At present a debate exists in the ornithological community as to whether TVs, as they are often called, hunt primarily by sight or smell. Unlike most birds, turkey vultures possess a strong sense of smell, which may help them find the pungent aromas emitted from their main food item, carrion. They also have excellent vision to help them see carcasses while they soar high above on rising columns of warm air, known as thermals.

Turkey vultures' carrion-eating proclivity plays an important role in desert ecosystems. In a landscape where decomposition occurs slowly, these scavengers help recycle nutrients by eating carcasses. The generic name, *Cathartes*, which comes from the Greek word for purifier or cleanser, alludes to this habit. Their lack of head feathers is an advantage, because a bird can easily clean itself after extracting its head from the inside of a carcass. A featherless head is also less prone to harbor insects or diseases.

Close-up

California Condors: Back from the Brink

Big, bald, and beautiful. It's the California condor (*Gymnogyps californianus*), brought back from the edge of extinction by a dedicated group of scientists working with the US Fish and Wildlife Service, the Los Angeles Zoo, and the San Diego Wild Animal Park. Since 1983, when the condor reintroduction program began, the number of condors has increased from 22 to 391 in late 2011. Of those, 209 are wild, with 113 in California, 23 in Baja California, and 73 in Arizona/Utah.

They have been sighted from Arches to Zion National Parks, though they are known to nest (cracks and crevices without a nest) only in Arizona, particularly in the Grand Canyon. Good places to see the birds in Utah include northwest of Zion's Kolob Terrace, north of Panguitch Lake, and on UT 14 at the Zion overlook.

During the last ice age, California condors roamed across the entire United States, but by the nineteenth century they were restricted to west of the Rockies, and by the middle twentieth century to California. Lead poisoning was, and still is, the primary culprit in the population decline, though historical records indicate that shooting also led to many bird deaths. (People used the birds' flight feathers to store gold dust.) The birds ingested the lead from the consumption of carrion, primarily mule deer and coyote.

Their diet also included cattle, sheep, mountain lion, and blue whale. They prefer fresh carcasses, which they find by visually locating other scavengers. Unlike their close cousins, turkey vultures, condors do not rely on aroma. Once a scavenger is found, they will push out previous diners, except for golden eagles with their rapier talons, and eat in groups. Their bald, or featherless, head and neck helps prevent food and bacteria from catching when they are neck deep in a rotting body.

California condors have the widest wingspan, at 9 feet, of any bird in North America, and are some of the heaviest with males up to 22 pounds. Only tundra and mute swans rival them; eagles by contrast peak out at about 10 pounds.

The condor breeding program began with a single captive and one wild bird. Wild populations were so dire by 1987 that biologists decided to capture the last wild bird and rely solely on the breeding program. Because the birds do not breed until six years old and generally lay an egg every other year, biologists removed eggs as soon as they were laid, which led to captive birds laying multiple eggs. Caretakers using condor hand puppets then raised the young birds. This prevents the birds from imprinting on and identifying with humans.

Condors have continued to be released yearly, which along with wild births has pushed the total population of northern Arizona and southern Utah to 73. Any bird that you see will also have a white, numbered tag on it. You can track down information on that specific bird at the Peregrine Fund website (http://peregrinefund.org/pages/conservation/condor-individuals.html).

PEREGRINE FALCON
Falco peregrinus
Falcon family (Falconidae)
Length 16 in., wingspan 41 in.

The Colorado Plateau's combination of cliffs for perching and nesting, open terrain for hunting, and swifts and swallows for food makes this ideal territory for peregrine falcons. The rising population of the bird in the post-DDT world reflects this peregrine utopia. At present more than 160 pairs of peregrines nest in Utah, compared with only two pairs in 1975.

Peregrines were removed from the federal list of endangered and threatened wildlife in August 1999.

Peregrines live year-round in canyon country, nesting alone or in pairs on the vertical cliffs. Pairs mate for life and they have an elaborate courtship ritual in which the pair will trap a bird, often a swift, between them in flight. As the swift attempts to elude the peregrines, they will fly along with the bird. Eventually the male grabs the swift and gives it to his mate—in flight. She lays two to six eggs, which both sexes will incubate.

With a top dive speed of more than 180 miles per hour, peregrines live by their speed. The hunt generally consists of a high-speed collision with a subsequent explosion of feathers, followed by the prey either falling to the ground or being caught in midfall by the peregrine. If the meal is not dead, the peregrine kills it with its beak.

Peregrines have a slate-blue back and wings. Dark bars cover the white chest. Their black head and neck looks like a hood, and their dark face marking looks like sideburns, although birders call it a mustache. Like all falcons they have long, pointed wings and a long tail, and make rapid, strong wing beats.

The closely related prairie falcon (*Falco mexicanus*) is similarly sized, lighter in color, with a white area between the eye and dark ear patch, and has a black center spot on its underwings. They live in hilly and mountainous areas of the West and hunt for small, mostly ground-dwelling animals.

CHUKAR
Alectoris chukar
Grouse family (Phasianidae)
Length 14 in.

WHITE-THROATED SWIFT
Aeronautes saxatalis
Swift family (Apodidae)
Length 6¹/₂ in.

The Utah State Fish and Game Department introduced this Asiatic partridge into Utah in 1936 to create a new population of game birds. The department held the first hunt in 1956. Chukars are ground-oriented birds, roosting on the ground and obtaining food by scratching with their feet or pecking with their bill. They thrive in the western United States by consuming their fellow alien invaders, cheatgrass, red-stemmed filaree, and Russian thistle. Chukars are abundant at Capitol Reef National Park.

Chukars are so named because of their *chuck-chuck-chuck* call, which increases to a chukar under duress. Both sexes use this rallying cry for locating one another. During mating season, males also call to alert other males of their location.

White-throated swifts may be confused with violet-green swallows. Both are insectivorous, nest on cliff faces, and fly fast and gracefully. The swallow has a solid white belly and shorter, wider wings (swift's wings are more pointed). A swallow's flight consists of flapping and gliding; swifts rock and flutter. In addition, swifts may be encountered zipping by people sitting on cliff edges.

Unlike the world of botany where bantering about scientific names is *de rigueur,* birders rarely utter complicated Latin names. White-throated swifts, though, offer a reason to learn the more formal names of birds. The generic epithet, *Aeronautes,* from the Greek for "air sailor," refers to the animals' flying lifestyle. As a group, swifts are considered to be the fastest birds in the world. The specific epithet, *saxatalis,* a Latin derivation meaning "rock-inhabiting," alludes to the animal's habit of constructing nests in cracks on vertical cliff faces, cementing grass and feathers together with saliva.

VIOLET-GREEN SWALLOW
Tachycineta thalassina
Swallow family (Hirundinidae)
Length 5¹/₄ in.

CLIFF SWALLOW
Petrochelidon phyrrhonota
Swallow family (Hirundinidae)
Length 5¹/₄ in.

Cliff Swallow

Violet-green Swallow

Violet-green swallows shoot through the clear desert air, catching a multitude of insects. Like swifts, swallows catch and eat on the wing, but are more likely to eat on a perch. They mostly nest in cracks in cliff faces and less often in tree cavities, usually at higher elevations. Unlike other swallows, they eschew colony living. When the sun hits them, green and purple light shimmers off their iridescent wings.

Another swallow, the cliff swallow, lives in colonies of gourd-shaped mud dwellings beneath overhangs. The bird often builds near water and close to marshes or meadows where it can exploit open airways. Like violet-greens, it also takes advantage of human habitats and constructs nests on buildings and bridges. Cliff swallows have dark wings with a cinnamon throat and rump.

COMMON RAVEN

Corvus corax
Crow family (Corvidae)
Length 24 in.

Wherever humans live, we notice ravens. The great black bird may represent evil, as in Edgar Allan Poe's "The Raven," or it may be a trickster, as in many Native American cultures. As one ornithologist wrote: "Humanity has never been indifferent to the presence of ravens." The cosmopolitan common raven ranges from western North America to northwestern Africa.

Do animals play? Ornithologists believe that ravens are one of the few animals that play. If in doubt, watch a raven somersault, dive, tumble, and flip through the air, or watch one sneak up on visitors and berate them for not giving it any food. Ravens are ubiquitous to canyon country, a black specter constantly watching from a cliffside nook or piñon pine.

Please note: Do not feed ravens or any other bird. It is not good for the birds.

Ravens are omnipresent and omnivorous, inhabiting the desert year-round and eating anything they find, whether it is carrion, a kangaroo rat, or birds' eggs. Their raucous cries, noisy wing beats, and communal habits make them a prominent part of the landscape.

Ravens closely resemble another common black bird, the American crow (*C. brachyrhynchos*). Crows are smaller and have a less stately bill, and they only caw as opposed to the raven's varied oral cacophony. Crows nest more often near riparian areas than ravens.

CANYON WREN
Catherpes mexicanus
Wren family (Troglodytidae)
Length 5³/₄ in.

ROCK WREN
Salpinctes obsoletus
Wren family (Troglodytidae)
Length 6 in.

Canyon Wren

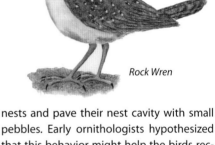

Rock Wren

The two canyon country wrens produce unmistakable evidence of their presence. Canyon wrens inhabit rocky canyons, nesting in cavities high on cliff faces. From high above, the wren's song gently descends the musical scale in a series of *tees* and *tews*. Along with the coyote's haunting call, it is one of the true songs of the canyon country.

The classic rock wren sign is the gravel walkway that leads to its nest. Some walkways run up to 10 inches in length. Rock wrens live in a labyrinthine world of crevices, nooks, passageways, and recesses. True to their name they even use rocks in their nests and pave their nest cavity with small pebbles. Early ornithologists hypothesized that this behavior might help the birds recognize their nest cavities from the multitude of holes found in cliff faces, or that the walkway kept "the young from falling into crevices or getting their feet caught in the same." To this day no one knows the real reason.

Both wrens are low, squat birds with cocked tails and mottled coloring. The rock's gray back and white chest separate it from the chestnut-backed, white-bibbed chest of the canyon wren. Both extract insects from crevices with their long, powerful bills.

Piñon-Juniper Woodland

MOURNING DOVE
Zenaida macroura
Pigeon family (Columbidae)
Length 12 in.

Desert birds that do not live near water generally obtain moisture by consuming insects and meat. Mourning doves are an exception, subsisting almost completely (more than 98 percent) on a dry resource, seeds. They obtain water by flying to it, usually during the morning or evening. One study found that doves can rehydrate in about 1 minute after not drinking for 24 hours. Members of the Columbidae family, which includes pigeons and doves, drink in a manner different from other birds, which must take a mouthful, raise their head, and let the water trickle down. Columbids drink by lowering their bill into water and sucking it up without having to raise their head.

In the morning hours, unmated male doves trying to attract females produce the plaintive *coo-oo, oo, oo, oo* sound ubiquitous to many desert environments. They can nest on the ground but more often build a haphazard stick nest in trees or shrubs. Mourning doves are most common in the summer.

GREAT HORNED OWL

Bubo virginianus
Owl family (Strigidae)
Length 22 in.

WESTERN SCREECH OWL

Megascops kennicottii
Owl family (Strigidae)
Length 8¹/₂ in.

Great Horned Owl

Illustration © Todd Telander

Owls are elegantly adapted to hunting at night. Their exceptionally large eyes contain a high proportion of light-gathering rods, facilitating vision in low-light situations. Furthermore, by having eyes located on the front of their heads, owls see with binocular vision like humans. This allows them to accurately gauge distance, especially important when your next meal is constantly moving.

The location of owls' ear openings also enhances their hunting abilities; one is higher than the other. Because of this feature, sound reaches their ears at slightly different times (on the order of microseconds or one-millionth of a second), which enables the birds to create a three-dimensional map of their acoustic space.

These adaptations contribute to making great horned owls extremely efficient hunters. They are also notorious for their ferocity and will eat other raptors, as well as skunks, but jackrabbits and cottontails make up the bulk of their diet. The "horns" are ear tufts. Listen for the distinct *Who's awake? Me too* call.

Another common desert owl, the western screech, does not screech. Instead, it produces a series of short whistles on one pitch at a steady tempo. It lives in tree cavities and often nests in towns. Like the much larger great horned owl, it has yellow eyes and ear tufts. Robert Kennicott (1835–1866) was a naturalist who explored Alaska, where he died under mysterious circumstances. His body was exhumed in 2001 and showed that he died of natural causes and not suicide as some claimed.

WESTERN SCRUB JAY
Aphelocoma californica
Crow family (Corvidae)
Length 11¹/₂ in.

PINYON JAY
Gymnorhinus cyanocephalus
Crow family (Corvidae)
Length 10¹/₂ in.

Scrub jays live in areas of low-growing, or scrub, vegetation. Common associations include oak thickets and piñon-juniper woodlands. They employ a powerful bill to obtain their varied diet, which includes eggs and young birds, spiders, scorpions, acorns, and nuts. They also may land on a deer and remove ticks. Like most members of the jay family they are noisy, producing a raspy *peent* or *shreep* call.

A gregarious bird, scrub jays are notorious as camp robbers, especially in national park campgrounds. Unlike pinyon jays, which form large flocks, scrubs are solitary. The scrub jay's flight pattern is undulating, as opposed to the pinyon's direct path. The overall blue coloring of the pinyon jay contrasts with the scrub jay's light gray chest.

Pinyon jays and piñon pines exemplify the interdependence between plants and animals. During autumn, hundreds of pinyon jays may congregate in a raucous, sociable group, collecting, eating, and caching piñon nuts. Like a well-trained Planters™ employee, the jays choose only the finest nuts, assaying each nut; scrutinizing it for a uniformly dark brown shell; and weighing and tapping it to eliminate light, hollow-sounding seeds, which indicate aborted embryos. Pinyon jays completely depend upon these nuts to the point that during low-nut years, their populations will crash.

Piñon trees also benefit from the jay's nut caching. Because the birds bury more nuts than they can consume, some will germinate. Jays aid the plants by dispersing seeds far from parent populations. Mass burial also facilitates self-selection of the fittest individuals, which must outcompete their neighbors.

Author note: *Pinyon, the official name for the bird, is used here, while piñon is used for the plant.*

JUNIPER TITMOUSE
Baeolophus ridgwayi
Titmouse family (Paridae)
Length 5³/₄ in.

Illustration © Todd Telander

BLACK-THROATED GRAY WARBLER
Setophaga nigrescens
Warbler family (Emberizidae)
Length 5 in.

Illustration © Todd Telander

Rarely does a juniper titmouse sit still. It spends its life moving constantly, chattering and scanning. It forages in the protective foliage of piñons and junipers and only ventures to the ground in open understory. Juniper titmice eat insects, fruits, and seeds. Their slight crest distinguishes them from many other "little gray birds." They are year-round residents and also may be found in riparian areas. The juniper titmouse was previously called the plain titmouse.

It is not uncommon to see juniper titmice in mixed-species foraging flocks. Many varieties of bird forage together for predator defense. More eyes and ears help detect potential predators. Mixed flocks also increase foraging efficiency because a group can overwhelm other foragers and take over a good food territory, which a single bird could not accomplish.

Black-throated gray warblers are fairly common when they migrate into southern Utah in the summer. They nest in piñon-juniper woodlands and subsist on insects found in these conifers. Unlike many other western warblers, black-throated grays lack yellow coloration except for a small spot between the eye and the bill. They have a black-and-white head with a gray-streaked back.

CHIPPING SPARROW
Spizella passerina
Warbler family (Emberizidae)
Length 5¹/₂ in.

Spring brings the chipping sparrow back to southern Utah. The two most common places to see the birds are in the piñon-juniper forest or in town on lawns, where they forage for grass seeds. Like many other sparrows, chippings primarily feed on the ground, eating seeds, insects, and spiders.

Many birders group chipping sparrows in the notorious group of LBBs, or little brown birds. They are easier to distinguish during breeding season with their chestnut head and white eyebrow patch. Habitat is a good key to distinguish chipping sparrows from Brewer's sparrows (*Spizella breweri*), which also have a distinct white eye ring. The chipping also has a white eye stripe above the eye, whereas the Brewer's does not. Look for chippings at higher elevations. Thomas Brewer (1814–1880) was a Boston oologist.

FISH

The Colorado River and its tributaries, including the Green and San Juan Rivers, drop more than 2 miles as they flow from mountains in Wyoming, Colorado, and New Mexico to the Gulf of California. The Colorado has seasonally variable temperatures and radical fluctuations in flow, historically ranging from a few thousand to nearly 400,000 cubic feet per second.

Only fourteen species of fish originally inhabited the unique ecosystem of the upper basin of the Colorado River. Three-quarters of these fish are found in no other river basin. At present, four of those fish are listed as endangered: bonytail chub, Colorado pikeminnow, humpback chub, and razorback sucker. More than forty alien species now live in these waters.

In the last 50 years, human changes to this river system have altered the seasonally variable flows, created large lakes behind dams, and led to hundreds of miles of cold water below the dams, all of which have contributed to habitat loss and a decline in species numbers.

The introduction of alien fish to the Colorado River has had a significant negative impact on the native fish, too. One study at the confluence of the Green and Colorado Rivers found that 95 percent of the fish species were nonnative. Channel catfish are particularly damaging as they eat young pikeminnows and the eggs and larvae of razorback suckers.

Although one rarely sees fish in the Colorado River, nine species are described in this section. The two most commonly encountered species are the carp and channel catfish.

Roundtail Chub

Carp

Channel Catfish

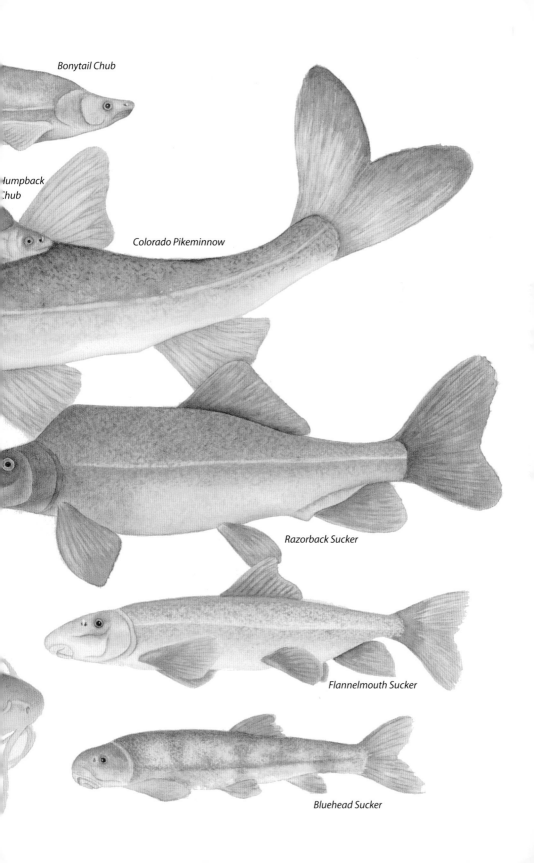

Bonytail Chub

Humpback Chub

Colorado Pikeminnow

Razorback Sucker

Flannelmouth Sucker

Bluehead Sucker

BLUEHEAD SUCKER
Catostomus discobolus
Sucker family (Catostomidae)
6–10 in., blue head, bluish gray back,
white belly

Blueheads are native to the upper Colorado River drainage system. Their preferred habitat is in the fast-flowing sections over cobbles, where they can use a cartilaginous chisel on their mouths to scrape algae and bugs off the bottom. The mouth of all members of this family is under the fish, allowing them to feed effectively on the bottom substrate. Blueheads are common and widely distributed.

FLANNELMOUTH SUCKER
Catostomus latipinnis
Sucker family (Catostomidae)
18–24 in., weight up to 4 lb., greenish-gray back and upper sides, lower sides yellow or orange-red

Flannelmouths are big river fish. They have not suffered as much of a population decline as other natives. Along with bluehead suckers they are the most common species caught in drift nets in the upper Colorado River. They inhabit shallow riffles as young and deep riffles as adults. Flannelmouths only have a short upstream migration. Like other suckers, they eat algae and insects off the river bottom. They may have been a primary component of the pikeminnow diet.

RAZORBACK SUCKER
Xyrauchen texanus
Sucker family (Catostomidae)
Up to 36 in., weight up to 16 lb., brownish green with whitish belly, abrupt bony hump on back

Razorbacks were once plentiful enough to be commercially harvested. Now they are limited to a large but dwindling population in Lake Mojave and smaller groups on the Green River near Dinosaur National Monument and on the Colorado River near Colorado National Monument. Razorbacks have a sleek body and a thin, humped back, excellent adaptations for the fast, turbulent water of the Colorado River. Similar to the other endangered native fish, razorbacks have been unable to adapt to the dam-caused changes and introduction of nonnative fishes.

CARP
Cyprinus carpio
Carp and minnow family (Cyprinidae)
Up to 30 in., weight up to 10 lb., large bronze scales, very short "whiskers"

Carp live in shallow water. During the spring and summer, they often congregate in groups to spawn in water less than 4 feet deep. They eat almost anything by taking in mouthfuls of the bottom substrate, gleaning invertebrates, and spitting out sediments, a process that tears up the fragile bottom, actively degrading habitat.

Carp are native to Asia. The US Bureau of Fisheries billed carp as the greatest food fish ever and shipped them across the country by rail following the Civil War. They reached Utah around 1888.

HUMPBACK CHUB
Gila cypha
Carp and minnow family (Cyprinidae)
Up to 20 in., olive-colored back, silver sides, white belly, small eyes, long snout that overhangs jaw

Humpback chub are so rare that they were not discovered by scientists until ichthyologist Robert Rush Miller found one in a collection at Grand Canyon National Park. They were federally listed as endangered in 1973. Humpbacks, as their name suggests, have an unusual dorsal hump found in no other fish. This feature, combined with their torpedo-shaped body, helped the fish survive in the turbulent, swift water found in the Colorado River canyons. Humpbacks, though, have not been able to adapt to the clear, cold, silt-free waters that flow out of the dams on the main body of the river. They are now limited to Desolation Canyon on the Green River, Black Rocks and Westwater Canyon on the Colorado River, and at the confluence of the Little Colorado and Colorado Rivers.

BONYTAIL CHUB
Gila elegans
Carp and minnow family (Cyprinidae)
Up to 20 in., olive-colored back, silver sides, white belly, large fins, streamlined body very thin in front of tail

Bonytails have been federally listed as endangered since 1980. At present, only a few 40- to 50-year-olds are found in Lake Mojave, below Hoover Dam. A few live in hatcheries, while 2,000 5- to 6-inch-long bonytails were stocked in the Colorado River near Moab in 1996–1997. They live in backwaters and eddies. Ichthyologists suspect that bonytails may have been an important part of the pikeminnow diet.

ROUNDTAIL CHUB
Gila robusta
Carp and minnow family (Cyprinidae)
10–14 in., weight 1–2 lb.

Roundtail chub numbers are down, but they are faring better than the other two *Gila* species in the system. They are protected in Utah because they are so hard to distinguish from their endangered relatives. Roundtails are carnivorous, opportunistic feeders that eat insects and other fish. They prefer murky waters and silty, sandy, gravelly, and rocky substrates.

COLORADO PIKEMINNOW
Ptychocheilus lucius
Carp and minnow family (Cyprinidae)
Historically up to 6 ft., weight more than 100 lb., present fish up to 2 ft., olive-green back, silvery white belly, mouth extends to back of eye

For the past few million years, until recently, Colorado pikeminnow reigned supreme in the Colorado River basin. In a typical year the fish migrated up to 200 miles through whitewater rapids to spawn in quiet, warm backwaters. Food was not a problem; if it was smaller, it was dinner. When you are a 6-foot-long fish and weigh over 100 pounds, everything is smaller. But life for this predator is not what it used to be.

Pikeminnow, once plentiful enough to be pitchforked out of irrigation canals in Arizona, have now been extirpated in more than 75 percent of their habitat. Dam-created habitat degradation has fragmented the fishes' historic migratory routes. Dam building has also severely curtailed the river's dramatic spring floods, which the fish require for spawning. Habitat loss and introduction of nonnative species created the perfect recipe for this species' decline.

Old-timers called pikeminnow "white salmon," a probable allusion to the fishes' migratory habits. The American Fisheries Society changed the name of the Colorado squawfish to Colorado pikeminnow in 1999 because the former name was offensive to many Native Americans and because *P. lucius* is a member of the minnow family and has a pikelike body.

CHANNEL CATFISH
Ictalurus punctatus
Bullhead catfish family (Ictaluridae)
Up to 36 in., weight 25 lb., spines on dorsal and pectoral fins for protection

Channel catfish were also introduced into the Colorado River around 1888. They live in moderately swift parts of the river system. During the day they hide in sheltered spots and feed in riffles at dusk. In early summer after a mayfly hatch, catfish, with their characteristic "whiskers," can be seen sucking bugs off the water's surface. Catfish eat anything, including the young of several native fish species. They are a significant contributor to the decline of native fish populations.

REPTILES

Lizards and snakes define deserts for many people. The deadly rattlesnake meandering up a sand dune, the elusive lizard darting under cover—these are the images we carry. There is some truth in this picture. Lizards are probably the most commonly seen animal in canyon country, after birds. With their varied diets of insects, arachnids (e.g., spiders and scorpions), and each other; and homes in trees, under rocks, and underground, reptiles are remarkably adapted and resilient. One species of lizard in particular, the western whiptail, may be seen scurrying about during the hottest part of a summer day.

Like all ectotherms, reptiles derive their body heat from external sources, which makes most reptiles active in the early morning and late afternoon, when temperatures are most comfortable. In the hottest part of the day, they stay in burrows or under rocks. During winter, most reptiles hibernate. The small side-blotched lizard, however, is able to come out of hibernation to take advantage of warm winter days.

Ectothermic animals have several advantages over endothermic animals (e.g., birds and mammals). Reptiles need less food than endotherms because they do not have to generate their own heat. One study found that "one day's food for a small bird will last a lizard of the same body size more than a month." During a drought, this is especially important, because food supplies may be scarce. Neither ectotherms nor endotherms tolerate temperatures of 100° or more. Lizards are often seen performing thermoregulatory dances on hot surfaces, lifting their legs or even using their tail as a lever to elevate the rest of their body off the hot surface.

Both snakes and lizards periodically shed their epidermis (commonly, but incorrectly, called the "skin") as they grow, although they take different approaches. Lizards slough off patches of epidermis, usually separately on the head, tail, and body. Shedding, or molting, occurs fairly regularly throughout the period of daily activity. Snakes, on the other hand, shed their entire epidermis at one time, a process that may take several hours to days. To accomplish this, a snake rubs its head or nose on a rock or stick until the old epidermis catches, then simply crawls out of the old, dry covering. In addition, rattlesnakes add a new rattle during each molt, which can occur several times a year; thus the number of rattles does not indicate a rattlesnake's age. Shedding occurs more often in young reptiles, during the time of greatest growth.

Reptiles play an important role in the desert food web. Without snakes, the fecund rodent population would quickly grow out of control. Lizards help control insect and arachnid populations and, in one case in Utah, were found to slow down an invasion of beet leafhoppers. In turn, snakes and lizards provide a hearty meal for many animals, including birds, rodents, and other small mammals.

Common and scientific names for reptiles and amphibians conform with the *Standard Common and Current Scientific Names for North American Amphibians and Reptiles*, Sixth Edition (SCCSNNAAR).

Lizards

During the summer, lizards are a common sight throughout this region. Their small size entices many people to try to catch them. Unfortunately, the pursuer often ends up with only a writhing tail and no lizard in his or her hands. This ability to lose a tail forms the lizard's first line of defense. In many species of lizard, the tail has weak fracture planes between the vertebra, allowing the tail to detach easily. After breaking off, the thrashing tail attracts the would-be predator, enabling the lizard to escape. In addition to having easily broken tails, some lizards have brightly colored tails (often found on young individuals), which further enhances the chance of losing only a tail instead of a life. There can be serious consequences, however, to losing one's tail.

Lizard tails serve numerous purposes, including locomotion and balance, social status, and fat storage. A long tail acts as a counterbalance, enabling a lizard to lift its forelegs when running. Lizards move more quickly on two legs than on four, and large lizards running on two legs can sprint up to 12 miles an hour. Studies show that females lose their tail more easily than males. Males need their tail for social status, which, if low, reduces their chances to mate. Researchers have also found that tail loss may slow a juvenile's acquisition of a home range, due to a lowered social standing. Fat stored in a tail provides a food source during periods of starvation and reproduction.

A healthy tail is critical for lizards. Do not attempt to catch lizards; you are only putting their lives at risk.

EASTERN COLLARED LIZARD
Crotaphytus collaris
Iguanidae family
3 to 4$^{1}/_{2}$ in. snout to vent length, 8–14 in. with tail, green body with yellow head, two black collars around neck

The bright green and yellow collared lizard stands out in a landscape of red rocks. These large lizards commonly perch on top of boulders, scanning their territory for prey. Large insects make up the majority of their diet, but these omnivores will also eat smaller lizards. Collared lizards catch their prey with a quick chase, often running on their hind legs with their forelimbs lifted. One study found that a full-grown lizard has a stride of 12 inches when running in this manner.

Male collared lizards will defend their territory with great vigor. They may chase and/or fight an intruder, but usually resort to an elaborate series of push-ups designed to display their colors. These lizards are the supermodels of the lizard world, seeming to show off their beautiful bodies, allowing humans to approach within a few feet and take pictures; however, they can and will inflict a painful bite.

Unlike short-lived species, such as *Uta stansburiana,* which invest a high amount of energy into one year of life, consumed by feeding and breeding, collared lizards instead spread out their reproduction over several years. They do not become sexually active until their second summer and then only produce two clutches per year. This life history pattern, which is more pronounced in larger lizards, usually indicates limited resources.

There is no western collared lizard. The common name arises because this species has the eastern-most distribution in the genus.

LONGNOSE LEOPARD LIZARD
Gambelia wislizenii
Iguanidae family

$3^1/_2$–$4^1/_2$ in. snout to vent length, $8^1/_2$–$15^1/_2$ in. with tail, variable coloration is generally tan to darker brown and temperature dependent; numerous small dark spots cover entire body

DESERT SPINY LIZARD
Sceloporus magister
Iguanidae family

$3^1/_2$–$5^1/_2$ in. snout to vent length, 7–12 in. with tail, pale yellow to yellowish brown with vague, dorsal crossbands or spots; both male and female adults have yellowish orange on head, most prominent scales of any *Sceloporus*

Unlike many lizard species, where the male has special breeding coloration, the female leopard lizard undergoes a dramatic color change during breeding season. After copulation, her undersides turn scarlet and red streaks shoot up her sides. This coloration remains for several weeks after she lays eggs.

Leopard lizards inhabit grasslands and open habitat, where they use their speed to capture grasshoppers and other lizards, including members of their own species. If chased, they retreat under shrubs or into rodent burrows. The specific name honors Frederick Wislizenus, a German physician who traveled in the Southwest in the late 1830s and 1840s. The generic name honors William Gambel (1821–1849), an American naturalist, who died at the age of 28 on an ill-fated winter crossing of the Sierra Nevada.

Throughout their range, desert spiny lizards inhabit a variety of habitats. In some areas they are primarily a tree- or shrub-dwelling species, only moving down onto the ground to capture prey. In canyon country, spiny lizards move about between shrubs, boulders, and canyon walls. Although these omnivores occasionally eat other lizards, beetles constitute the majority of their diet.

An arboreal lifestyle has led to several adaptations. Tree-dwelling *Sceloporus* species have shorter hind legs than ground-dwelling *Sceloporus*. Climbing species tolerate a narrower range of temperature variation. When an arboreal species needs to cool down, it only has to move slightly to find shade. In addition, they do not have to expend energy, which alters body temperature, running from rock to rock or shrub to shrub.

NORTHERN PLATEAU LIZARD
Sceloporus tristichus
Iguanidae family
$1^5/_8$–$3^1/_4$ in. snout to vent length, 4–7 in. with tail, gray, brown with lengthwise stripes, blue on throat usually divided into two patches

Sceloporus lizards are commonly called swifts or blue bellies due to the blue markings found on the undersides of males. During mating, the males employ an elaborate series of movements including bowing, head bobbing, flattening of the sides, and push-ups, all oriented toward displaying their blue markings. Similar gestures are also used during territorial displays.

These common lizards scamper amongst rocks and shrubs throughout the day, using their long claws for climbing. Like many lizards, plateau lizards have catholic diets that include spiders, beetles, ticks, and other small arthropods. They were formerly known as eastern fence lizards.

SAGEBRUSH LIZARD
Sceloporus graciosus
Iguanidae family
$1^7/_8$–$2^5/_8$ in. snout to vent length, 5–$6^1/_4$ in. with tail, gray, brown with blotches on upper side, rust-colored behind forelimbs, small scales

Sagebrush lizards inhabit areas with scattered shrubs and open ground. In the canyonlands region, they often occur at higher elevations than most other lizards. They do not venture far from the protective refuge of bushes, rock outcrops, or rodent burrows. Although sagebrush lizards are primarily ground dwellers, preferring gravelly soils, they will climb shrubs or boulders in pursuit of prey. They primarily eat insects but may indulge in spiders and scorpions.

The sagebrush lizard closely resembles the plateau lizard in appearance, but it has an entirely blue throat and rust or light orange on its sides.

SIDE-BLOTCHED LIZARD
Uta stansburiana
Iguanidae family
$1^1/_2$–$2^3/_8$ in. snout to vent length, 4–$6^3/_8$ in. with tail, brownish with blue-black blotch behind forelimbs, no distinct blue belly markings

Side-blotched lizards have a typical daily lizard lifestyle of morning and evening basking interrupted by occasional feeding. Like most lizards, they are opportunistic feeders, attacking any suitable prey when encountered. When not basking or feeding, they retreat to cooler spots under plants or rocks. During winter, however, when most lizards are hibernating, side-blotched lizards take advantage of their small body size, which facilitates quick warming, to move around on warm days.

Side-blotched lizard populations have essentially an annual turnover with an individual normal life expectancy of about 5 months, although they can live for 2 years. They quickly reach sexual maturity and can produce several clutches of three to four eggs. Side-blotched lizards have evolved this life history to take advantage of abundant food resources (see eastern collared lizard, page 160, for comparison). In low food production years, though, fewer clutches are laid.

The common name refers to the dark blue or black spot located behind each forelimb, which is a key identification characteristic. The specific name honors Captain Howard Stansbury, who led a US government mapping expedition to the Great Salt Lake in 1849. His vast collection included plants, reptiles, birds, and mammals.

TREE LIZARD
Urosaurus ornatus
Iguanidae family
$1^1/_2$–$2^1/_4$ in. snout to vent length, $4^1/_2$–$6^1/_4$ in. with tail, brown to gray body with light-edged darker crossbands on back

Despite their common name, tree lizards do not live in trees. They prefer to forage on boulders, cliffs, and shrubs in a riparian habitat. Males usually perch higher than females, allowing them to search for mates and potential territorial intruders. Females remain closer to the ground to search efficiently for food needed during egg production. After breeding season, females perch higher because males no longer harass them.

Tree lizards have similar habits to the side-blotched lizard, and at one time herpetologists placed them in the same genus, *Uta*. Although one might expect fierce competition between these lizards (due to their similar size, habits, and habitats), each species exploits separate microhabitats or has a slightly different diet. For example, tree lizards remain closer to the water's edge than side-blotched lizards.

To identify a tree lizard, look for a series of interconnecting Y-shaped crossbands on its back.

MOUNTAIN SHORT-HORNED LIZARD

Phrynosoma hernandesi
Iguanidae family
2¹/₂–4 in. snout to vent length, short, stubby, reddish horns; coloration generally similar to background soil color

Due to the low nutrient value of ants, their primary food source, horned lizards have evolved extremely large stomachs, which make up 13 percent of their body weight. This large gut has led to a short, round body instead of the usual long, skinny lizard body. As a result, horned lizards do not run very fast. They rely on their coloring, which generally matches the surrounding soil, as their first line of defense against predators. If discovered by a predator, a horned lizard can quickly inflate its body with air, so that it resembles a tiny, spiny, armored tank.

One well-known horned lizard trait, squirting blood from its eyes, is not practiced by short-horned lizards. This defensive feat only occurs in Texas-, coast-, and regal-horned lizards, all of which live south and east of canyon country. Those lizards can shoot a thin stream of blood as far as 4 feet.

Short-horned lizards have the widest distribution of any horned lizard, ranging from Canada to Mexico and living at elevations up to 11,000 feet. They have adapted to cold climates by giving birth to live young (five to twenty-three at a time), an unusual trait among horned lizards. Live birth provides several advantages over laying eggs. The warmth of the pregnant female ensures that the young develop safely and much more quickly. In contrast, cold soil exposes eggs to dangerously low temperatures. Live-born young are larger and have more time to locate a safe place for brumation as winter approaches.

The closely related desert horned lizards (*P. platyrhinos calidiarum*) have reportedly been seen in Glen Canyon National Recreation Area and Zion National Park. The desert variety inhabits shrubby semiarid or arid regions, while the short-horned lizard is found in open plant communities of the piñon-juniper and higher elevation forests.

DESERT NIGHT LIZARD
Xantusia vigilis
Xantusiidae family
1 1/2–1 3/4 in. snout to vent length, 4–6 in. with tail, olive, gray speckled with black, vertical pupils with no eyelids

Until recently, night lizards were considered uncommon, but this may not be the case. Now herpetologists believe that night lizards are secretive, spending almost all of their time under vegetation, especially yucca. In 1857 a Hungarian working for the US Army, John Xantus, discovered this species near Bakersfield, California. Spencer Baird, one of the nineteenth century's most important cataloguers of birds and reptiles, named the night lizard after Xantus.

Night lizards possess many unusual characteristics. Instead of laying eggs, females give birth to one or two live young, which after much prodding and nipping emerge upside down and tail first. After birth the female eats the fetal membrane, a trait unknown in other American lizards. The animal's life expectancy is 4 years, and some individuals live for at least 9 years. And unlike most lizards, night lizards are darker during the day and lighter at night, reflecting their nocturnal habits.

WESTERN WHIPTAIL
Aspidoscelis tigris
Teiidae family
2 3/8–4 1/2 in. snout to vent length, 8–12 in. with tail, gray, brown with a network of black markings that form rows lengthwise on back

One commonly sees western whiptails darting and dashing around in search of food during summer days. This active foraging technique is uncommon among western North American lizards; most lizards employ the "sit-and-wait" hunting method. This species' common name comes from its tail, which is up to 2 1/2 times as long as the body. Whiptails flick their tails from side to side as they run, providing attractive objects for predators. It's always better to lose a tail than a life.

Western whiptails constantly use their exceptionally long, forked tongues to probe for airborne chemicals. One study found that they flick out their tongue an average of 456 times each hour. The Jacobson's organ, a chemosensory organ also found in snakes, sends this chemical information directly to the brain for processing. Whiptails may use this information for food seeking, sexual recognition, courtship, or communication, unlike other lizards that rely on color and body gestures for most communication.

PLATEAU STRIPED WHIPTAIL
Aspidoscelis velox
Teiidae family

2¹/₂–3³/₈ in. snout to vent length, 8–12 in. with tail, 6 to 7 dorsal stripes, light blue tail, whitish below

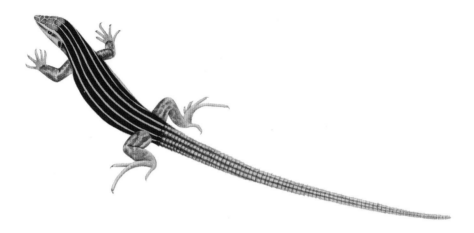

No males occur in this species. Females produce unfertilized, but viable, eggs—all clones of the mother. This process, known as parthenogenesis (Greek for "virgin birth"), offers several advantages. Because all individuals are female, plateau striped whiptails can reproduce at a more rapid rate than species that have both sexes, half of whom cannot lay eggs. Parthenogenetic lizards can colonize new territory more easily, because it only takes one individual to create a new population. Clones, however, are more susceptible to disease and less adaptable to changing environmental conditions.

Plateau striped whiptails evolved through the mating of two different species, which produced mostly sterile males and females; however, a few females must have been capable of reproducing by themselves. Six of the twelve species of whiptail in the Southwest reproduce parthenogenetically.

Snakes

Eleven species of snake occur in southeast Utah, ranging in size from 15 to 72 inches. Most only come out at night, avoiding the heat of a summer day (most snakes cannot tolerate temperatures above 100°F). They live in a variety of habitats, including streamsides, grasslands, rocky slopes, and piñon-juniper woodlands.

All serpents are carnivorous and can swallow objects much larger than themselves. Prey is secured in several different manners. Rattlesnakes and night snakes inject a toxin to subdue prey. Gopher and rat snakes seize their meals and squeeze them to death, while racers hold their quarry down with their coils. Garter snakes simply bite their prey, overpower it, and swallow.

Snakes use several different sensory organs to locate prey. They possess well-developed eyesight, although it is most useful at close range.

Please note: Most snakes will try to avoid you, but if you harass them, snakes can and will bite. Rattlesnakes are the only snake that can inject a potentially fatal venom. Most studies, however, show that only about one-third of all rattler bites inject a dangerous quantity of venom; roughly one-third of all bites inject no venom, while the other one-third only inject a minute amount. If you are bitten, remain calm and go to the nearest medical facility. Do not apply ice. Do not use a tourniquet. Do not make an incision and try to suck out the venom.

One further note: Do not pick up a rattlesnake even if it is dead. A recent study described five people who were bitten by snakes that they had recently killed. One victim had to have a finger amputated. All of the victims were males between the ages of 20 and 35, who are statistically the most commonly bitten people, especially when they have been drinking.

WESTERN RACER
Coluber mormon
Colubridae family
33–54 in., usually less than 36 in., no markings, uniformly colored brownish olive with yellow belly; juveniles have dark blotches similar to gopher snake

These active, fast-moving snakes inhabit open habitats of piñon-juniper or sagebrush. Although principally ground dwelling, they climb trees with ease and celerity. When hunting, racers hold their head and neck above the ground. They kill by using a loop of their own body to hold down prey.

Females lay white, leathery eggs under rocks, rotting logs, or in moist sand in early summer. When the young break out of the eggs, they do not look like adults at all. Instead, bold blotches and spots cover the juvenile racers. This coloration eventually fades after 2 or 3 years.

As cooler weather sets in, racers migrate to communal den sites. Once at the site they may remain outside for a few weeks. They often den with striped whipsnakes, gopher snakes, night snakes, and garter snakes.

STRIPED WHIPSNAKE
Masticophis taeniatus
Colubridae family
36–60 in., black to brown with four narrow stripes that run length of body, top two more distinct than bottom ones

The whipsnake is one of the fastest-moving snakes in canyon country. It inhabits piñon-juniper woodlands and sage flats, hunting during the day for lizards, snakes, and small rodents. The striped whipsnake moves

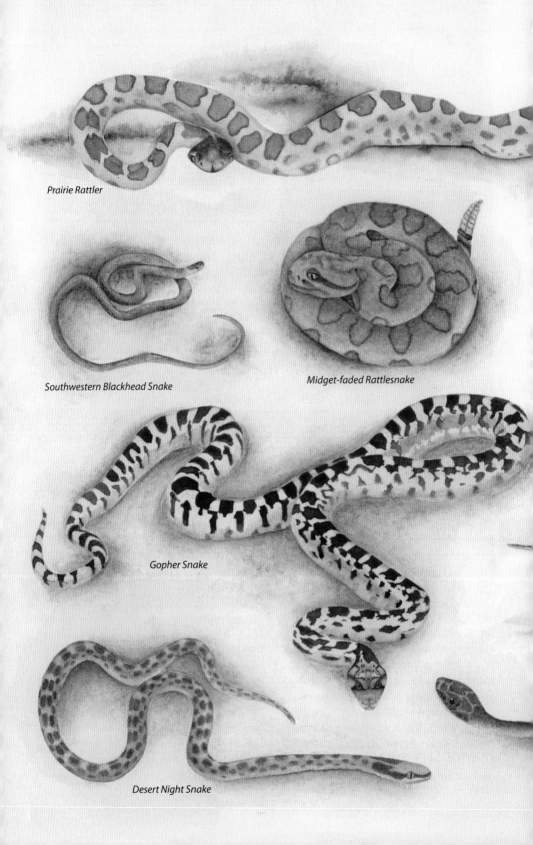

Prairie Rattler

Southwestern Blackhead Snake

Midget-faded Rattlesnake

Gopher Snake

Desert Night Snake

Striped Whipsnake

Great Plains Rat Snake

Western Terrestrial Garter Snake

Blackneck Garter Snake

Western Racer

equally well on the ground or through the foliage of shrubs and trees. If captured, it may inflict a bite that can puncture the skin. The snake is not venemous.

GREAT PLAINS RAT SNAKE
Pantherophis emoryi
Colubridae family
36–72 in., varied color but usually light gray with dark-edged brown blotches on back, pair of neck blotches unite to form a spear point between eyes on top of head

This species primarily occurs in the Great Plains region of the United States, but a distinct subspecies inhabits the Colorado River basin of Utah and Colorado. Like the garter snakes, rat snakes may void their anal scent glands when distressed. They frequent a variety of habitats and are primarily ground dwellers. During the summer months they emerge from burrows at night to search for small mammals, which they kill by constriction. For many years, this rat snake was known as *Elaphe guttata. Emoryi* honors William H. Emory, a topographic engineer who worked on both the Mexican-US and Canadian-US borders.

GOPHER SNAKE
Pituophis catenifer
Colubridae family
30–72 in., ground color, usually light brown to yellowish with darker blotches

In his book *Desert Solitaire,* Edward Abbey befriended a gopher snake to help keep rattlesnakes away from his trailer in Arches National Monument. It worked. In contrast, many people indiscriminately kill gopher snakes because their body coloration resembles that of rattlesnakes and because they vibrate their tail and hiss when threatened. In dry leaves the vibrating tail produces a rattlelike sound.

Gopher snakes kill their prey, which includes squirrels, mice, and birds, by constriction. They incapacitate their prey by one of three methods: a simple holding down or pinioning, a pinion with a non-overlapping loop, or fully encircling coils. Prey handling depends both on size and prey type; larger and/or more active species receive more attention. Obtaining a larger meal must be weighed against the consequences of being more vulnerable to predation.

A diurnal species, gopher snakes are one of the most commonly seen snakes in canyon country. They live in a variety of habitats, ranging from piñon-juniper to open grasslands to rocky slopes. They are also known as bullsnakes, though like many common names, it isn't clear why. One herpetologist told me that he had heard that it could be because the snakes have "bullish," or aggressive, behavior or because they are "strong as a bull."

SOUTHWESTERN BLACKHEAD SNAKE
Tantilla hobartsmithi
Colubridae family
7–15 in., uniformly tan or brown with distinct black cap on head

These small, burrowing snakes live beneath rocks, logs, or fallen yucca in the piñon-juniper ecosystem. Southwestern blackhead snakes are so thoroughly adapted to a subterranean lifestyle that their eyes are almost rudimentary. Their miniature skulls facilitate slithering through the smallest cracks. They eat worms, millipedes, and burrowing insect larvae.

Blackheads are relatively well adapted to cool weather for this genus, which predominantly lives in the tropics. Cold winters, though, will drive them several feet down into the ground.

Hobart Muir Smith wrote more papers on herpetology, at least 1,600, than anyone else.

MIDGET-FADED RATTLESNAKE
Crotalus concolor
Crotalidae family
24–30 in., tan to creamish body, with barely discernible darker blotches

GREAT BASIN RATTLESNAKE
Crotalus lutosus
Crotalidae family
36–60 in., light brown, dark dorsal blotches with margin in black

PRAIRIE RATTLESNAKE
Crotalus viridis
Crotalidae family
36–48 in., greenish coloration, large, rounded, and well-separated brown blotches with a white margin

These three species were long described as three subspecies of the widely distributed western rattlesnake (*Crotalus viridis*, now separated into two species *C. oreganus* [northern Pacific rattlesnake] and *C. viridis* [prairie rattlesnake]): the midget-faded (*C.v. concolor*), Great Basin (*C.v. lutosus*), and prairie (*C.v. viridis*). They are extremely hard to tell apart; it is usually better to rely on location instead of color or patterns. Prairie rattlesnakes are the most widely distributed subspecies, ranging from Canada to Mexico. Midget-fadeds only inhabit the drainages of the Colorado and Green Rivers in eastern Utah and southern Wyoming. In this area, the midget-faded occurs in Arches and Canyonlands National Parks but interbreeds with the prairie at Natural Bridges National Monument. The Great Basin species ranges from western Utah across most of Nevada.

Although midget-fadeds are one of the smallest rattlesnakes, they employ an extremely toxic venom. The neurotoxic venom attacks the body systemically, producing respiratory problems. As with most rattlesnakes, a full venom injection occurs in only about one-third of all bites. These nonaggressive snakes inhabit small burrows and rock crevices, and can form dens of several hundred hibernating individuals during winter.

During the day rattlesnakes stay cool in the shade of a shrub or tree. At night they hunt for food, using their loreal pits, heat-sensitive depressions located slightly behind the nostrils, to locate prey. The loreal pits detect changes in temperatures well enough to allow a snake to locate a mouse up to a foot away in complete darkness. Most rattlesnakes' coloration makes them hard to see, but they will warn you with a high-pitched rattle if you approach too closely.

Studies in Wyoming show that prairie rattlesnakes emerge from dens in early April and migrate up to 12 miles in almost straight lines in search of their main prey, deer mice (*Peromyscus maniculatus*). Local populations migrate shorter distances due to rougher terrain and a more evenly distributed prey base.

After hibernation, prairie rattlesnakes separate into two distinct groups: males and non-pregnant females, which migrate from the den; and pregnant females, which form a communal birthing area. Rattlesnakes give birth to live young in the late summer and remain with their progeny until the newborn snakes shed their first layer of epidermis, a process that takes 2 to 3 weeks. The female then leaves a scent trail for the young to use to find their way back to the hibernation area.

Rattlesnakes kill their prey through venom secreted from two retractable fangs. The fragile fangs are constantly replaced throughout a snake's life. Similar to most reptiles, rattlesnakes employ a "sit-and-wait" method of hunting, but on occasion will go in search of food. If the victim is small enough, the snake will simply kill it and swallow it. If the quarry is too large, a rattlesnake will bite it, injecting venom, let the victim escape, and then locate it after it dies.

DESERT NIGHT SNAKE
Hypsiglena chlorophaea
Dipsadidae family
12–26 in., light-colored with numerous small dark spots and a pair of larger dark blotches on neck, vertical pupils

An aptly named serpent, the night snake spends the daylight hours under rocks or plant debris, only coming out during the nocturnal hours. It subdues its prey with a mildly toxic saliva that is secreted from enlarged teeth in the back of the upper jaw. The bite is not poisonous to humans. Night snakes find their prey—lizards, toads, and insects—throughout their rocky habitat.

BLACKNECK GARTER SNAKE
Thamnophis cyrtopsis
Natricidae family
16–43 in., whitish-yellow middorsal stripe, two black blotches at back of head

Blackneck garter snakes are aquatic habitat specialists, rarely traveling far from water. They employ two different hunting methods, dependent upon water and prey availability. In spring, with abundant water and habitats, blackneck garter snakes forage widely to locate relatively sedentary prey. In summer, when prey is restricted to only a few deep pools, the snakes use a "sit-and-wait" method to obtain active frogs and tadpoles.

During the cooler months of April or May, blackneck garters may be seen basking on streamside rocks. If pursued, they usually enter the water, where they swim on the surface instead of underwater. Captured individuals sometimes discharge excrement and the contents of their anal scent glands, which generally deters most aggressors.

WESTERN TERRESTRIAL GARTER SNAKE
Thamnophis elegans
Natricidae family
18–43 in., dull-colored with well-defined, yellowish middorsal and side stripes

Terrestrial garter snakes range throughout the western United States from sea level to mountains. Some are primarily terrestrial and others principally aquatic. Our local subspecies does not require permanent water, but is seldom found far from a source, which it will enter to escape from a predator by swimming below the water surface. They feed on amphibians, small mammals, fish, and insects.

Unlike most snakes, garter snakes give birth to live young. In midsummer, four to nineteen young work their way out of a translucent sac inside the female. The 5- to 7-inch-long snakes look exactly like the adults. The name garter snake supposedly came about because the striped pattern resembled the pattern found on garters designed to hold men's socks in place.

AMPHIBIANS

A desert amphibian may seem like an oxymoron, but several different species thrive in canyon country. The common image of amphibians is an animal that lives both in water and on land; however, during their adult stage they may only inhabit one environment or the other. A more precise definition of amphibian (Greek for "two lives") is an animal that has two distinct life stages: a larval form and an adult form. Consider the difference between a tadpole and an adult toad. In a desert environment, amphibians exploit ephemeral water sources such as seeps, potholes, and seasonal streams to deposit their eggs, which do require water. During their adult stage they can move away from water but usually remain near these water sources or burrow underground, only crawling to the surface during the rainy season.

Three groups of amphibians inhabit southeastern Utah: salamanders, toads, and frogs. The tiger salamander has smooth, moist skin and clawless toes. True toads typically have horizontal pupils, no teeth, warty skin, short legs for hopping, and parotoid glands (big lumps behind the eyes that can secrete a whitish toxin). Spadefoot toads, which are members of a distinct family, have vertical pupils, teeth in the upper jaw, and indistinct or absent parotoid glands. Frogs have smooth skin and long legs for jumping. Male frogs and toads are generally smaller than females and have a voice; the female voice is either weak or absent. Canyon country batrachians (frogs and toads) are not poisonous to humans (although the parotoid toxin can irritate the eyes and mucous membranes). They won't give you warts.

RED-SPOTTED TOAD
Anaxyrus punctatus
Bufonidae family
1¹/₂–3 in., olive-gray brown with reddish
warts, parotoids small and round

It is a fine little toad of very neat, compact appearance. It frequently gives a pleasant birdlike chirp in captivity.
—Wright and Wright,
Handbook of Frogs and Toads

Red-spotted toads live near permanent and intermittent water sources. Summer storms control their breeding habits. After a rainstorm, males emit a high-pitched trill to attract females. Following a brief mating, the female lays gelatin-covered eggs, which sink to the bottom of pools and hatch in only a few hours. Tadpoles metamorphose into adulthood in 40 to 60 days, racing against the fleeting life of a desert pothole.

Although they are primarily nocturnal (they cannot tolerate temperatures above 95°F), these little toads can sometimes be found during the day hopping around or squatting in water. While squatting, they are absorbing water through their pelvic patch, a translucent piece of skin that stretches from the hind legs partway up the abdomen. Red-spotted toads are able to lose up to 40 percent of their body water and still survive.

Author note: *Many toads formerly in the genus* Bufo, *including Woodhouse's, red-spotted, and Great Plains, were placed in the new genus* Anaxyrus. *Some herpetologists reject this decision and stick with the old name. I used* Anaxyrus *because of its use in the SCCSNNAAR checklist.*

WOODHOUSE'S TOAD
Anaxyrus woodhousii
Bufonidae family
1³/₄–5 in., gray to yellowish brown with distinct white dorsal stripe, prominent cranial crests

The distinct white stripe down the back of a Woodhouse's toad makes it one of the easiest amphibians to identify. They inhabit canyons, streams, and marshes, wherever moisture is sufficient. During the day they may burrow in the soil, waiting to emerge during the cooler hours of the night.

In this region of diverse habitats, Woodhouse's toads have evolved several different breeding techniques. In ponds or creeks, where mating only lasts a few days, larger males are more successful. In areas where mating occurs over a longer period, males with higher call rates reproduce more successfully. In contrast, in a dense accumulation of males, males reduce their call rate and tend to call when their neighbors do not. It appears this behavior would allow a female to evaluate and select a mate.

The common name honors Samuel Woodhouse, a Philadelphia physician and naturalist, who traveled west several times collecting specimens. See red-spotted toad, page 174, for genus name change.

GREAT PLAINS TOAD
Anaxyrus cognatus
Bufonidae family
2–4¹/₂ in., buffy olive with large, symmetrical, dark dorsal blotches

An uncommon and nocturnal toad, the Great Plains toad only moves about during the day in cloudy weather or during the breeding season. It excavates a shallow burrow, where it can remain for several weeks during dry conditions. This medium-size toad only breeds after rains and when air temperature reaches 54°F or greater. Females lay eggs in early April, and metamorphosis occurs in about 45 days.

Thomas Say, a naturalist from Philadelphia, described the Great Plains toad in 1821. He found them along the Arkansas River while employed on Stephen Long's expedition to the Colorado Rockies. See red-spotted toad, page 174, for genus name change.

GREAT BASIN SPADEFOOT TOAD
Spea intermontana
Scaphiopodidae family
1¹/₂–2¹/₂ in., dusky brown with ash gray streaks, glandular boss between the eyes, vertical pupils, no parotoid gland

Hearing the raucous cacophony of male spadefoots is one of the great joys for many desert denizens. This toad requires a combination of heavy rain and warm temperatures to trigger its emergence from its underground burrow. During its short time on the surface, the spadefoot locates water (usually temporary potholes), rehydrates, starts a feeding frenzy (eating up to 55 percent of its body weight in a single night), and participates in a mating orgy. When this concludes, it disappears back into the ground.

The sprint from egg to adulthood of a spadefoot toad is one of the quickest metamorphic cycles of any amphibian. The eggs hatch within a few days, and tadpoles transform to adulthood in less than 14 days. During the tadpole stage, fierce competition occurs for the scarce resources, and cannibalism is common. Some tadpoles even crawl out of the ephemeral pools with their tail still attached.

During adulthood spadefoots spend the vast majority of their time underground; they sometimes remain buried for over a year. They use the spade on the underside of their rear legs to slowly wriggle and dig into the ground. In their burrow they will shed successive layers of skin to form a permeable covering that allows for water absorption. Spadefoots can store up to a third of their weight as diluted urine in their bladder. Furthermore, these toads can absorb water from surrounding soil by concentrating urea, creating an osmotic differential and causing water to move into their body.

The closely related New Mexican spadefoot (*S. multiplicata*) lacks the prominent glandular boss or bump between the eyes.

BULLFROG
Lithobates catesbeianus
Ranidae family
3¹/₂–8 in., greenish or gray brown,
conspicuous eardrum

One of the earliest descriptions of an animal in the United States is that of a bullfrog. Mark Catesby, for whom the species was named, wrote in the 1730s: "The Noise they make has caused their name; for at a few Yards Distance their Bellowing sounds very much like that of a Bull a quarter of a mile off." Bullfrogs, though, are not native west of the Rocky Mountains; they were introduced into Utah sometime after the turn of the century. Some herpetologists believe that this omnivorous species has contributed to a decline in native frog species by eating eggs and other tadpoles.

Bullfrogs seldom venture far onto land; they usually sit on shore or remain submerged with only their eyes protruding above the water surface. When frightened, they emit a loud *eeep* before leaping into the water. Bullfrogs are an extremely fecund animal, laying up to 20,000 eggs, which hatch within 2 weeks. They can remain as tadpoles for up to 2 years, growing to 5 inches or more in length. Adults live for 4 to 5 years or longer. If you happen to catch one, they will usually "play dead" and then leap away when you least expect it.

Author's note: *Many toads formerly in the genus* Rana, *including bullfrog and northern leopard frog, were placed in the new genus* Lithobates. *Some herpetologists reject this decision and stick with the old name. I used* Lithobates *because of its use in the SCCSNNAAR checklist.*

NORTHERN LEOPARD FROG
Lithobates pipiens
Ranidae family
2¹/₄–4 in., green with darker oval spots, rimmed in lighter color

CANYON TREEFROG
Hyla arenicolor
Hylidae family
1¹/₄–2 in., prominent toe pads, skin color matches surroundings with scattered small, darker splotches

Northern leopard frogs range from northeastern Canada to California, the widest distribution of any North American amphibian. In southern Colorado they live above 11,000 feet. Despite this wide distribution, herpetologists believe there has been a population decline, but need to acquire more data. Several environmental changes have been implicated for this decline, including competition with or predation by bullfrogs, habitat alteration, and nonnative fish predation.

These frogs live near bodies of permanent water that have rooted aquatic vegetation. Northern leopard frogs emerge from winter hibernation at the bottom of ponds in March and remain active until October. Males emit a 2- to 3-second-long snorelike call to attract females. The female attaches the 2- to 5-inch-wide egg mass to vegetation several inches below the water surface. Eggs hatch in less than 2 weeks, and tadpoles become adults several weeks later. See bullfrog, page 177, for genus name change.

Canyon treefrogs depend upon camouflage to protect themselves from predators. They blend in so well that you can overlook them even when staring directly at them. They rarely venture far from water during the day and usually sit motionless in cracks, under boulders, or behind vegetation. They are active at night, sometimes traveling up to 200 feet from water. Breeding occurs from March to July and eggs are laid singly in quiet water. The tadpoles, which can grow to 2 inches, metamorphose in 6 to 10 weeks.

Similar to most desert toads and frogs, canyon treefrogs can tolerate high temperatures and severe desiccation. A warmer body offers several benefits, including increased rates of food digestion, protection against bacterial infection, and control of external parasites. Dehydration also helps control parasites. Bloodsucking mites, which live on treefrogs, will leave the surface of a desiccated frog.

Salamanders

TIGER SALAMANDER
Ambystoma tigerinum
Ambystomatidae family
3–6 in. snout to vent length, up to 12 in.
with tail; black with spots, bars, or blotches
of yellow or white

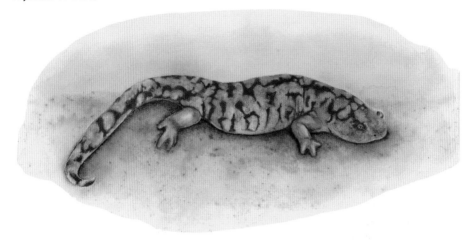

Few people see the largest desert amphibian, the tiger salamander. Similar to their batrachian relatives, tiger salamanders require water for breeding; thus, they spend the majority of their lives in burrows, only emerging when water is abundant. Once on the surface, they migrate (often dozens move together) at night to temporary pools or streams for feeding and mating.

Tiger salamanders have evolved two lifestyles to survive in a desert environment. In ephemeral pools, the larvae, which have large heads, four legs, and frilled external gills, feed on invertebrates, tadpoles, and other salamander larvae. Salamanders may metamorphose into adults in their first year of life or wait until their second or third year. This allows the larvae to grow larger, exploiting resources and reducing the energy required for growth as an adult.

However, some populations of tiger salamander do not depend upon rainfall but live in stock ponds. In this environment, the larvae may never change into the adult form. Instead, they become sexually mature as larvae and continue to take advantage of the plentiful resources of their artificial water refuge. No other amphibian in canyon country has evolved this same lifestyle.

INSECTS AND ARACHNIDS

Insects and arachnids are both arthropods or "jointed-leg" animals. Other arthropods include crabs, shrimps, millipedes, centipedes, and the extinct trilobites. Arthropods make up about 85 percent of all animal life in terms of number of different species. The class Insecta makes up 90 percent of all arthropods. This includes earwigs, bedbugs, spittlebugs, and boll weevils, along with beetles and butterflies, to name just a few of the more than 100,000 insect species in the United States.

The smaller group, class Arachnida, which includes spiders, ticks, mites, harvestmen, and scorpions, is characterized by animals with eight legs and two body regions, the abdomen and the cephalothorax, and no antennae. They grow by molting their exoskeleton. They were one of the first groups of animals to colonize land roughly 400 million years ago. Most species are terrestrial.

Insects have six legs, three distinct body regions (a moveable head, a rigid thorax, and a flexible abdomen), a pair of antennae, and, in most species, two pairs of wings. All insects go through a metamorphosis from egg to adult. The grasshoppers, true bugs, and lice, to name a few, have a nymph stage between egg and adult. The nymph looks similar to an adult but is sexually immature and usually lacks wings. They grow by molting their exoskeleton. With each molt the wing pads increase in size. Dragonfly, mayfly, and stonefly nymphs, however, differ from adults more than most other insects that mature through this process, which is known as "simple" metamorphosis.

About 80 percent of all insect species develop through complex or complete metamorphosis. Their four-stage life consists of egg; larva or grub, when they are active and feeding and look nothing like the adult; pupa, when they are encased in a mummy-like cocoon or chrysalis; and adult, when the wings unfold. Caterpillars are the larval stage of butterflies and moths, while maggots eventually become flies, and grubs metamorphose into beetles.

Canyon country insects and arachnids range in size from microscopic mites to 5-inch-long scorpions. They live from several days to 15 to 20 years. They live underwater; underground; and in plants, burrows, and nests. While a few damage crops and bother animals, including humans, most are beneficial. Bees and other flower-visiting insects are essential for pollination of many plants. In addition, little decomposition would occur without insects.

Despite some people's perception that a vast bug conspiracy exists, no insect or arachnid is waiting for a tasty human to come along. They evolved long before humans. The best defense is rather simple; leave them alone and they will leave you alone. You can help yourself by not putting your fingers in cracks or prodding webs or nests, by checking your shoes before putting them on if you left them outside at night, and by remaining calm if you encounter one.

A note on venom and poison: These terms have different meanings. Venom must be injected via fangs, spurs, spines, or harpoons. Poison, in contrast, is absorbed or ingested; you must touch or eat the animal or plant to feel the effects of the toxin.

If you are stung or bitten, however, do not panic. Try to positively identify your assailant. If it was a wasp, bee, black widow or brown recluse spider, or scorpion, or if you develop allergic reactions, go to a hospital. Otherwise most bites are more painful than life threatening. If you are unsure or uncomfortable, seek professional help.

This section describes a few of the colorful, common, or controversial insects and arachnids found in the Southwest.

Butterflies and a Moth

Beloved yet often overlooked, butterflies are one of the few types of insects that people universally seem to like. They are beautiful, do not bite or sting, and are graceful in flight. They are also diverse and abundant with around 200 species in Utah and more than 330 in Arizona. Butterflies can be found throughout canyon country from riparian zones to open desert to mountaintops. They are one small part of the order of insects known as Lepidoptera, or "scaly wing." These scales, or modified hairs, are what give lepidopterans color, either through pigments or by reflecting color.

Moths make up the much larger part of the order, outnumbering butterflies at least fifteen to one. They are easy to tell apart. Butterflies have clubbed antennae, fly strictly during the day, and are brightly colored. Moths usually fly at night, lack clubbed antennae, and are typically drab in color. They also tend not to hold their wings vertically over their bodies.

Both pass through a complete metamorphosis from egg to larvae to pupae to adult. Eggs are typically less than a millimeter wide but if looked at under a magnifying lens reveal a complicated architecture. They are generally laid singly on a host plant, which the larvae, or caterpillar, can consume. Larvae have two goals: eat and don't get eaten. During the several weeks of life as a caterpillar, they can grow a hundredfold in size, passing through several molts, known as instars. To protect themselves, many larvae have hairs that can be painful to birds, and even to humans.

After reaching its full size, the caterpillar will use silk to secure itself in a secluded spot where it forms the pupa. As a pupa, it is essentially dormant and has little to no interaction with its surroundings. Unfortunately, there is no easy way to distinguish butterfly and moth caterpillars and pupae from each other.

This cycle of life takes weeks to years to accomplish. Butterflies can enter into a state called diapause, where they basically turn off all life functions. They can diapause as eggs, larvae, pupae, or adults. This phase is weather dependent. Most butterflies, though, live less than a year and spend only a few weeks as an adult.

TWO-TAILED SWALLOWTAIL
Papilio multicaudatus
Papilionidae family
Wingspan 3.5–4.5 in.

BECKER'S WHITE
Pontia beckeri
Pieridae family
Wingspan less than 2 in.

One of a number of large yellow butterflies, the two-tail is the biggest in the region and characterized by the twin tails on each hind wing. Other swallowtails include the anise (*P. zelicaon*) and western tiger (*P. rutulus*), both predominately yellow, and the indra (*P. indra*) and black (*P. polyxenes*), both black. Two-tails are canyon denizens, where their strong and active flight grabs one's attention. When you do see one, it is probably a male out in search of a female. Also look for them nectaring at damp spots.

Larvae are Granny-Smith-apple green with yellow eye spots rimmed in black. This fake face may help deter predators. Caterpillars can further discourage attackers by everting an orange prong, or horn, from behind their head, which emits a citrus smell.

Lepidopterists understand naming animals. Those with the name white have white wings, those with sulphur in their name are yellow, and those with blue have blue wings. There are even a couple called commas because of the white punctuation mark on their wings. Of course distinguishing these bugs down to species level can be taxing, but at least you often have a head start.

The moss green venation coloring on the ventral wings of these medium-size flyers is not technically green but consists of black and yellow scales. One study found that Becker's whites fluoresce under UV light, which may aid in species recognition. They produce multiple broods during their summer flight season. Mustards are the preferred host plants.

Ludwig Becker was a German naturalist who died on an expedition in Australia.

CABBAGE WHITE
Pieris rapae
Pieridae family
Wingspan less than 2 in.

CHECKERED WHITE
Pontia protodice
Pieridae family
Wingspan less than 2 in.

One of most common butterflies of the urban environment, cabbage whites are native to Europe. Called "ravenous and destructive," they were first collected in Quebec in 1860 and quickly spread across the entire continent. The main concern was that they outcompeted native species of *Pieris* and that they ate crops such as cabbages. They also eat kale, broccoli, and Brussels sprouts.

Cabbage whites fly year-round and can produce multiple broods across several seasons. Their wing tips look to be dipped in ink, which then left dots on the dorsal fore wing, two on females and one on males. The ventral surfaces are light yellow.

A resident species of warmer climates and one able to fly during the hotter parts of the day, checkered whites inhabit open areas, often in disturbed habitat. They, and other white butterflies, have evolved a novel thermoregulatory posture called reflectance basking, in which the wings act as solar reflectors bouncing heat to the butterfly's body. This helps provide enough warmth to allow flight.

Like other whites, their larval food plants are predominately mustards, including domestic and native, such as tansy mustard and pepperweed. The scientific name *protodice* comes from the Latin for "first season" in reference to their early season appearance. The closely related and very similar-looking western whites (*P. occidentalis*) may also be seen in canyon country.

ORANGE SULPHUR
Colias eurytheme
Pieridae family
Wingspan less than 2 in.

PAINTED LADY
Vanessa cardui
Nymphalidae family
Wingspan less than 3 in.

Lepidopterist and writer Bob Pyle says that another member of this genus, the pale clouded sulfur, "is the best candidate for the Original Butterfly: a ubiquitous, butter-colored European insect much like this one that suggested the name *butterfloege* in Old English." The sulphurs are indeed butter hued and extremely hard to tell apart without a careful inspection, though the orange sulphur is distinctly more orange than other species.

Also known as alfalfa sulphur, they can form dense swarms on alfalfa, clover, and locoweeds. Like other sulphurs, they fold their wings over their backs when they land so seeing one with wings spread is a rare sight. They have been known to hybridize with clouded sulphurs (*C. philodice*), though the orange's ability to fluoresce in UV light generally helps females distinguish their true mates.

A truly cosmopolitan species, found on all the continents except Antarctica, painted ladies have a wider distribution than any other butterfly. They are one of three species of lady butterflies that have colorful and similar markings and that occur in the region. The others are the American lady (*V. virginiensis*) and the West coast lady (*V. annabella*). The name "lady" comes from an early name for the species, *belladonna,* or "pretty lady."

Painted ladies are in irruptive species, meaning they can appear by the millions in certain years. All of these are migrants coming out of the south as they do not overwinter in colder climates. When they arrive, they can cover rabbitbrush and thistle in great patches of salmon and blotchy brown and white beauty. Look for them hilltopping or around taller trees, catching the late evening sun. They occur in all habitats throughout canyon country.

MOURNING CLOAK
Nymphalis antiopa
Nymphalidae family
Wingspan more than 3 in.

WEIDEMEYER'S ADMIRAL
Limenitis weidemeyerii
Nymphalidae family
Wingspan less than 3¹/₂ in.

Big and beautiful, mourning cloaks are one of the easiest butterflies to recognize. No other species looks like it and it is the only native species that may be seen year-round. They are velvety black with a yellow border, which fades to white over time. Unlike most butterflies, mourning cloaks can overwinter as adults.

Look for them nectaring on the sap of poplars or on fruit trees in orchards. They also have a very conspicuous caterpillar, black with a row of orange spots on their back, as well as black spines. Large groupings of larvae on willows or cottonwoods are common.

Often found in the mountains of canyon country, Weidemeyer's admirals also occur along streams and in open woodlands. At rest, their black wings with one continuous line of white form a stark contrast to most any place they stop. The common name may refer to this singular band, which suggests a military stripe of rank, or it may allude to the male's propensity to have a favorite perch from which he defends his territory. Some compare this to an admiral defending a harbor.

Larvae overwinter in a hibernaculum, which they form by wrapping themselves in a leaf and silk. They emerge in spring to become adults. Look for them on aspen or willows. They may also be found sipping mud, or other less tasteful items, such as dung. They are probably in search of sodium.

John William Weidemeyer made the first official collection of this species in the middle 1800s.

VARIEGATED FRITILLARY
Euptoieta claudia
Nymphalidae family
Wingspan less than 2$^{1}/_{2}$ in.

SATYR COMMA
Polygonia satyrus
Nymphalidae family
Wingspan less than 2$^{1}/_{4}$ in.

One of many fritillary butterflies, most of which present challenges to distinguish, the variegated has a wide habitat tolerance from urban to desert to mountain. They have the characteristic pattern of yellowish to orange wings above peppered with black bars and dots. This is the only species in the genus in the area; most others are classified as *Speyeria,* the greater fritillaries, and characterized by being larger and having silvery metallic spots below. Variegateds do not overwinter in areas of hard frost so often are migrants into this region and certainly farther north. Look for them and other frits wherever violets grow.

The *Nymphalidae,* or brush-foot family, gets its name from the front two legs, which are about half the size of the back four. In addition, hairs cover the legs so that they look like wee brushes. Bob Pyle writes that "lepidopterists know the brush-foots as 'smart' butterflies—perceptive, highly responsive, agile, and adaptable."

This is a butterfly of great contrast with golden orange and black splotched upper wings and muted undersides that look like bark. The common name alludes to a small, white crescent on the underside. Satyr refers to their preference for forested environments, though they are more often found along riparian areas. Another common name, anglewing, describes the wings, which look almost as if someone has taken bites out of them. Satyr commas are the most common desert member of this genus. Look for them in areas of nettles, but when they land, they may disappear into the background.

JUBA SKIPPER
Hesperia juba
Hesperidae family
Wingspan less than 1¹/₄ in.

YUCCA MOTH
Tegeticula altiplanella
Prodoxidae family
Wingspan about an inch

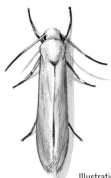

Illustration © Todd Telander

The common name for this very large group of butterflies comes from their skipping flight pattern, as if they are bouncing along through the air. Skippers are generally dull colored, with short, often hooked or curved antennae, and somewhat triangular wings. Most are small, and most cannot hold their wings completely spread out. When they land, the forewings stick up at 45 degrees to their body.

The tiny caterpillars are often found on bunchgrasses such as ricegrass and needle-and-thread, where they make nests of rolled plant and silk. Adults feed on nectar on rabbitbrush and are strongly territorial, at least the males are.

The juba skipper name appears to be a corruption of the name of the area where they were first collected, near California's Yuba River.

Yucca moths are nifty examples of the beauty of evolution. The females have specially adapted tentacles that allow them to collect the sticky pollen grains of yuccas, which they then fashion into a compact ball and store under their head. The female then flies to another yucca plant and deposits a single egg into the flower's ovary. Before flying away, she uses her tentacles again, removes a small quantity of pollen, and deposits it on the plant's stigma. A week or so later, the moth's eggs hatch and the larvae begin to feed on the seeds maturing in the ovary but not on all them, thus allowing the plant to benefit, too. Larvae overwinter in silken, subterranean cocoons. No other species pollinate yuccas.

Long thought to be a single species, the yucca moth, *Tegeticula yuccasella,* was recently reclassified into more than a dozen distinct species. Curiously, two don't pollinate; they are cheater species that simply deposit eggs.

All varieties are white with dark bodies. They rest in the flowers during the day and become active shortly after sunset. Attracted to UV light, they remain mobile for 2 to 4 hours after dark.

Dragonflies and Damselflies

Masters of flight, dragonflies can fly forward and backward, at speeds up to 60 mph. They hover. They nab prey in flight and mate in flight, even escaping from predators while so engaged. Dragonflies are some of the most conspicuous insects in canyon country, active during the day, rarely very far from water.

Dragonflies and damselflies are members of the order Odonata, or "toothed jaw." They first evolved their four flight wings around 300 million years ago and have remained little changed in the past 200 million years. (The largest dragonflies lived 280 million years ago and had a 29-inch wingspan.) Of the two groups, damselflies have thinner abdomens, a hammer head with eyes wide apart, and hold their wings parallel to their abdomen. Both have colorful bodies and often colorful eyes.

With their excellent flight skills, odonates are also first-rate predators, either sallying forth from a perch to nab a meal or chasing down prey, a practice known as hawking. Hawking dragonflies can often form large groups, flying precise paths. They catch insects and other dragonflies with their legs, which form a scoop.

Larvae are also fierce predators, consuming insects, small fish, and tadpoles. They remain as larvae for a few weeks to a few years. An adult's life span is generally 5 weeks though some live for 10 weeks.

Perhaps their most infamous skill is mating. There is little polite about it with males swooping in and pouncing on females, sometimes going so far as to knock them to the ground. Males may also inadvertently attempt to mate with females of a different species. Once he has successfully found the right partner, he uses specially modified parts on the end of his abdomen to grasp the female behind the neck. Once linked he transfers sperm to secondary genitalia under the forward end of his abdomen. She then extends her abdomen under his to receive the sperm.

Known as a wheel, this sexual position is unique in the insect world. While in tandem, they often remain in flight, during which the male typically spends most of his time removing another male's sperm before depositing his package.

VARIEGATED MEADOWHAWK
Sympetrum corruptum
Libellulidae family
Length 4–4$^1/_2$ in., wingspan 2$^1/_2$–3 in.

Illustration © Todd Telander

As the name implies, this species has a wide range of coloring, from gray to light pink to gold. The key identifying feature is a row of white-rimmed black dots running down the side of the abdomen. Also, look for two diagonal stripes that end in a yellow dot on the thorax. They have a tan to ivory face with light brown eyes.

Variegated meadowhawks both sally and hawk after insects. They tend to sally out from ground-level perches, often from grass stems, and hawk over ponds. Look for them along slow-moving streams and near ponds. Like several other species in the genus, *S. corruptum* migrate and can sometimes be found in large numbers during this movement. No one knows the origin of the specific epithet *corruptum*.

TWELVE-SPOTTED SKIMMER
Libellula pulchella
Libellulidae family
Length 2 in., wingspan 3$^1/_2$ in.

These are easily distinguished by the three black spots found at the leading edge of each wing. Other skimmers have four total spots (*L. quadrimaculta*) and eight spots (*L. forensis*). Twelve spots have a brown body, whitish spots between the black spots, and a yellow-brown face.

Inhabiting open ponds and streams with good sunlight, this is an aggressive species, with males actively defending their territories from other dragonflies and other intruders. They tend to perch higher up in vegetation. Unlike some species, the females will oviposit after breaking out of the wheel mating position. The generic name comes from the Latin for "little book," in reference to how the open wings are spread. *Pulchella* means "pretty little one."

BLUE-EYED DARNER
Rhionaeschna multicolor
Aescnidae family
Length 2¹/₂–3 in., wingspan 3¹/₂–4 in.

Illustration © Todd Telander

COMMON GREEN DARNER
Anax junius
Aescnidae family
Length 2¹/₂–3 in., wingspan 3¹/₂–4 in.

Illustration © Todd Telander

Common and colorful, these are some of the most conspicuous dragonflies of canyon country. They have a classic dragonfly flight pattern of hovering and rapid changing of direction, usually just a few feet above water, though females may forage away from water.

With their pale blue face and bright blue eyes, the males are one of the most beautiful bugs. Females tend to be more drab and can have a multicolored pattern.

The common name darner alludes to a notion that dragonflies could sew your eyes shut, which also led to the folk name "devil's needle." Another false belief is that dragonflies have a venemous sting. They cannot sting, and neither larvae nor adults can inflict much of a bite.

A slightly misleading common name as these insects are green only on the thorax; the face is yellow-green and the abdomen sky blue. The closely related *A. walsinghami* is the largest North American dragonfly. The scientific name *Anax* refers to the great size of these species. It means "lord" or "master."

Green darners are a migratory species, moving out of the south and arriving in spring, often before other species arrive. In Russia, this arrival is reflected in their common name "scout." There are also resident populations where the larvae overwinter. Look for green darners over ponds and in evening swarms.

Males are notorious for their belligerent behavior against other males mating with females. High-speed film footage shows males "ramming, pulling, and biting the escorting male, who tries to defend himself by beating his wings, clinging to plants, vibrating his body in sudden spasms, and biting his attacker in return."

AMERICAN RUBYSPOT
Hetaerina americana
Calopterygidae family
Length 1¹/₂ in., wingspan 2¹/₂ in.

Part of a genus found primarily in the neotropics, American rubyspots are a typical damselfly with their narrow body and habit of holding their wings directly over their bodies, as opposed to spreading them out like dragonflies. (One group of damselflies, the spreadwings, however, contradicts this general rule. The great spreadwing [*Archilestes grandis*] occurs in canyon country. They can be distinguished from dragonflies by the slender abdomen and yellow line on the thorax.) Other common damselflies are bluets, with their brilliant blue and black bodies.

American rubyspots look a bit like Christmas time with an iridescent green body and red head and thorax, complemented by the red wing spots. Females have an unusual capacity to oviposit while completely submerged. One study found they can remain underwater for up to an hour, with a male patrolling above her and chasing away potential mates.

CONE-NOSED KISSING BUG
Triatoma sp.
Reduviidae family
1/2–1 in., black with elongated
cone-shaped head

Commonly known as assassin bugs, Walpai tigers, and kissing bugs, these 1-inch-long bugs are bloodsuckers. They usually live in wood-rat nests, where they have a ready source of blood, but the adults are attracted to light and often end up inside people's homes. They spend the day out of sight in cracks and crevices and then emerge at night to seek a blood meal. The kissing bug's common name comes from its propensity to suck blood from a person's exposed face or neck.

The bite generally forms a large welt (up to 3 inches wide) and can cause swelling or a systemic reaction. A severe reaction leads to anaphylaxis. In South and Central America, *Triatoma* carry Chagas disease, which affects the nervous system and heart and can be deadly if left untreated. (Many people have speculated that Charles Darwin contacted Chagas disease when he was in Chile. He was bitten by a *Triatoma* bug, but without exhuming his body there is no way to know if he had the disease.) The disease is spread when the victim rubs the insect's fecal material, which carries the parasite, into the wound, eye, nose, or mouth. If you are bitten, wash well around the bite and do not smash the insect on your body.

VELVET ANT
Dasymutilla sp.
Mutillidae family
$1/2$–1 in. long, females wingless, densely covered with orange, red, yellow, or black hairs

Most of us have been warned not to judge a book by its cover. You should not judge insects that way either. Velvet ants look like hairy, extravagantly colored ants, which might be fun to pick up. Do not be fooled. They are actually wasps that have a particularly painful sting; one common name is "cow-killer." The orange, yellow, or red wingless females, which are encountered more often than the winged males, are often seen scurrying across the ground.

Velvet ants are active during the day and may be some of the first to hit the trail and last to settle in for the night. They retreat midday by burrowing under debris or climbing into plants. Nectar is the preferred food. If you see a walking velvet ant, you can be assured that it is a female, which is probably searching for other ground-nesting wasps or bees on which to deposit their eggs. When they hatch, the larvae will consume their hosts before pupating into adults.

Over 150 species of velvet ants occur throughout North America, although this is a rough number. Three commonly seen species in this region should be *Dasymutilla bioculata* (also reddish), *D. vestita* (red to orange), and *Pseudomethoca propinqua* (golden). The latter two parasitize bees and are more common on harder packed soil, versus *D. bioculta,* which prefers sand wasps and open sandy areas. There are probably around ten more diurnal species and about thirty nocturnal species.

HORSEFLY
Tabanus sp.
Tabanidae family
Up to 1 in. long, bodies black, eyes often with green stripes, wings clear, antennae short

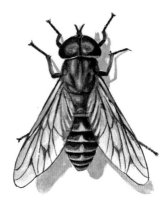

Illustration © Todd Telander

The bigger and faster cousin of deerflies, horseflies inflict a painful bite. Larvae, which can be up to 2 inches long, can bite as well. They are also cannibalistic, which may aid humans by reducing the density of individuals.

To aid in their phlebotomous ways, horseflies secrete an anticoagulant into the wound. This prevents clotting and enables them to slurp up to 200 mg of blood in 1 to 3 minutes. They require approximately ten visits to complete one blood meal. Researchers have begun to study the anticoagulant for potential human uses.

DEERFLY

Chrysops sp. (over 75 species in North America)

Tabanidae family

1/2 inch long, a common species, *C. discalis,* has pale yellow and black markings with darkish patches

Illustration © Todd Telander

A notorious biter, and a relatively slow flier, deerflies are an ironically easy pest to swat. Of course, your satisfying kill occurs because the fly, always a female, has taken a nice nip out of you. She does so not by puncturing your skin as a mosquito does but by using her scissorlike mouthparts to cut into you, which facilitates her sucking up the flowing blood. Males cannot bite; they feed on nectar.

Deerflies are about the size of a housefly. After overwintering in wet soil near ponds and streams as larvae, adults emerge in spring and fly through the summer. They are visual bugs, attracted to dark, moving objects, and to carbon dioxide. Warm, low-wind, sunny days are when they are most active, primarily attacking the head, neck, and shoulders. If the situation is dire, some people have turned to various patches and traps, many of which are bright blue and coated in sticky material that prevents flies from escaping.

Deerflies are a principal vector of *Francisella tularensis,* the bacteria that causes tularemia. The disease, which had an outbreak in Utah in 2007, produces chills, fever, muscle pain, and joint stiffness. Because deerflies can feed on multiple hosts, they can trigger acute outbreaks of tularemia. Tularemia seldom kills but is not pleasant.

BITING MIDGE

Culicoides sp. and Leptoconops sp.

Ceratopogndae family

Less than 1/4 inch long

Illustration © Todd Telander

Gnats, no-see-ums, punkies, #*@$ bugs. We know these voracious little biters by many names. Entomologists prefer biting midges, particularly for the main genus, *Culicoides,* found in southern Utah. More than a dozen genera with over 100 species live throughout the region. All of them require water in some form during the larval stage. Water may be on vegetation, in pools, in wet soil, or springs, to name a few locales.

Most *Culicoides* are crepuscular or nocturnal feeders but will come out on overcast and/or calm days. *Leptoconops,* in contrast, come out and bite during the day. Only a handful of experts can tell the different species apart.

While many of us may hate biting midges, we should rejoice that our most common local varieties do not transmit disease. Plus, the most important pollinators of cacao are biting midges. As with all biting midges, only the males are the pollinators; females are the bloodsuckers. And if that doesn't excite you, one species has the fastest recorded wing beat of any insect, at 1,046 beats per second, and another has been found in 120-million-year-old Lebanese amber. In addition to biting humans, midges attack all varieties of animals from caterpillars to birds.

MOSQUITO

Fifty species in the state, including many in the genera Culex, Ochlerotatus, Aedes, and Anopheles

Culicidae family

Larvae, up to $1/2$ inch long; adults $1/8$ to $1/3$ in. long, brown to dark brown

Illustration © Todd Telander

Mosquitoes exemplify one of the pleasures of teasing out the meaning of scientific names. Consider two of the genera found in canyon country. *Anopheles* is the Greek word for "troublesome" and *Aëdes* is their word for "disagreeable," two of the best descriptors of mosquitoes. Add to these specific names such as *excrucians* (tormenting), *provocans* (provoking), and *vexans* (annoying) and you can understand that those who study and name mosquitoes recognize the bugs' aggravating lifestyle. The name of *Culex pipiens*, or the common house mosquito, comes from the Roman term for piping, in reference to their whining flight.

Mosquitoes have two basic life plans. Some have short lives dependent upon temporary water from rain or flooding. They are typically diurnal and deposit eggs in soil that might not be wet for some time. Some produce a single brood and some as many as ten generations of biters. One species, *Aedes vexans,* is notorious for their huge, post-flooding numbers. Fortunately, they do not survive long in hot, dry weather.

Other mosquitoes rely on permanent or semi-permanent water sources. These species often hibernate in buildings or under bridges. They become active after sunset and can remain active till dawn. *Culex* species of mosquito that have this habit are known vectors of West Nile virus and Western and St. Louis encephalitis. They are aggressive biters, though *C. pipiens* typically favor birds over humans.

The eggs hatch in the water, becoming wiggling larvae. They breathe through a siphon-like tube near their rear ends. After a week or so of feeding, they develop into a nonfeeding pupal stage, characterized by a tumbling movement through the water.

Once out of the water and flying as adults, mosquitoes begin to torment animals. The goal, at least for females, is to acquire sustenance for their eggs. They do this by injecting their proboscis into our skins and sucking our blood. To aid in finding blood, they pump saliva into our bodies. Males do not bite but do have another singular goal; they hang out near us and our warm, carbon dioxide-spewing bodies with the hope of finding a mate. They do so by using their "bottlebrush" antennae to hone in on the pitch of her wingbeats. Post-mating, she goes in search of us for our protein-rich blood, and he usually dies.

When not mating or trying to mate, both females and males visit flowers to steal pollen. They are known to pollinate only a few plants including the orchid *Platanthera obtusata*, which grows in northern Utah.

On a positive note, mosquito larvae and adults feed many animals including bats, birds, dragonflies, tadpoles, and fish. And finally, some claim that the town name Moab is a corruption of a Paiute word—*moapa*—for mosquito, in reference to the mosquito-rich areas along the Colorado River.

Non-biting Insects

DARKLING BEETLE
Eleodes sp.
Tenebrionidae family
1 in., black

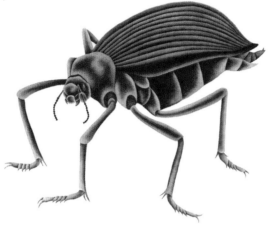

Beetles in the genus *Eleodes* are known as darkling or pinacate beetles, and colloquially as stinkbugs or clown beetles. Pinacate comes from the Aztec *pinacatl,* for "black beetle." Darkling is a common name applied to several genera and over 1,400 species within the family Tenebrionidae. *Eleodes,* derived from the Greek term for "olivelike" describes the general body shape and jet-black coloration.

More than 120 species are in the genus in the western United States occurring across ecosystems from open dunes to shrubs to mountains. Many are about 1 inch long, and all eat dead plant material and fungi. None are venomous, although a few varieties can spray a noxious liquid from the end of their abdomen. This leads to their typical defensive pose of head down and rear end pointing up. Most would-be predators leave the darkling beetle alone when threatened with this fearsome stance, but grasshopper mice simply grab the beetle, jam its behind into the sand, and eat the front end. You occasionally find these half-eaten beetles in sandy areas.

Pinacate beetles are one of the great walkers of the beetle world and can be encountered throughout the year. From spring to autumn they are crepuscular and nocturnal, but come fall they revert to a more diurnal lifestyle. Studies have shown that they are probably in search of food, which they can find by odor.

ANTLION
Myrmeleon sp.
Myrmeleontidae family
Larva, $1/2$ in. long, wide abdomen with long, curved jaws; adult, $1^1/2$ in., slender wings

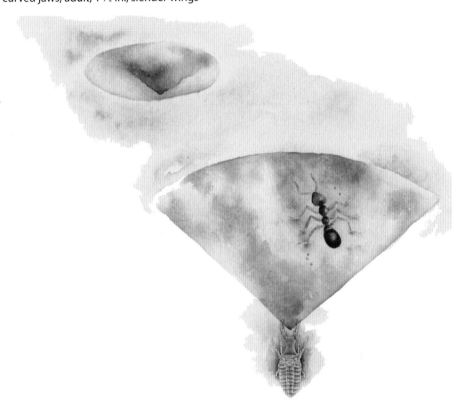

Antlions are rarely seen, but their homes are extremely common. The larvae construct conical pits to trap ants. When an ant crawls or stumbles into the pit, it creates an avalanche of sand, sending the victim to its death, for the antlion larva lurks underground at the nadir of the pit. When the ant hits bottom, the larva uses its elongate jaws to grab the ant and pull it underground. Antlions kill their prey by injecting a paralyzing venom and then sucking out the contents of its body. The carcass is then flicked out of the pit.

Antlions are also known as doodlebugs, because of the path they make when moving to a new burrow. Burrows are made by backing around in ever-tighter circles, pushing out dirt with their jaws.

Except for their clublike antennae, adult antlions resemble drab damselflies. They eat little or nothing at all, are poor fliers, and are active only at night. The goal of their 1-month adult life is reproduction.

CADDISFLY

More than 10,000 described species worldwide

Hydrotilidae family

$3/16$–$1^1/_2$ in. long larval cases covered in debris; adults $1/_{10}$–$1/_5$ in. long of common species

Illustration © Todd Telander

Entomologist Glenn Wiggins has written "caddisflies are remarkable animals close at hand, to be seen and appreciated by any who are interested in the ways the world works." Few bug larvae build such elaborate homes. Made of plant debris and bits of rock held together by silk secreted from its mouth, the tubular enclosures not only protect the larvae but also have a hydrologic function, altering the flow of water to the benefit of the inhabitant. The enclosures, or cases, may be permanent or toted around by the caterpillar-like larvae. The portable case makers use bits of debris and will add material at one end and trim the other. Permanent cases are usually attached to rocks and can be a variety of shapes from tubes to funnels to cocoonlike. Some are also constructed as a net in cracks or between rocks and catch floating plant and animal debris. Larvae and adults are an important food source for fish, particularly for trout. Adults look a bit like moths and are mostly nocturnal.

One study in the Grand Canyon found that the most abundant caddisflies were in the family Hydroptilidae, or microcaddisflies. The adults are no more than $1/_{10}$ to $1/_5$ inch long. The larvae make what are known as purse cases, which resemble domes. Genera include *Ochrotrichia*, *Hydroptila*, and *Oxyethira*.

There is some confusion over the origin of the common name. Shakespeare referred to caddisses, or a worsted tape or binding, in *The Winter's Tale*. Historically, cloth vendors were described as caddice men. The *Oxford English Dictionary* adds that caddis refers to wool or worsted yarn, but exactly how the term came to be applied to the insects is unclear.

JERUSALEM CRICKET

Stenopelmatus sp.

Stenopelmatidae family

1–2 in. long, straw colored with black stripes on abdomen, spiny legs, large jaws, large bald head

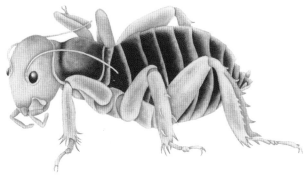

Jerusalem crickets always incite an exclamation in those who see one lumbering across the desert floor. Who would not exclaim when they saw a 2-inch-long "bug" with a head that looks eerily humanlike? Despite its appearance and its large jaws, the Jerusalem cricket is not venomous though it can inflict a painful bite. Nor is it a member of the cricket family but is closely related.

According to entomologist David Weissman, Jerusalem crickets play a central role in desert food webs by serving as meals for bats, skunks, and foxes, and by consuming plants and dead animals. Primarily nocturnal, they may sometimes be encountered during the day. Look for them under rocks, plant debris, and logs. Jerusalem crickets typically take about 20 months to mature from egg to adult with typical adults living another 2 to 6 months. During their larval stage, they molt multiple times, each time eating their cast skin.

Similar to crickets, Jerusalem crickets have a call song tied to temperature. Both sexes produce the call, which is a drumming sound, by beating their abdomen on the ground at up to forty drums per second. They use sensory organs in their legs to detect the impulses, some of which are audible to humans. Each species has its own specific drum pattern, which appears to aid males and females in locating each other.

In the western United States, there may be as many as 100 species of *Stenopelmatus* with at least six in southern Utah. For many years, entomologists described most American Jerusalem crickets as *S. fuscus*. Weissman's research has shown this to be incorrect; *S. fuscus* is limited to northwest New Mexico and northeast Arizona. At this time, the most common Utah species has not been named.

Jerusalem crickets have many common names including skull insect, "child of the earth," and potato bug. First used scientifically by entomologist Vernon Kellogg in 1905, the name Jerusalem is controversial. One entomologist believes that it "arose from a mixing of Navajo and Christian terminology," because the Navajo called the bugs "skull insects" and early Franciscan priests in the area knew of a cliff in Jerusalem known as Skull Hill. In contrast, the term may have simply developed because Jerusalem was a common nineteenth-century swear word, leading another entomologist to write about someone "turning over a rock and in surprise, shouting 'Jerusalem! What a cricket.'"

SCORPION
Variety of species
Class Arachnida
$1/2$–5 in., generally brown or tan, eight legs, with long tail, and large front appendages that end in a pincer

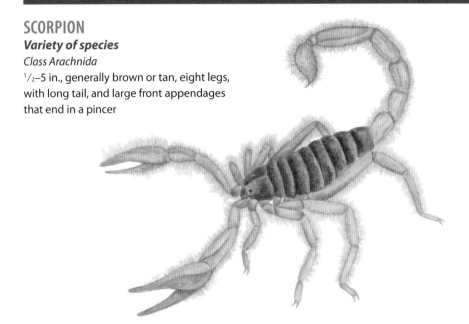

Scorpions are one of the most feared desert inhabitants. Although many people believe that scorpion stings (scorpions do not bite) can kill a human, most stings are no worse than that of a bee. In the United States only one species, which occurs in southern Arizona, has a venom that can kill a human. Even our largest scorpion, the giant desert hairy scorpion, has a mild sting.

Scorpions began their long adventure on land more than 400 million years ago. Along with spiders, they were one of the first animals to move onto land. Although they have remained practically unchanged in that time, they are an extremely successful group. Scorpions live in forests, grasslands, seashores, and deserts and inhabit all the continents except Antarctica. Only a few insects and spiders (principally tarantulas) reach a greater size in the world of terrestrial arthropods. In addition, their average life span of 2 to 10 years (some species can live for 25 years or longer) is greater than most other insects and arachnids.

Scorpions employ sophisticated sensory capabilities, similar to the methods used by seismologists in locating earthquakes, to locate prey. Hairs and slits on the scorpion's legs detect subsurface vibrations, and by determining the magnitude and direction of wave propagation, a scorpion can locate its prey. They are opportunistic eaters with liberal tastes that include insects, spiders, and other scorpions.

Unlike most other terrestrial arthropods, scorpions give birth to live young. Mating occurs after an elaborate dance in which the male tries to position the female over a spermatophore that he has deposited on the ground. Gestation times range between 3 and 18 months. Females give birth to an average of 30 young. After birth the newborn climb on the mother's back, where they remain until their first molt.

People rarely see scorpions because they are nocturnal and spend the majority of their time in burrows or under rocks. Scorpions can be seen quite easily at night, though, because their exoskeleton fluoresces (glows) under black or ultraviolet light. However, one word of caution: Remember that other animals, like rattlesnakes, do not glow and often forage at night as well.

At least six species inhabit southern Utah. The biggest are the two, hard-to-distinguish species of giant desert hairy scorpion (*Hadrurus spadix* and *H. arizonensis*) at up to 5$^1/_2$ inches long including tail. They have a dark brown back and live in burrows in a variety of habitats in arroyos and rocky areas. The most common scorpion is the boreal or northern scorpion (*Paruroctonus boreus*), which ranges from British Columbia to Nebraska. Average adult length is 2 inches. They are mostly found in sandy flats.

Spiders

TARANTULA
Aphonopelma sp.
Theraphosidae family
Up to 6 in. legspan, eight legs, brown to black, hairy body

In the 1700s in southern Italy, an epidemic known as tarantism spread throughout the populace. The unfortunate people suffered through "grotesque and unnatural gestures and extravagant postures," ultimately resulting in death. The only cure was music that induced a series of movements known as the tarantella dance. All of this was supposedly brought about by the bite of a tarantula.

Tarantulas, however, do not occur in southern Italy; between 10 and 20 species live in the United States. This much feared spider, with a legspan of up to 6 inches, rarely bites and has a mild venom that does not affect humans. Tarantulas do not employ webs to catch prey; instead they go in search or wait just inside their burrow for a meal to wander by. They eat frogs, lizards, and insects, secreting enzymes that break down soft tissues, allowing the victim's insides to be sucked dry.

Although they seldom bite, tarantulas can create a cloud of hairs by scraping their abdomen. These urticating hairs are especially irritating to the eyes and nose.

Juvenile males and females are indistinguishable until their final molt, which does not occur until their eighth year. Males do not live long after mating. A female, on the other hand, can live for up to 25 years.

After the final molt, usually in the fall, the male goes in search of a mate. He must be careful because the larger female may eat him instead of mating with him. If mating occurs, the female will deposit roughly 800 eggs on a silk sheet that she then forms into a bag. She may carry the egg bag out of the burrow to warm it. Incubation lasts 2 to 5 months, depending on temperature and humidity. The young leave the burrow a few days after hatching and go in search of a new burrow. Juvenile mortality is high as they make a good meal for rodents, birds, scorpions, and snakes.

Besides humans, the tarantula's main predator is the tarantula hawk (*Pepsis* sp.), a large wasp with a metallic blue-black body and orange wings. It can grow up to 3 inches long. The females are the hunters, and after mating, they run about searching for a tarantula who will become the food source for the *Pepsis* young. When the female *Pepsis* finds a tarantula, she attacks and stings the spider, paralyzing it. She then drags the immobilized tarantula to a burrow and deposits an egg on it. After hatching, the *Pepsis* larva eats the still-living tarantula. The tarantula has to be living; a dead tarantula would dry out and not be a food source. All members of this wasp family, Pompilidae, have a similar lifestyle, paralyzing spiders and using them as food for their larvae.

BLACK WIDOW SPIDER
Latrodectus hesperus
Theridiidae family
Female up to 1½ in., black with red hourglass on abdomen; male ⅓ in., gray with stripes and blotches, no hourglass

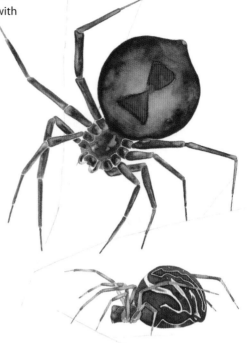

Black widow spiders are relatively common in canyon country. To find one, look in protected areas, such as rock cracks and crevices or under logs, for a sprawling web that ends in a more densely made, tubelike opening. Inside the funnel the timid female waits for food and a mate. The jet-black females have the well-known red hourglass on their abdomen, while the much smaller males are grayish with stripes and blotches. Despite their reputation, females do not actively attack males after mating. Instead, males generally crawl away from females and simply go into another part of the web

to die. One could view this as a noble sacrifice, for the male provides food to the female and hence to his progeny.

Black widows also have a reputation for their poisonous bite—this one is well deserved. The neurotoxin contains seven different proteins and is one of the most highly toxic of all venoms. The bite does not hurt, but symptoms, which include intense pain, vomiting, and nausea, manifest quickly. Few people die from the bite, but children and the elderly should be cautious. Antivenin is available and hospitalization is highly recommended.

Close-up

Life in Desert Potholes

If you spend much time in canyon country, you will begin to notice that a miraculous ecosystem emerges after desert rains. What appeared to be lifeless, dirt-filled pits now begin to teem with activity. Tiny organisms, eggs, and larvae that have lain dormant in the soil burst forth with great exuberance from these potholes. In a few hours to days, crustaceans, beetles, and insect larvae begin to wriggle and squirm in the shallow pools.

Pool size and temperature are the key determining factors in what organisms inhabit a pothole. Even shallow depressions that only have a thin black coating of soil contain algae and rotifers, microscopic animals that eat algae and in turn are eaten by worms and crustaceans. If sediment is present, mites have a home. Gnat larvae and other minute organisms live in slightly larger pools. As the pool size increases, tadpoles, fairy shrimp, clam shrimp, and tadpole shrimp become prevalent. In the largest pools backswimmers, predaceous diving beetles, and midge larvae predominate.

These pothole creatures have adapted to withstand the extremes of a high desert. During the long, dry periods, organisms must be able to withstand soil temperatures that can reach 140°F (60°C) in the summer, and then remain frozen for many weeks during the winter. When there is water, an organism only has a few weeks to complete its life cycle before it dies.

Several lifestyles have evolved to cope with these extremes. Many organisms have a dormant stage in which they can resist the long periods of desiccation. They are protected by an eggshell, exoskeleton, or a coating of waterproof mud. Other organisms can tolerate an almost complete loss of water in their cells, and then rehydrate and regain all body functions in less than 1 hour after a good rainstorm. Some creatures live in more permanent water sources and only take advantage of potholes when water is present.

No matter what method they use to survive, most pothole organisms need to have a short life cycle. Red-spotted and spadefoot toad eggs can hatch in less than 24 hours, and take 2 to 3 weeks to develop from tadpole to toad. Compare that with a bullfrog, which may remain in its tadpole stage for up to 2 years. Fairy shrimp and tadpole shrimp complete their life cycles in less than 2 weeks. Smaller organisms have even shorter life cycles.

The survival of pothole organisms depends upon their ability to make use of the slow, natural water cycle between periods of desiccation. Unexpected changes can kill, so if you need water, only take a little from each pothole and leave the rest. **Do not jump into or swim in potholes because body oils, insect repellent, and sunblock damage this fragile ecosystem. The animals' tenuous grip on life can easily be snuffed out when feet or tires crush them during their dry, dormant period.** When that happens, we lose one of the most interesting ecosystems in the desert.

DESERT POTHOLES

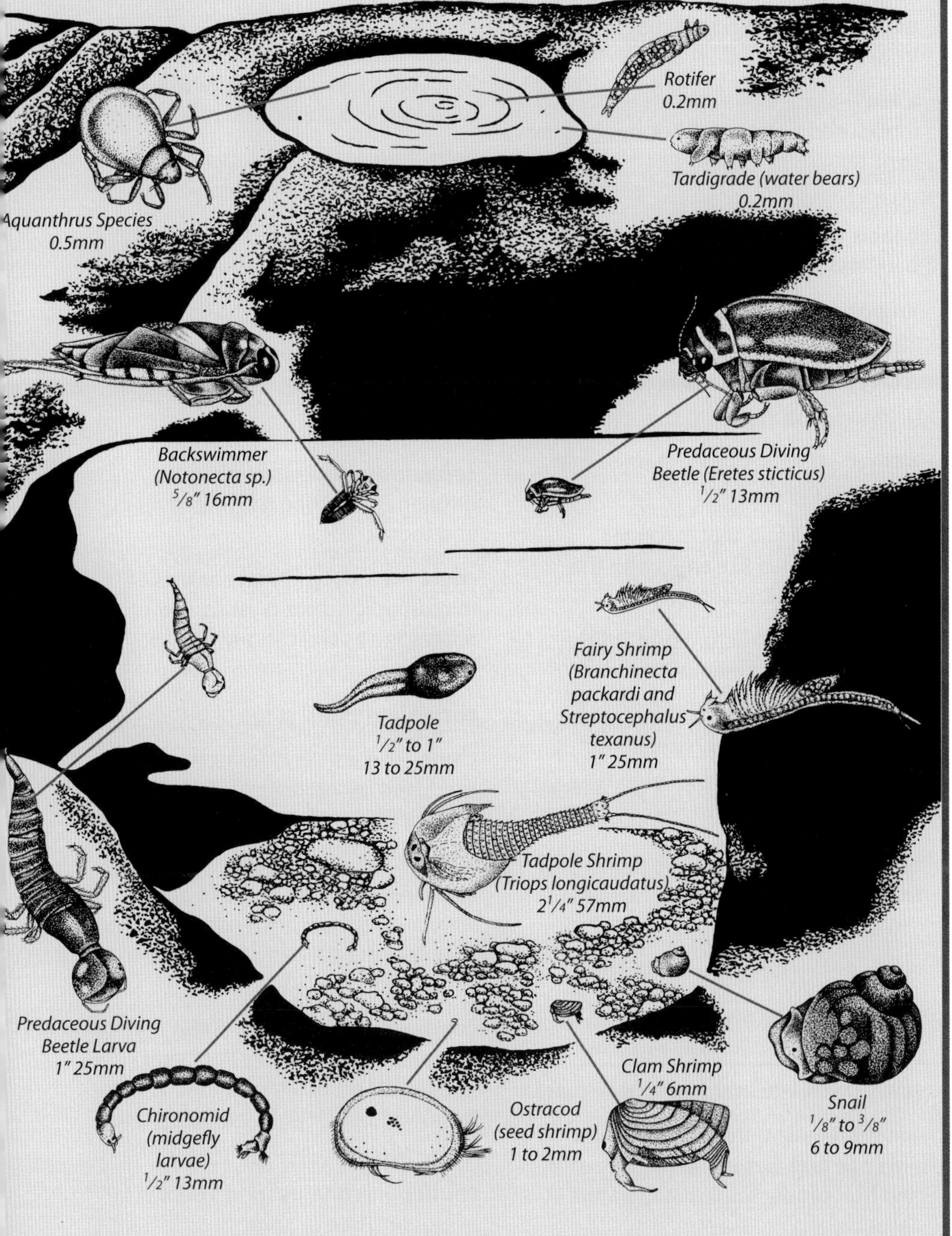

Rotifer
0.2mm

Tardigrade (water bears)
0.2mm

Aquanthrus Species
0.5mm

Backswimmer
(Notonecta sp.)
5/8" 16mm

Predaceous Diving
Beetle (Eretes sticticus)
1/2" 13mm

Fairy Shrimp
(Branchinecta
packardi and
Streptocephalus
texanus)
1" 25mm

Tadpole
1/2" to 1"
13 to 25mm

Tadpole Shrimp
(Triops longicaudatus)
2 1/4" 57mm

Predaceous Diving
Beetle Larva
1" 25mm

Chironomid
(midgefly
larvae)
1/2" 13mm

Ostracod
(seed shrimp)
1 to 2mm

Clam Shrimp
1/4" 6mm

Snail
1/8" to 3/8"
6 to 9mm

GLOSSARY

accipiter—"true hawks" with long tails, relatively short, rounded wings (e.g., Cooper's, sharp-shinned, and goshawk)

adventitious—any root that originates from a stem

alien—a nonnative species either introduced purposefully or by accident (e.g., tamarisk)

altricial—born naked, blind, deaf, and unable to walk (e.g., many rodents, bats, and shrews)

angiosperm—a flowering plant

annual—a plant that germinates, flowers, and sets seed in a single growing season

anther—the part of the stamen that produces pollen

anticline—a fold that is convex upward (shaped like an A) with the oldest rocks in the center

antler—bony structure protruding from forehead of members of deer family

apetalous—having no petals

arkose—sandstone rich in the minerals feldspar and quartz

arroyo—a stream channel that is only occupied by water during the rainy season or after a rainstorm

aspect—the direction a slope faces

basin—an extensive depressed area into which the adjacent land drains

batrachian—relating to frogs or toads

biennial—plant that completes its life cycle and dies in 2 years; flower and fruit production usually occurs in second year

brackish—partially salty water

bract—a reduced or modified leaf associated with a flower

brumation—ectothermic equivalent of hibernation

buteo—medium to large raptors with long, broad wings and relatively short, wide tails (e.g., red-tailed hawk)

call—bird vocalization, generally innate and used for a specific function like alerting or locating

calyx—usually greenish whorl of sepals collectively, from the Greek for "cup"

catkin—an inflorescence that consists of dense, erect spikes of tiny, apetalous flowers

cephalothorax—arachnid body division comprising the united head and thorax

chert—a rock type that consists of microscopic quartz crystals, sometimes referred to as chalcedony, flint, or jasper

chrysalis—pupal stage of butterflies

clone—genetically identical young produced by asexual or vegetative reproduction from a single parent (e.g., aspen and plateau striped whiptail)

cocoon—protective case of many larval forms that surrounds the pupa; silky or other covering formed by many animals for their young

composite—a member of the Asteraceae plant family (formerly known as Compositae) characterized by flower head that resembles a single flower (e.g., daisies and sunflowers)

conifer—a cone-bearing, usually evergreen, tree or shrub

corolla—collectively, the flower parts (petals) interior to the calyx

cotyledon—a seed leaf; the specialized leaf first produced by a plant after germinating from a seed

crepuscular—active at dawn or dusk

cross-beds—inclined beds of depositional origin in sedimentary rocks formed by wind or water currents

cruciform—shaped like a cross

deciduous—a shrub or tree that drops its leaves after the growing season, not evergreen

diapir—a body of salt that has pushed up the surrounding rock into an anticline and pierced through it

dicot—short for dicotyledon, a plant that produces two seed leaves

dioecious—two homes: plants that have male and female flowers on separate plants

disjunct—a local population geographically separated from other populations of the same species (e.g., Douglas fir trees growing in the Island in the Sky district in Canyonlands National Park 30 miles and 3,000 feet lower in elevation from the nearest population of Douglas firs)

disk flower—small, tubular flowers in the central part of the flowering head of many Asteraceae family flowers

diurnal—active during the day

dorsal—pertaining to the back

ectotherm—cold-blooded; body temperature responds directly to the temperature of the surrounding environment

ecotone—the boundary between two ecological communities

endemic—restricted to a geographic region (e.g., the humpback chub is only found in the Colorado River basin)

endotherm—warm-blooded; internal regulation of body temperature

eolian—deposited by wind

evapotranspiration—water loss from soil and plants

evergreen—plants that bear green leaves year-round, not deciduous

exotic—see "alien"; some people prefer exotic instead of alien

extinct—plants or animals that have no living members on the planet

extirpation—elimination of a group of plants or animals from a specific area

extrusive rock—rock formed from lava or other volcanic material ejected onto the surface of the earth

fault—a fracture in a rock or on the earth's surface where there has been relative displacement; can be any size from microscopic to many miles long

fauna—animal assemblage in a geographic area

filament—stalk of a stamen

flora—plant assemblage in a geographic area

forbs—broadleafed (nongrass) herbaceous plants

form—shallow depression occupied by rabbits and hares

fruit—the ripened ovary of a plant

genus—a taxonomic group of closely related species (plural: genera)

gneiss—a coarse-grained metamorphic rock characterized by banding and parallel alignment of minerals

granite—coarse-grained intrusive igneous rock composed of silica-rich minerals

gymnosperm—seed-bearing vascular plants that reproduce by clusters of cones, generally wind-pollinated

hare—jackrabbits; differ from rabbits in having generally larger ears, tail, and legs

harvestmen—also known as daddy longlegs; unlike spiders they only have two eyes, and their cephalothorax and abdomen are broadly joined so it appears to be one piece

herbaceous—nonwoody plants

herpetology—the study of reptiles

hibernation—condition of torpor in winter

hirsute—covered by hairs

hoodoo—a strangely eroded column of rock

horn—bony outgrowth from skull covered in keratin, they grow continuously through life

hypha—branching, threadlike structures of fungus responsible for feeding, growing, and reproduction (plural: hyphae)

ichthyology—the study of fishes

igneous rock—a rock formed by the solidification of magma or lava

inflorescence—a cluster of flowers

intrusive rock—rock that cooled within the earth

laccolith—an igneous intrusion that forces apart two layers of strata and forms a mound-shaped body much wider than it is thick

lacustrine—a lake or pond ecosystem

lagomorph—pikas, rabbits, and hares

larva—an insect, amphibian, or other preadult form of an animal that differs strongly from the adult form

lava—magma that reaches the surface

lek—form of animal display in which males with exaggerated plumage strut and vocalize in front of females who choose a mate based on this display

limestone—a sedimentary rock composed mainly of calcium carbonate

magma—molten rock

metamorphic rock—a rock whose original mineralogy, texture, or composition has been changed due to pressure and/or temperature (e.g., gneiss or marble)

monocot—monocotyledon, having one cotyledon; plants characterized by floral parts in threes (e.g., lilies)

monoecious—"one house": male and female reproductive parts on the same plant

monotypic—characterized by a single species

native—plant or animal that originated in the region in which they live

nectar—a watery, sugar-rich solution secreted by plants to attract pollinators

niche—role of a species within a community

nocturnal—active at night

parotoid gland—large swellings on the side of the head of some amphibians, sometimes poisonous

perennial—a plant that normally lives for more than 3 years

petal—flower part generally surrounded by the calyx, colorful and showy to attract pollinators

photosynthesis—process by which plants use the sun's energy to convert carbon dioxide and water into carbohydrates and oxygen

pinnate—a compound leaf having smaller leaflets arranged along either side of a central axis

pistil—female organ of plant consisting of stigma, style, and ovary

pollen—microscopic particles that contain male reproductive cells

precocial—born with full coat of hair, and can see, hear, and move around, at least somewhat (e.g., deer and jackrabbits)

pupa—third stage of complete metamorphosis of insect; insect enclosed in a case

raptor—a member of the hawk or owl orders, often synonymous with birds of prey, but does not include all predators; does include accipiters, buteos, eagles, falcons, harriers, kites, ospreys, owls, and vultures

rhizomes—underground stems that produce new plants and roots

riparian—the ecosystem along a stream or river

rut—annual period of sexual activity in some mammals

sandstone—a sedimentary rock composed of sand-size particles

scat—animal feces

sedimentary—rock formed by the deposition of material by wind, water, or ice, or by chemical means

sepal—outermost whorl of floral leaves, generally green

siltstone—a sedimentary rock composed of silt-size particles

song—bird vocalization generally learned, females rarely sing, males sing either to attract a mate or to defend territory

spine—firm, sharp-pointed, modified leaf

stamen—male or pollen-producing part of flower

stigma—part of pistil receptive to pollen

style—slender stalk that connects ovary to stigma

syncline—a V-shaped fold with the youngest rock strata at the center

taproot—a vertical root that extends deep into the ground

tepal—petals and sepals that are indistinguishable from each other

torpor—considerably reduced metabolic rate with subsequent slow breathing and heart rate; body temperature drops down near the ambient temperature

woody—trees or shrubs

FURTHER READING

GEOLOGY

Baars, Don. *Canyonlands Country: Geology of Canyonlands and Arches National Parks.* Lawrence, Kans.: Cañon Publishers, 1989.

———. *The Colorado Plateau: A Geologic History.* Albuquerque: University of New Mexico Press, 1983.

Blakey, Ron, and Wayne Ranney. *Ancient Landscapes of the Colorado Plateau.* Grand Canyon, Ariz.: Grand Canyon Association, 2008.

Chronic, Halka. *Pages of Stone: Geology of Western National Parks and Monuments: Grand Canyon and the Plateau Country.* Seattle: Mountaineers Press, 1988.

———. *Roadside Geology of Arizona.* Missoula, Mont.: Mountain Press Publishing Co., 1986.

———. *Roadside Geology of Utah.* Missoula, Mont.: Mountain Press Publishing Co., 1990.

Doelling, Hellmut, Charles Oviatt, and Peter W. Huntoon. *Salt Deformation in the Paradox Basin.* Salt Lake City: Utah Geological and Mineral Survey Bulletin 122, 1988.

Fillmore, Robert. *Geologic Evolution of the Colorado Plateau of Eastern Utah and Western Colorado.* Salt Lake City: University of Utah Press, 2011.

Hintze, Lehi. *Geologic History of Utah.* Provo, Utah: Brigham Young University Geology Studies Special Publication 7, 1988.

Stokes, William Lee. "Geology of Utah." Salt Lake City: Utah Museum of Natural History and Utah Geological and Mineral Survey Occasional Paper 6, 1986.

Weigand, Del L., ed. *Geology of the Paradox Basin.* Rocky Mountain Association of Geologists Field Conference Guidebook, 1981.

PLANTS

Benson, Lyman, and Robert A. Darrow. *A Manual of Southwestern Desert Trees and Shrubs.* Tucson: University of Arizona Press, 1945.

Buchmann, Stephen L., and Gary Paul Nabhan. *The Forgotten Pollinators.* Washington, D.C.: Island Press, 1996.

Coombes, Allen J. *Dictionary of Plant Names.* Portland, Ore.: Timber Press, 1985.

Dunmire, William, and Gail Tierney. *Wild Plants of the Pueblo Province.* Santa Fe: Museum of New Mexico Press, 1995.

———. *Wild Plants of the Four Corners.* Santa Fe: Museum of New Mexico Press, 1997.

Durant, Mary. *Who Named the Daisy? Who Named the Rose? A Roving Dictionary of North American Wild Flowers.* New York: Congwood & Weed, Inc., 1976.

Elmore, Francis. *Shrubs and Trees of the Southwest Uplands.* Tucson, Ariz.: Southwest Parks and Monuments Association, 1976.

Fagan, Damian. *Canyon Country Wildflowers.* Helena, Mont.: FalconGuides, 1998

Lamb, Samuel H. *Woody Plants of the Southwest.* Santa Fe: The Sunstone Press, 1975.

Leake, Dorothy Van Dyke, John B. Leake, and Marcelotte Leake Roeder. *Desert and Mountain Plants of the Southwest*. Norman: University of Oklahoma Press, 1993.

Martin, William C., and Charles R. Hutchins. *Spring Wildflowers of New Mexico*. Albuquerque: University of New Mexico Press, 1984.

McDougall, Walter Byron. *Grand Canyon Wildflowers*. Flagstaff, Ariz.: Museum of Northern Arizona, 1964.

Moore, Michael. *Medicinal Plants of the Mountain West*. Santa Fe: Museum of New Mexico Press, 1979.

Mozingo, Hugh Nelson. *Shrubs of the Great Basin: A Natural History*. Reno: University of Nevada Press, 1987.

Nabhan, Gary Paul. *Gathering the Desert*. Tucson: University of Arizona Press, 1985.

Nelson, Ruth Ashton. *Plants of Zion National Park: Wildflowers, Trees, Shrubs, and Ferns*. Springdale, Utah: Zion Natural History Association, 1976.

Taylor, Ronald J. *Sagebrush Country: A Wildflower Sanctuary*. Missoula, Mont.: Mountain Press Publishing Co., 1992.

Vines, Robert A. *Trees, Shrubs and Woody Vines of the Southwest*. Austin: University of Texas Press, 1960.

Welsh, Stanley L. *Flowers of Canyon Country*. Moab, Utah: Canyonlands Natural History Association, 1977.

———. "On the Distribution of Utah's Hanging Gardens." *The Great Basin Naturalist* 49, No. 1 (1989): 1-29.

———. *Wildflowers of Zion National Park*. Springdale, Utah: Zion Natural History Association, 1990.

Welsh, Stanley L., et al. *A Utah Flora*. Provo, Utah: Brigham Young University, 1993.

Whitson, Tom D., et al. *Weeds of the West*. Newark, Calif.: The Western Society of Weed Science, 1992.

MAMMALS

Armstrong, David. *Mammals of the Canyon Country*. Moab, Utah: Canyonlands Natural History Association, 1982.

Barnes, Claude T. *Mammals of Utah*. Kaysville, Utah: Inland Printing Company, 1922.

Durrant, Stephen D. *Mammals of Utah, Taxonomy and Distribution*. Lawrence: University of Kansas, 1952.

Findley, James S. *The Natural History of New Mexican Mammals*. Albuquerque: University of New Mexico Press, 1987.

Fitzgerald, James P., Carron A. Meaney, and David M. Armstrong. *Mammals of Colorado*. Niwot: University Press of Colorado, 1994.

Hoffmeister, Donald Frederick. *Mammals of Arizona*. Tucson: University of Arizona Press, 1986.

Olin, George. *Mammals of the Southwest Mountains and Mesas*. Globe, Ariz.: Southwest Parks and Monuments Association, 1961.

———. *50 Common Mammals of the Southwest*. Tucson, Ariz.: Western National Parks Association, 2000.

Stall, Chris. *Animal Tracks of the Southwest States*. Seattle: The Mountaineers, 1990.

Warren, Edward Royal. *The Mammals of Colorado, Their Habits and Distribution.* 2d ed. (rev). Norman: University of Oklahoma Press, 1942.

Zeveloff, Samuel I. *Mammals of the Intermountain West.* Salt Lake City: University of Utah Press, 1988.

REPTILES AND AMPHIBIANS

Cox, Douglas, and Wilmer Tanner. *Snakes of Utah.* Provo, Utah: Brigham Young University, 1996.

Degenhardt, William G., and Charles W. Painter. *Amphibians and Reptiles of New Mexico.* Albuquerque: University of New Mexico Press, 1996.

Heymann, M. M. *Reptiles and Amphibians of the American Southwest.* Scottsdale, Ariz.: Doubleshoe Publishers, 1975.

Jones, Lawrence, and Rob Lovich, eds. *Lizards of the American Southwest: A Photographic Field Guide.* Tucson, Ariz.: Rio Nuevo, 2009.

Klauber, Laurence M. *Rattlesnakes: Their Habitats, Life Histories, and Influences on Mankind.* Abridged by Karen Harvey McClung. Berkeley: University of California Press, 1982.

Stebbins, Robert C. *Peterson Field Guide to Western Reptiles and Amphibians.* Boston: Houghton Mifflin Co., 1966.

Wright, A. H., and A. A. Wright. *Handbook of Frogs and Toads.* Ithaca, NY: Comstock Publishing Co., 1933.

———. *Handbook of Snakes.* Ithaca, NY: Cornell University Press, 1957.

FISH

Sigler, William, and John W. Sigler. *Fishes of Utah: A Natural History.* Salt Lake City: University of Utah Press, 1986.

BIRDS

Clark, William. *A Field Guide to the Hawks of North America.* Boston: Houghton Mifflin Co., 1987.

Cunningham, Richard L. *50 Common Birds of the Southwest.* Tucson, Ariz.: Southwest Parks and Monuments Association, 1990.

Dunn, Jon L., and Jonathan Alderfer. *National Geographic Society Field Guide to Birds of North America,* 6th ed. Washington, D.C.: National Geographic Society, 2011.

Ehrlich, Paul R., David S. Dobkin, and Darryl Wheye. *The Birder's Handbook: A Field Guide to the Natural History of North American Birds.* New York: Simon & Schuster Inc., 1988.

Gray, Mary Taylor. *Watchable Birds of the Southwest.* Missoula, Mont.: Mountain Press Publishing Co., 1995.

Ryser, Fred A. *Birds of the Great Basin: A Natural History.* Reno: University of Nevada Press, 1987.

Sibley, David Allen. *The Sibley Guide to Birds of Western North America.* New York: Knopf, 2003.

INSECTS AND ARACHNIDS

Cranshaw, Whitney, and Boris Kondratieff. *Bagging Big Bugs.* Boulder, Colo.: Fulcrum Publishing, 1995.

Hubbell, Sue. *Broadsides from the Other Orders: A Book of Bugs.* New York: Random House, 1993.

Polis, Gary, ed. *The Biology of Scorpions.* Stanford, Calif.: Stanford University Press, 1990.

Russo, Ron. *Field Guide to Plant Galls of California and Other Western States.* Berkeley: University of California Press, 2006.

Werner, Floyd, and Carl Olson. *Learning About and Living With Insects of the Southwest.* Tucson, Ariz.: Fisher Books, 1994.

GENERAL

Abbey, Edward. *Desert Solitaire: A Season in the Wilderness.* New York: Ballantine Books, 1971.

Evans, Howard Ensign. *Pioneer Naturalists: The Discovery and Naming of North American Plants and Animals.* New York: Henry Holt and Co., 1993.

Harper, Kimball, et al., ed. *Natural History of the Colorado Plateau and Great Basin.* Niwot: University Press of Colorado, 1994.

Larson, Peggy. *A Sierra Club Naturalist's Guide: The Desert of the Southwest.* San Francisco: Sierra Club Books, 1987.

MacMahon, James. *The Audubon Society Nature Guides: Deserts.* New York: Alfred A. Knopf, Inc., 1985.

Mutel, Cornelia Fleischer, and John Emerick. *From Grassland to Glacier: The Natural History of Colorado.* Boulder, Colo.: Johnson Books, 1984.

Tweit, Susan. *The Great Southwest Nature Factbook.* Bothell, Wash.: Alaska Northwest Books, 1992.

———. *Seasons in the Desert: A Naturalist's Notebook.* San Francisco: Chronicle Books, 1998.

Whitney, Stephen. *A Field Guide to the Grand Canyon.* New York: Quill, 1982.

Zwinger, Ann Haymond. *The Mysterious Lands.* New York: Truman Talley Books, 1990.

———. *Run, River, Run: A Naturalist's Journey Down One of the Great Rivers of the American West.* New York: Harper and Row, 1975.

———. *Wind in the Rock: The Canyonlands of Southeastern Utah.* New York: Harper and Row, 1978.

INDEX

ABOUT THE AUTHOR

David B. Williams is a freelance writer and naturalist. His books include *Cairns: Messengers in Stone, Stories in Stone: Travels Through Urban Geology,* and *The Seattle Street-Smart Naturalist: Field Notes from the City.* He lived in Moab for 9 years, where he worked as a park ranger at Arches National Park and as a program coordinator and instructor for Canyonlands Field Institute. He now lives in Seattle.

ABOUT THE ILLUSTRATORS

Gloria Brown grew up in Colorado, studied art in San Francisco and Chicago, then worked in The Hague, Copenhagen, and New York City. During the mid-1990s she was publication specialist for Canyonlands Natural History Association in Moab, Utah. Gloria has illustrated several nature books for children. Her watercolors have been shown in the Southwest, including "The Pages Come Alive," an interpretive exhibit of art from this book at Kolb Studio in Grand Canyon National Park. She lives and works in an 1880s mining cabin along the Continental Divide.

Todd Telander is a naturalist/illustrator/artist living in Walla Walla, Washington. He has studied and illustrated wildlife since 1989, while living in California, Colorado, New Mexico, and Washington. He graduated from the University of California at Santa Cruz with degrees in biology, environmental studies, and scientific illustration, and has since illustrated numerous books and other publications, including Falcon Pocket Guides and Scats and Tracks (both FalconGuides) series. His wife, Kirsten Telander, is a writer, and they have two sons, Miles and Oliver. His work can be viewed online at www.toddtelander.com.

ABOUT CANYONLANDS NATURAL HISTORY ASSOCIATION

Canyonlands Natural History Association (CNHA) was established in 1967 as a not-for-profit organization to assist the scientific, educational, and visitor service efforts of the National Park Service (NPS), the Bureau of Land Management (BLM), and US Forest Service (USFS).

CNHA's goals include enhancing each visitor's understanding and appreciation of public lands by providing a thorough selection of quality educational materials for sale in its bookstore outlets. A portion of CNHA's proceeds, including profit from this publication, are returned directly to our public land partners to fund their educational, research, and scientific programs. Bookstore sales support the agencies' programs in various ways, including free publications, outdoor education programs for local school districts, equipment and supplies for ranger/naturalists, exhibits, and funds for research. Since our inception in 1967, CNHA has donated over 8 million dollars to our public land partners.

The Discovery Pool

CNHA established the Discovery Pool in 2006 to provide our federal partners with financial support for eligible scientific studies conducted within their administrative boundaries.

The goals for use of the Discovery Pool grants are:

- Encourage the scientific research that makes up the backbone of interpretive and educational programs, including resource management or protection surveys and monitoring.
- Provide matching funds that may assist federal partners in obtaining larger grants.
- Promote an understanding of the intricate cultural and natural resource complexities found on federally administered lands.

CNHA Membership

People protect that which they understand. With visitor use demands escalating and agency funding declining, CNHA's role in assisting in the agencies' educational efforts will continue to expand. Those wishing to support CNHA and our mission are invited to join the association's membership program. (Membership dues and other contributions are tax deductible to the extent provided by law.)

For more information about CNHA, the Discovery Pool, our membership program or our products, please visit us online at www.cnha.org or call (800) 840-8978.

CANYONLANDS
Natural History Association

Your next adventure begins here.

falcon.com